EFFECTIVE ECONOMIC DECISION-MAKING by NONPROFIT ORGANIZATIONS

EFFECTIVE
ECONOMIC
DECISION-MAKING
by NONPROFIT
ORGANIZATIONS

DENNIS R. YOUNG, EDITOR

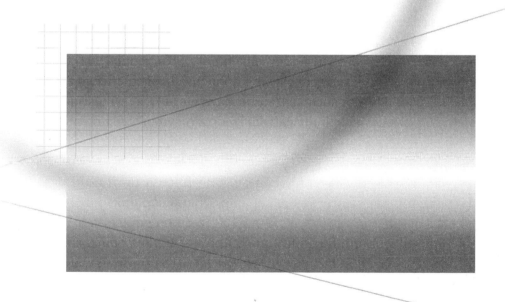

THE FOUNDATION CENTER

 NCNE

Library of Congress Cataloging-in-Publication Data

Effective economic decision-making by nonprofit organizations / Dennis
R. Young, editor ; sponsored by the National Center on Nonprofit
Enterprise [and] The Foundation Center.— 1st ed.
       p. cm.
The contents of this book derive from the work of eight task forces,
which deliberated prior to the inaugural conference of the National
Center on Nonprofit Enterprise (NCNE) in January 2002, and produced
reports that served as the basis of conference discussions.
Includes bibliographical references and index.
    ISBN 1-931923-69-8 (pbk.)
  1. Nonprofit organizations—Finance—Management—Congresses. 2.
Charities—Finance—Management—Congresses. 3. Fund
raising—Management—Congresses. I. Young, Dennis R., 1943- II.
National Center on Nonprofit Enterprise. III. Foundation Center.
    HG4027.65.E345 2004
    658.15—dc22
                                                    2004024303

Table of Contents

Acknowledgments vii

Preface xii

Foreword by Larry J. Wilker xv

   1. Introduction and Overview
     Dennis R. Young 1

PART 1: CORE OPERATING DECISIONS

   2. Pricing in the Nonprofit Sector
     Sharon M. Oster, Charles M. Gray, and *Charles Weinberg* 27

   3. Compensation in Nonprofit Organizations
     Anne E. Preston 47

   4. Outsourcing by Nonprofit Organizations
     Avner Ben-Ner 67

PART 2: RESOURCE DEVELOPMENT

   5. Fundraising Costs
     Joseph J. Cordes, Patrick M. Rooney 83

   6. Investment and Expenditure Strategies
     Marion R. Fremont-Smith 101

PART 3: NEW DIRECTIONS

   7. Nonprofit Commercial Ventures and Their Funding Agents' Responses
     Howard P. Tuckman 121

   8. Institutional Collaboration
     James E. Austin 149

   9. Internet Commerce and Fundraising
     Dov Te'eni, Julie E. Kendall 167

   10. The Seven Insights of Effective Nonprofit Economic Decision-Making
     Dennis R. Young 191

About the Authors 219

About the National Center on Nonprofit Enterprise 220

Index 221

Acknowledgments

This book was made possible by several foundations that supported the development of the National Center on Nonprofit Enterprise (NCNE) and helped fund its inaugural conference in January 2002. Special thanks go the W.K. Kellogg Foundation and the Rockefeller Brothers Fund, which underwrote much of the initial development of the center, to the David and Lucile Packard Foundation, which provided the lead grant for the inaugural conference, and to the John C. Whitehead Foundation for continuing support. In addition to these contributors, generous funding for the inaugural conference was received from the Carnegie Corporation, the Charles Steward Mott Foundation, the Community Foundation of the National Capital Region, the Morino Institute, the Surdna Foundation, and an anonymous source.

The contents of this book derive from the work of eight task forces, which deliberated prior to the inaugural conference and produced reports that served as the basis of conference discussions. These reports were subsequently revised and are available on NCNE's Web site. The revised task force reports in turn served as the basis for eight of the chapters in this book. Given this history, members of these task forces are acknowledged for their multiple, important contributions to the contents of this book. The members of the task forces are as follows. (Those designated with asterisks also participated in the conference):

Task Force on Pricing:

*Sharon M. Oster, Yale University, Chair
*Charles M. Gray, University of St. Thomas
*Charles Weinberg, University of British Columbia
 Robert Cahen, Mandel Jewish Community Center of Cleveland
*Victor Gelb, Victor Gelb Inc.
 Gary Jonas, Venture Philanthropy Partners
 Gordon Winston, Williams College

Task Force on Compensation:

*Anne E. Preston, Haverford College, Chair
 Carolyn Ban, University of Pittsburgh
*Elizabeth Boris, The Urban Institute
 Jan Masaoka, CompassPoint
*Thomas McKenna, University of Pennsylvania
*Myron Roomkin, American University
*Mary Lou Stricklin, Visiting Nurse Association of Cleveland
*Cheryl A. Young, National Broadcasting Company

Task Force on Outsourcing:

*Avner Ben-Ner, University of Minnesota, Chair
*Roger Stough, George Mason University
*Kirsten Gronbjerg, Indiana University
*Mario Tonti, Beech Brook Children's Services
 Les Silverman, McKinsey & Company
 Jason Saul, What Works
*Mary Anne Waikart, St. Albans School
 Kathy O'Regan, New York University

Task Force on Fundraising Expenditure:

*Joseph J.Cordes, George Washington University, Co-Chair
*Patrick M. Rooney, Indiana University, Co-Chair
*Rita Feurst-Adams, Charitable and Philanthropic Management Counsel
*Dean Gladden, Cleveland Play House
*Richard Pogue, Dix & Eaton
*Mara Patermaster, Combined Federal Campaign
 Claude Rosenberg, RCM Capital Management
 James Greenfield, The Alford Group

Task Force on Investment and Expenditure of Funds:

*Marion Fremont-Smith, Harvard University, Chair
*Eugene Steuerle, The Urban Institute
Jeffrey Bradach, The Bridgespan Group
Kent Chabotar, Bowdoin College
Larry Fies, The Irvine Foundation
Regina Herzlinger, Harvard University
Malcolm Rogers, Boston Museum of Fine Arts
John C. Whitehead, AEA Investors

Task Force on New Ventures and Venture Philanthropy:

*Howard P. Tuckman,, Rutgers University, Chair
*Alan Abramson, The Aspen Institute
*Ed Robinson, Community Wealth Ventures
*Louise Myers, IONA Senior Services
Terri Freeman, Community Foundation of the National Capital Region
Greg Dees, Duke University
Vanessa Kirsch, New Profit, Inc.
Mclinda Tuan, Robert Enterprise Development Fund
Burton Weisbrod, Northwestern University

Task Force on Institutional Collaboration:

*James E. Austin, Harvard University, Chair
*Joseph Galaskiewicz, University of Arizona
*Ben Shute, Rockefeller Brothers Fund
*John Garrison, JR Garrison, Inc.
*Craig Smith, Harvard University
Carol Cone, Cone Communications, Inc.
Roxanne Spillet, Boys and Girls Clubs

Task Force on Internet Commerce and Fundraising:

*Dov Te'eni, Bar Ilan University, Chair
*Julie Kendall, Rutgers University
*Arthur (Buzz) Schmidt, Guidestar
*Sean Milliken, MissionFish
Bruce Kingma, Syracuse University
Tae Yoo, Cisco Systems

Several other individuals also made outstanding contributions to the success of this project, especially Peter Frank for overseeing the task forces and helping to assemble the material for each of the chapters and the final manuscript; Sarah Masters, Tanya Suphatranand, and Dana Ross for their superb efforts in organizing, overseeing, and following up the work of the conference; Dwight Burlingame for his help and guidance throughout this project; Richard Steinberg for his comments and contributions on various chapters; Claudia Holtzman for keeping us organized and helping with the editing; Lisa Tradewell for her expert assistance in editing the manuscripts; an anonymous reviewer for his/her substantive suggestions on each chapter, and Rick Schoff for his shepherding of the book through to publication. Finally, thanks are due to the members of NCNE's board of directors for their ongoing guidance and support, and to the members of NCNE's Institutional Consortium for their participation in this project and the confidence they have expressed in the future of the National Center on Nonprofit Enterprise.

Preface

This book is the first major publication of the National Center on Nonprofit Enterprise (NCNE). NCNE was founded in 1998 to "help nonprofit organizations make wise economic decisions." The Center is based on the premise that nonprofit organizations need to deploy their resources ever more wisely in the contemporary world of increasing competition and scarce resources, and that in order to do so they need more sophisticated ways of thinking about their economic decisions—not just simply adopting standard business methods but adapting basic business and economic reasoning to the special circumstances of nonprofit institutions.

Eight of the chapters in this book are based on the work of interdisciplinary task forces commissioned by NCNE to examine a wide spectrum of nonprofit economic decision-making issues. The net for these task forces, and for this book, was cast widely. Hence, the general lessons learned are applicable to nonprofit organizations across a broad spectrum of experience—large and small nonprofits, service-producing and advocacy-focused organizations, and member-driven associations as well as board-driven corporations. As a practical matter, however, the book will be most useful to managers of public-serving, charitable [501(c)(3) and 501(c)(4)] organizations, especially those that employ paid staff and manage significant sums of money, as contrasted with small, entirely volunteer-based organizations. While the economic reasoning employed here is universal, the examples and applications are concentrated within that domain.

After the introductory chapter, the book is divided into three parts. The first part examines core operating decisions that face almost any organization, nonprofit or otherwise: How should an organization price its services? How should it compensate its workers? What kinds of activities should it administer itself (in-house) versus outsourcing them to external suppliers? These may be questions common to all kinds of organizations, but as the three chapters in this part of the book attest, the answers for nonprofits can be quite different.

The second part of the book addresses resource development issues peculiar to nonprofits; specifically, how much should be spent on raising charitable contributions, and how should endowments and other nonprofit funds be invested and disbursed? These questions are too rarely addressed with hard-headed scrutiny and careful analysis, yet as the chapters in this part of the book suggest, they have numerous important implications for the success of nonprofit organizations.

The third part of the book addresses three important contemporary strategic dimensions of nonprofit resource development and deployment. First, how does a nonprofit organization decide whether to undertake a new programmatic venture, and from the funding point of view, how does a foundation or other funder determine which nonprofit venture initiatives should be supported? Second, we recognize that many new nonprofit ventures entail the engagement of business and government partners in various types of institutional collaborations. What principles should guide nonprofits in entering such arrangements? Finally, we appreciate that many new venture activities, as well as fundraising initiatives, now take place via the Internet. Hence, we address the new questions that face nonprofits in this modern venue of communication and commerce. As the chapters in this third part of the book imply, the efficient pursuit of new ventures, institutional partnerships, and Internet participation constitute a strong strategic nexus for nonprofits, clearly influencing the effectiveness with which they will be able to deploy their resources in the future.

Having traversed a relatively wide spectrum of economic decision-making activity, we take the opportunity in the final chapter of the book to synthesize some overall observations. These take the form of seven lessons of effective nonprofit economic decision-making. These lessons are intended as both a general summary of the findings of earlier chapters, and a reflection on what is common to the deliberation of nonprofit economic issues in their various manifestations. As such, we hope this analysis can serve as a beacon for addressing a wide variety of nonprofit economic decision-making issues in the future - not just those addressed in the few chapters here but many other important decisions, that in one way or another, influence the deployment of valuable resources. These include decisions about securing, changing, and managing physical facilities, purchasing insurance, undertaking alternative forms of programming, joining umbrella associations, engaging consultants, expanding or contracting the scale of operations, engaging in franchising, training staff, managing collections, and so on. By trying to understand what is common to various manifestations of nonprofit economic decision-making, we hope that this book helps establish a strong beginning for a stream of continuing inquiry and guidance that will help nonprofits become more effective economic and social institutions as time goes on.

Dennis R. Young
Chief Executive Officer, National
    Center on Nonprofit Enterprise
April, 2003

Foreword

Every organization presents unique challenges to its managers. In the for-profit world the goal is clear—maximize returns to shareholders in the form of increasing stock value and dividends. So too, must the nonprofit manager maximize value to shareholders. However, in the nonprofit world, there are different kinds of shareholders whose definitions of value vary. While balancing these differing perceptions of value, the nonprofit manager works in a difficult environment, serving many masters, almost always in the glare of the public eye, and chronically short of resources. These circumstances remind me of a sign I saw in a nonprofit administrator's office that said, "Put your ear to the ground, keep your eye on the ball, your shoulder to the wheel, and try to work in that position!"

Shareholders of nonprofit enterprises are not just the clients or patrons whom the organization serves. Trustees, funders, staff, and government officials all have vested interests and agendas that may or may not be in alignment with the mission of the organization. The manager must try to balance those often conflicting agendas to keep the organization on course to serve its social mission.

Nonetheless, today's nonprofit managers are expected to practice responsible and informed economic decision-making to maximize the effectiveness with which their organizations employ their valuable resources. These managers are obligated to appreciate "nonprofit" as a form of organization but not as a managerial goal. As such, there is much that can be learned from the for-profit world, but it must be remembered that nonprofit organizations work for a larger social purpose. Nonprofits represent the community, the greater good, which is articulated in the mission, and decision-making must be made with that as well as with good business practice in mind. This is the most difficult balancing act of all—practicing wise economic decision-making to advance the mission, while balancing the conflicting agendas of trustees, funders, staff, and government.

This is not an easy road to travel. As managers we must have the fortitude to stay true to mission and yet be open to opportunities, and to be flexible and creative in order to avoid or withstand the whiplash forces that can sway us from mission. Nonprofit managers need to apply efficient business practices but we cannot just borrow principles and practices wholesale from business. Those principles and practices need to be specially suited for nonprofit organizations. Our bottom line is our social mission, not profit, and we must employ financial and economic strategies specifically designed to efficiently support *that* bottom line.

The National Center on Nonprofit Enterprise and the authors and contributors to this volume have begun to construct an important body of knowledge and a set of useful, practical guidelines to support the work of nonprofit managers. This work is based on informed analysis, practical experience, and acute appreciation of the special character of nonprofit organizations. As such, it is invaluable and I hope that it will continue to be developed, refined, and elaborated far into the future.

Larry J. Wilker
Co-Founder, President, and CEO of
Show on Demand, Inc. and
TheaterDreams

CHAPTER 1

Introduction and Overview

Dennis R. Young

It has always been important for nonprofit organizations to use their resources wisely. Nonprofit organizations require a special trust between those who supply their resources and use their services, and those who manage them. Donors of money, time, and gifts-in-kind want to know that their gifts are not wasted or misused. The public at large wants assurances that public expenditures made to purchase services from nonprofit organizations are properly expended and a good bargain, and that the tax privileges granted to these organizations are justified. Consumers who utilize the services of nonprofit organizations want to feel that they are well served and that they too are receiving the best value for whatever fees they pay. These consumers are often quite vulnerable, with limited ability to look out for themselves, or they are represented by caretakers with limited means to oversee the services received by those for whom they have responsibility.

Nonprofits serve combinations of stakeholders who count on the organization to act responsibly and to do the right thing, especially where behavior and performance cannot easily be closely monitored. In this sense, leaders and managers of nonprofit organizations have moral and legal obligations to make the best use of the resources entrusted to them. As David H. Smith puts it, ". . . the *moral* duties of trustees of nonprofit institutions derive from the unique structure of their relationships with beneficiaries and founders." (1995, 125) Since the beginnings of our republic, this special trust relationship with charitable and philanthropic organizations has been understood. Benjamin Franklin, known both for his scrupulous economic practices and his charitable enterprises, virtually personified both the sacredness of philanthropic stewardship and the importance of efficiency in the use of charitable and public resources (Hammack 1998 70–84).

While the moral imperative of responsible stewardship of nonprofit resources is timeless, in recent years the urgency of efficient deployment of these resources has increased considerably. The reason for this is closely related to the basis on which economists attribute value to resources—the concept of *scarcity*. In short, many of the resources that nonprofits deploy in carrying out their work are becoming increasingly scarce over time, hence more valuable, hence more important to manage in the most effective way possible.

Before examining this proposition directly, let us first consider what the idea of scarcity really means. A resource may be extremely useful and important to people's lives, but if it is plentiful—that is, if additional quantities of the resource can be obtained easily—it has little economic value at the margin. However, as such a resource becomes less freely available it becomes more valuable. For example, clean water in a remote mountain setting with plentiful lakes and rivers has no (marginal) economic value, but if industry moves in and begins to pollute the water supply, clean water becomes more scarce and hence more valuable (and worth investing in its maintenance). By contrast, in the 1970s, electronic pocket calculators were useful and rare, and highly valued, selling for several hundred dollars each. Now such calculators are almost literally a dime a dozen, not because they are less useful, but because they are so common and easy to obtain.

The resources associated with nonprofit organizations are more like clean water than pocket electronic calculators—they have generally become more scarce and hence more valuable over time. Consider volunteer effort. While Americans continue to volunteer at impressive rates, they generally have less time to do so than they had twenty or thirty years ago. In particular, women, who have historically constituted the backbone of American volunteerism, are much more engaged in the paid labor market than they were in earlier times. Moreover, the number of nonprofit organizations has increased considerably over the same period, making volunteering a scarcer, more valuable resource for them. From 1987 to 1998, the estimated number of hours formally volunteered in the United

States increased only six percent, while the number of nonprofit organizations increased by 27 percent. It is not surprising, therefore, that the estimated value of hours volunteered increased by 51 percent over this period (Weitzman et al. 2002). In short, volunteer time has become more scarce, hence more valuable, and hence more important to manage effectively.

The same may be said for paid labor utilized by nonprofit organizations. As Anne Preston (1990) has pointed out, nonprofits have historically depended heavily on woman for their leadership and staffing. In some sense, the nonprofit sector has been a sector of opportunity for women at times when opportunities for women's advancement was limited by closed doors and glass ceilings in the business sector. But times have changed, and many new opportunities have opened up for women in the economy at large. So, even though there are now more women in the labor force, women's talent has become a scarcer, more valuable resource for nonprofit organizations, not fully compensated by crossover of some men into the nonprofit sector from the business sector. Overall, average wages paid by nonprofit organizations increased by 52 percent between 1987 and 1998, and by 180 percent between 1977 and 1998 (Weitzman et al. 2002). After accounting for inflation, these figures represent increases of approximately 16 percent and 32 percent, respectively, in "real terms," reflecting the increasingly competitive nature of the nonprofit labor market.

Similar arguments can be made for the various sources of funding available to nonprofit organizations. Charitable donations, for example, constitute approximately 20 percent of the revenues received by nonprofit organizations in the United States. Giving of money has increased steadily in absolute terms since the 1960s, generally following the growth of the overall economy, at the rate of approximately two percent of personal income (Weitzman et al. 2002). Again, however, nonprofit organizations have also grown quickly, both in their number and size. In particular, while charitable contributions increased fourfold between 1977 and 1998, the size of the nonprofit sector as gauged by its expenditures has grown almost six-fold in this same period (Weitzman et al. 2002). Clearly, demands for nonprofit services have grown rapidly, so much so that nonprofits have had to finance these imperatives by shifting to other means. Where charitable giving represented more than 26 percent of the revenues in charitable organizations in 1977, it constituted under 20 percent in 1997 (Weitzman et al. 2002). The flat growth of charitable revenues combined with the increasing number of nonprofits seeking those revenues, has led to intense competition among nonprofits for charitable funding and serious investments in fundraising efforts. In short, charitable funds have become more scarce, hence more valuable to nonprofit organizations. Add to this the fact that charitable resources, freely given to underwrite the public mission of a nonprofit, lie at the heart of such an organization, even if they do not constitute the bulk of its funds. This is essentially what Burton Weisbrod (1988) argues, that qualification for tax exemption be based on an organization's "collective index," i.e., its ratio of donated to other revenues. In any case, charitable resources have become more valuable to nonprofit organizations and so their effective stewardship has become all the more urgent.

Many also argue that government funding of nonprofit organizations has become scarcer too. Here, the history is mixed and complex (Salamon 1999, Salamon 1995, Abramson, Salamon, and Steuerle 1999, and DeVita 1999), but the general pattern was that nonprofits in the United States experienced a significant expansion in the 1960s and 1970s, driven in large part by a major infusion of government funding associated with the Great Society programs initiated by the Johnson administration. Since the late 1970s, however, government has put the brakes on such expenditures, in some cases reversing their levels. There has been some backing and filling, with state and local governments picking up some of the slack from federal cutbacks in the 1980s, as well as shifting of some nonprofit services from social service funding programs that were being reduced, to health funding programs that continued to expand. Generally, however, government funds have become more challenging to secure, involving more competition among alternative suppliers (both for-profit and nonprofit) and increased administrative resources to satisfy government reporting and accountability requirements (Smith 1999). Though the share of public benefit [501(c)(3) and 501(c)(4)] nonprofit organization revenues derived from government increased from 26.6 percent in 1977 to 31.3 percent in 1997, these figures are explained mostly by increases in the health care sector (e.g., Medicare and Medicaid), where the government share rose from 32.4 percent to 42.2 percent over this period. Corresponding figures for social services and arts organizations show declines in government shares, while government shares in the education sector remained fairly constant at around 20 percent (Weitzman et al. 2002). Again, the increasing scarcity of government funds in most areas of the nonprofit sector magnifies their value and mandates their effective stewardship. Even in health care, increased government funding is outpaced by cost inflation.

Scarcity of philanthropic and government funds has driven nonprofit organizations more and more squarely into the marketplace of business and commerce (Young and Salamon 2002). Revenues from fees, charges, commercial ventures and the like, now constitute more than half of all revenues received by United States nonprofit organizations, although this proportion varies considerably by area of service and some of it is underwritten by government subsidy programs (Salamon 1999). With government voucher programs included, Burton Weisbrod (1998) estimated that public benefit [501(c)(3)] nonprofit organizations increased their reliance on commercial income from 69 percent in 1987 to 73.5 percent in 1992. More than half the growth in nonprofit revenue between 1977 and 1996 has been financed through fees (Salamon 1999). As a result, nonprofits compete more fiercely for the consumer dollar, sometimes head to head with for-profit businesses. Here too, increasing scarcity plays a part. Museums and performing arts organizations compete for the dollars people are willing to allocate for culture and recreation. Y's and JCC's compete with each other and with health clubs for the dollars people are willing to spend on physical fitness. Nonprofit home health organizations compete head to head with for-profit firms for the home health care market. Private universities compete for tuition dollars among themselves, with public universities, and even with some new for-profit institutions of higher education. And nonprofit organizations in social and rehabilitation services operate for-profit businesses designed to train and employ disadvantaged workers while they compete for general consumer business. As nonprofits become a more integral part of the world of business, they are learning that market share isn't so easy to build—consumer dollars too are a scarce commodity, becoming more valuable by virtue of both their importance in the overall balance of nonprofit finances and their increasing vulnerability to competition. These funds too must be considered scarce, valuable, and requiring more effective stewardship.

Given this overall picture of resource scarcity, many nonprofits are driven by the mantras to create endowments and reserve funds that would serve as safe havens in the competitive jungles in which they now struggle to survive and grow. In theory, such funds can provide a margin of safety when economic conditions threaten the viability of the organization, providing steady streams of income when other revenue sources turn sour. Even here, however, the concept of scarcity imposes itself. Endowments must be created by allocating scarce resources to the increasingly competitive domain of charitable fundraising. More importantly, endowments require allocating scarce donations to investment markets rather than current charitable uses. And existing endowment resources must be invested wisely in order to ensure that the value of these resources does not dwindle over time. Recent declines in the stock market reflect the difficulty of this challenge during economic downturns, and many organizations have suffered large losses. Moreover, the concept of unrestricted funds, available for discretionary use by nonprofit organizations, is itself under attack.

Donors now want more say over how funds are used, especially endowments—truly unrestricted funds are becoming even scarcer. In addition, nonprofits are no longer an exclusive domain for accumulating tax-exempt resources for dispensation to charitable uses. In particular, for-profit securities firms, such as Merrill Lynch, Fidelity Investments, and Charles Schwab, offer this option to investors with full discretion over how such funds are dispensed. In short, investment revenues derived from accumulated funds have become both more competitive and more valuable to nonprofit organizations.

There are two things that nonprofits can do to address the scarcity of resources with which they are confronted. First, they can seek to address that scarcity directly by competing more effectively for their shares of the economic pie. Second, they can become better at using existing resources to accomplish their goals more efficiently. This book is about both of those approaches, though the latter approach is probably the one that needs the most attention. There are lots of books and consultant resources that will tell you how to raise more funds, position yourself in new markets, undertake new and profitable ventures, recruit and train new people, or seek out additional volunteers. There are few references that can tell you how to use the resources you have at hand in the most effective way to address your mission or to leverage them in a manner that will help you expand the resources available to support that mission. That is the general focus of this book - to offer some general direction, in key areas of nonprofit organization decision-making, for nonprofit managers and leaders seeking to use the resources they have at hand in the most effective possible way. To achieve this purpose we apply some very basic intuitive principles of economic analysis. We adapt these ideas to the nonprofit context and translate them into common-sense terms that every manager should be able to appreciate.

We start with the very basic notion that nonprofit organizations are businesses in the sense that they must compete in various marketplaces and must make financial ends meet. Unlike government, they do not have the power to tax, and they can go bankrupt. But they are more complex than businesses of similar magnitudes because they have multiple ways in which to support themselves—through charitable means, through government support, through investments, and through sales of goods and services in the marketplace.

And nonprofits differ from commercial business in another way that is of primary importance: they are judged by how well they accomplish their charitable or public service missions, not how well they perform financially. Strong financial performance is instrumental to success only as it contributes to mission success; it should not be a stand-alone nonprofit goal in itself. There are a number of ways in which this realization is important. First, it emphasizes the primacy of mission and identifies mission as the touchstone for making all significant non-profit economic choices. Second, it reflects the key fact that nonprofits and commercial organizations are different in a critical way that impacts the choices that they make. While both types of organizations should be equally concerned with using their economic resources effectively, they will often make different choices in similar circumstances because their ultimate goals are different. They will often make different pricing decisions, different decisions about employee compensation, different investments, undertake different kinds of new ventures, engage in different kinds of collaborations, and so on, because they are measuring their success by their impact on a social mission rather than by profitability.

That said, nonprofits can make their special economic choices using many of the same principles of economic analysis as businesses do. Fundamental notions of economic analysis and strategy—such as thinking at the margin, accounting for opportunity and transactions costs, determining comparative (or competitive) advantage in the marketplace, achieving gains from trade, diversifying to hedge against risk, computing market value, determining present value by adding up costs and benefits and discounting them over time, pricing to generate revenues and ration consumption, differentiating products to exploit alternative tastes and willingness to pay, offering product mixes to address synergies among alternative products, or accounting for interactions (cross-elasticities of demand and crowd out effects) between different product lines are all generic considerations that apply conceptually to nonprofit as well as for-profit organizations. However, nonprofits are unused to applying such ideas, and they must be wary not to simply adopt the answers that businesses have reached.

Below, we briefly review some of the forgoing concepts and illustrate how they apply in special ways to nonprofits. In subsequent chapters, these ideas are liberally applied to a wide spectrum of nonprofit economic decisions, in order to provide guidelines and advice in pursuing effective economic decisions along multiple dimensions of managerial responsibility. Our treatment here is not meant to be definitive or comprehensive. The intent is to encourage nonprofit decision-makers to think along certain logical lines that will help them to analyze and make critical choices.

The remainder of this chapter provides a cross-cutting overview along the two dimensions referenced above: areas of nonprofit decision-making and concepts of economic analysis. We offer a tour of the book that explains the various economic analysis concepts and describes the domains of economic decision-making that nonprofits must address. We also explain how the application of economic logic can often lead nonprofits to unique conclusions about how to use their resources most effectively.

Domains of Nonprofit Economic Decision-Making

Part 1 of the book is concerned with core operating decisions that nonprofit managers face in most areas of service provision. Virtually all nonprofit organizations face three types of decisions: how to compensate workers, whether and how to price services, and whether to carry out particular functions inside the organization or contract them to outside suppliers.

Part 2 of the book examines two major resource development functions and issues that most nonprofit organizations face: spending to raise charitable funds, and investing funds and making expenditures from invested funds.

Part 3 of the book considers new strategic directions that many nonprofit organizations are now exploring in order to expand their resources and more effectively address their missions. These include three interrelated strands of activity: new ventures and philanthropic "investing" in these ventures; collaborations with business, government, and other nonprofits; and undertaking commerce and fundraising on the Internet.

Core Functions

Setting prices is perhaps the most fundamental of economic decisions. Economists have long studied the various functions of prices and how they influence economic behavior and performance. In Chapter 2, Sharon Oster, Mel Gray, and Charles Weinberg illustrate that nonprofits are concerned with many of the same considerations about pricing as for-profit firms, but there are also fundamental differences in nonprofit versus for-profit thinking about pricing.

For example, prices serve as rationing or gatekeeping devices, allowing those willing to pay the price to consume the service, and preventing others from doing so. Here is the first key difference between nonprofits and for-profit businesses. For-profits want to exclude those who cannot pay the price necessary for the firm to make a profit. In order to fulfill the organization's mission, nonprofits often want to be inclusive so that they can ensure that as many people as possible (from their target populations) benefit from their services. Nonprofits often must consider whether to even charge a price, and when they do, they may decide to price low and incur a loss.

Second, prices serve as a means of generating revenue. This is the prime function of prices in a for-profit business. It is also an important consideration for nonprofits, but nonprofits face a more complex decision. In some cases, they may decide that prices must be low or zero, and losses must be incurred because the service is so fundamental to the mission. In other cases, they may decide that prices can be set at levels that would generate profits, and to use those profits to subsidize mission through other means.

Third, prices can serve as regulators of behavior in ways that matter to a non-profit. If charging a modest price induces the client of a counseling service to take it more seriously, then price can actually contribute to mission rather than limit mission-related benefits. For-profits would rarely care about such benefits, except perhaps as a selling strategy; e.g., for-profits might charge extra high prices in order to signal that the good or service they are selling is of exceptional quality.

Just as decisions on whether and how much to charge yield different answers for nonprofits versus for-profits, based on similar considerations, so too will decisions on how to differentiate pricing schedules or bundle prices together for different goods or services. In their efforts to maximize profits, for-profit businesses often try to practice price discrimination among different classes of consumers in order to "milk the demand curve," i.e., to take advantage of the fact that certain classes of consumers are willing to pay more for essentially the same product than others. Differential airline fares for business and personal travel illustrate this strategy. Nonprofits also have reasons to differentiate their pricing schedules, but the goal is usually to accommodate certain groups of consumers who would otherwise not be able to afford the service. If some consumers can be convinced or induced to pay more, less advantaged consumers can be included at loss-incurring prices—a practice incompatible with profit-making business strategy, except possibly as a come-on to bring customers in before raising prices to profitable levels.

Similarly, both nonprofits and for-profits may choose to bundle the pricing of multiple services together into packages. As Oster, Gray, and Weinberg observe, nonprofits might do this to enhance various mission-related benefits such as inducing members of arts organizations to sample performances or art works they might not normally be attracted to. For-profits might undertake a similar strategy, but only if they thought the demand for the package would be greater than that for the individual parts, leading to increased profits.

Similar commonalties and differences between nonprofits and for-profits occur in the realm of compensating employees. Here, nonprofits often must decide whether to pay employees or to rely on volunteers. For-profits rarely ever consider this choice. Clearly then, there are benefits of working for nonprofit organizations that can eliminate the need for monetary compensation, just as there are reasons that nonprofits may choose not to charge for their services. Still, as Anne Preston explains in Chapter 3, market wage is a useful concept for helping to determine what to pay workers in both the nonprofit and for-profit sectors.

The market wage level for a given type of employee stems from the equilibration of supply and demand in a particular labor market. Since the business sector is much larger than the nonprofit sector, market wages will generally reflect what individuals with particular skill sets and experiences can command in that sector (except for very specialized labor skills that are largely confined to the nonprofit and/or public sectors). It remains to ask, however, whether nonprofits should necessarily offer that wage level. Preston explains that several factors may compel nonprofits to depart from offering the market wage. She introduces the notion of *labor donations,* which reflects the fact that nonprofits can offer a number of valuable nonpecuniary benefits that may attract certain workers even if the monetary wage is below market. Not the least of these benefits relates to the fact that nonprofit organizations carry out public service work, which workers themselves intrinsically value. Pure volunteerism represents the extreme where those non-pecuniary benefits completely overwhelm the need for monetary compensation. Preston also points out that egalitarian cultures in nonprofit organizations may influence compensation decisions as well. In particular, while individuals working different jobs within the organization may command vastly different sums in the labor market at large, notions of fairness may dictate that the internal differentials be less severe.

Compensation decisions also revolve around the very basic economic concept of incentives. A fundamental assumption in business economics is that people will adjust their behavior in response to material incentives. In particular, they will tend to work harder or more effectively if faced with performance incentives that reward them for more or better work. The concept of offering performance incentives and bonuses is a commonly accepted, relatively noncontroversial notion in for-profit business. It also applies to nonprofit work, but as Preston points out, nonprofits must approach performance incentives differently, for several reasons. First, they must be careful not to encourage self-serving behavior that can be detrimental to mission. For example, if incentives depend on measurements, then the measurements themselves can distort behavior if the intrinsic quality of the work cannot be fully captured by quantitative measures. This is a common experience with the kinds of services that nonprofit organizations provide. (For example, "teaching to the test" does not capture the full quality of educational performance.) Second, nonprofits must avoid inequities that may result from the fact that certain kinds of work within the organization are more easily measurable, and hence more amenable to incentives, than other kinds of work. The classic application here is fundraising, which is easily amenable to incentives compared to direct service work with clients, which is often not easy to measure. Third, nonprofits must avoid allowing material incentives to become so important that they begin to attract workers to the organization who are primarily driven by material motives, which might distort the internal atmosphere and orientation of the organization, or create severe tensions within it. Given these complications in the nonprofit realm, Preston suggests that performance incentives be kept within narrow bounds, but also that collective, organizationwide, rather than individual, incentives be emphasized so that behavior correlates more closely with organizational mission.

Outsourcing is a third core function common to both nonprofit and for-profit organizations, and subject to analysis using common economic concepts. As Avner Ben-Ner discusses in Chapter 4, a number of such concepts are helpful in guiding decisions of whether to perform certain kinds of work within the organization (in-house) or to contract it out to external suppliers. The idea of *opportunity cost* applies here, for example. Opportunity cost represents the value of a resource in its next best alternative use: this is the true cost of any resource that is expended in the course of an economic activity. For example, if a manager decides to contract out a particular function, he or she will have to spend time overseeing contractors—time that might have been better spent focusing more tightly on the core internal functions of the organization. Thus, the decision to contract out depends in part on whether the benefits of contracting out overwhelm the additional opportunity costs of contract supervision—namely the benefits forgone by neglect of core activity. It is unclear whether such opportunity costs are different in a nonprofit than a for-profit organization, but they may very well be. Attention to mission is the heart of nonprofit work. If the nonprofit manager loses that focus in the process of overseeing contractors, the opportunity cost could be extremely high.

Ben-Ner reasons that nonprofits should never consider contracting out functions that constitute the core of its mission-related work because such a practice calls into question the very rationale for a nonprofit's existence. Abandoning that position would indeed entail very high opportunity costs. Ben-Ner employs the basic economic concept of comparative advantage to explain this position—a nonprofit's *comparative advantage* is to produce services that have the characteristics of public goods or which require consumers' trust in circumstances where they face an informational disadvantage. If nonprofits contract out these functions, they are in essence abandoning their *raison d'être*. Just as a for-profit business should keep in-house that which it does more efficiently than other businesses, a nonprofit should do the same. For example, if parents choose a nonprofit day care supplier for their children because they have confidence in its judgments about the kind of care their children will receive, that day care organization should avoid contracting out that care to an outside vendor. While this sounds obvious, Ben-Ner points out that organizations can (and do) consider outsourcing almost any function.

Clearly then, there are some outsourcing choices to be avoided if nonprofits are to preserve their special roles and functions in society. Within those boundaries, however, other concepts of economic analysis are equally useful to both nonprofits and for-profits in guiding their outsourcing decisions. The notion of economic incentives plays a role similar to that in compensation decisions. Under the contracting option, organizations must ask if they can draw up contracts that provide sufficiently explicit terms to ensure that contractors behave in the manner desired, or whether they would be better off relying on the incentives and controls that can be implemented only if the operation were maintained in-house. Such a determination requires the analysis of what economists call *transactions costs* by asking: Is it more costly to do business in the context of the marketplace through contracting or through internal processes of the organization? Again, there is some suggestion that the same analysis will yield different answers for nonprofits versus for-profits. For example, because nonprofits provide services that are harder to measure or evaluate with quantitative performance indicators, it is more difficult for them to implement effective contracts. Thus, in some cases they may favor in-house operation. On the other hand, for those conventional business functions—ranging from bookkeeping and maintenance of computer systems, to building and grounds maintenance—outsourcing may very well be a nonprofit's best choice.

Resource Development Functions

While nonprofit organizations typically support themselves from multiple sources of revenue, the classical source of revenue and the one almost uniquely associated with nonprofits is charitable fundraising. Giving and fundraising for favored causes can be an emotional and tradition-bound activity, but it is nonetheless subject to careful economic examination. Joe Cordes and Patrick Rooney suggest in Chapter 5 that fundraising activity is often insufficiently scrutinized and hence frequently carried out in an inefficient way that wastes valuable resources.

Fundraising is a nonprofit activity that does not have a direct for-profit equivalent, so nonprofits are in some sense truly unique in applying economic principles to this area of economic decision-making. Yet, there are important interconnections and parallels with for-profit activity. For example, the outsourcing decision is critical to fundraising. Should a nonprofit organization raise its own funds, or contract out to for-profit telemarketers and consultants? Lessons can be drawn here from Ben-Ner's chapter. The fundraising function comes close to the heart of a nonprofit's *raison d'être* and comparative advantage. People who give to a nonprofit organization do so because they trust that their contributions will be used to support the organization's mission. Support for the organization may be undermined if contributors learn that high proportions of contributed funds go into the pockets of fundraisers. Yet frequently, even when contracted fundraisers retain most of the take, it may be efficient for nonprofits, especially small ones, to engage them. Fundraising firms that exploit *economies of scale* and *specialization* can simply be more efficient than small nonprofits with less professional development capacity. Hence, the outsourcing decision for fundraising can be a difficult one for nonprofits, weighing the likely levels of revenue return in the short run against the more amorphous losses associated with loss of donor confidence in the long run.

Within the context of fundraising operations, there is another close, even paradoxical parallel between nonprofits and for-profits. In essence, and perhaps within certain cultural and ethical constraints, fundraising is essentially a for-profit activity within the nonprofit organization. Indeed, the very point of fundraising is to maximize net revenues. A successful fundraising operation should therefore emulate the business guidelines of a for-profit business. There is no clearer demonstration of this than by application of the economic concept—*analysis at the margin.* As Cordes and Rooney show, nonprofits can be misled by attention to average costs of fundraising, when they should be focusing on the margin. In order to maximize net returns of fundraising, nonprofits should continue to invest in fundraising activity as long as a dollar spent yields at least a dollar in return—even if the investment drives up the average cost of raising a dollar. Alternatively, nonprofits should reduce their fundraising expenditures if the yield on the marginal dollar spent is less than a dollar in return—even if a so-called "fundraising goal" has not been met. Nonprofit fundraising appears to be traditionally driven by concepts of gross fundraising goals and average costs of fundraising, rather than the more efficient approach of balancing costs and revenues at the margin.

That said, Cordes and Rooney also note several complications that make marginal calculations difficult in practice. First, calculating returns to fundraising can be more complex than computing returns to an ordinary business investment. Expenditures made now may yield returns months or years later. Nonprofits must account for these delays in determining what the yield on another dollar spent really is. As Cordes and Rooney put it, fundraising costs may have to be *amortized* over long periods of time. Second, opportunity costs, which may even exceed the dollars spent explicitly on fundraising activity, must be taken into account. For example, the top personnel of a nonprofit organization—university presidents, orchestra conductors, or chief executive officers—are often directly involved in fund development, raising the question of what is lost in terms of their attention to other aspects of the organization's mission. Moreover, fundraising activity often involves considerable volunteer effort—a real resource that must be evaluated in terms of its value in this context versus in other activities. Finally, fundraising activity must account for possible losses in other revenue streams. Economists call this *crowding out*. For example, if a nonprofit is successful in raising additional charitable funds, government may be able to drive a harder bargain in paying for contracted services. Alternatively, fundraising may have positive *crowding in* effects that increase its returns, e.g., when additional paying customers are drawn to an organization that can portray itself as a charitable success.

Finally, Cordes and Rooney observe that the very concept of efficiency in fundraising, and its parallel with profit maximization at the level of the individual organization, may be called into question in the nonprofit world. They distinguish between *organizational efficiency* and *social efficiency* in fundraising, noting that from a societal point of view, it may be sensible to discourage fundraising competition among nonprofits in favor of fundraising collaboration so that total net charitable revenue for the community is maximized rather than that for any individual organization. In the business world, such collaboration would generally be frowned upon as anticompetitive. In the nonprofit world, it is encouraged through federated fundraising appeals. For the federated fundraising organization, such as a United Way or a Jewish Community Federation, the logic of net revenue maximization—equating marginal costs and returns at the margin—continues to apply at the community level, although difficult decisions need to be made about the allocation of the funds raised. Nonprofits that participate in federated appeals (assuming they have a choice) face a different calculation: what share from the federated fundraising campaign makes it worthwhile for the organization to participate? Here, the organization must know its own calculus of fundraising returns on different levels of expenditure and compare its potential with that promised from the joint campaign. Other factors may also be involved, such as supporting a larger community mission embodied by the federated organization. In all, the calculation of net returns to fundraising, while benefiting from the business analog, must reflect these various complexities of the nonprofit context.

The same is true of the decisions nonprofits make in investing the funds they maintain in endowments and other types of accounts. On their face, these decisions closely parallel the types of decisions made by private investors and financial institutions. As Marion Fremont-Smith instructs in Chapter 6, the concept of *total return,* while relatively new to the lingo of nonprofit organizations, still applies. Given recent changes in the law, nonprofits now have the flexibility, and indeed are mandated, to pursue returns on their investments that account for growth in the capital value of securities as well as dividend or interest income. Moreover, in pursuing total return on their investments, nonprofits should attend to the same basic principles of portfolio analysis as private sector investors do. In particular, investments should be diversified to hedge against risk, and portfolios should be designed to reflect the risk profile of the organization.

But, as with other areas of economic decision-making, there are complications and complexities in the nonprofit world that cause nonprofit investment decisions to diverge from their for-profit counterparts. For example, in the nonprofit case, diversification is often constrained by donor requirements—a practice that can put the financial health of nonprofit institutions at considerable risk. Moreover, it is often not clear whose risk preferences should be reflected in a nonprofit organization's decisions—those of the donor, the beneficiaries of nonprofit services, the particular trustees who govern the organization, or the general public? This is an area requiring more intensive scrutiny and research.

The nature of alternative investments may also differ for nonprofits compared to business or private investors. The relationship between a particular investment and the mission of the nonprofit organization is especially important. This relationship can play out in several ways. Ethical considerations may preclude otherwise lucrative investments. For example, a health care organization would not want to invest in a tobacco company. Moreover, the nonprofit may wish to consider program-related investments, which directly contribute to the organization's mission but may entail larger risks or lower financial returns than alternative investments. Here, the nonprofit must weigh the opportunity costs: what will be lost in mission-related terms if the extra financial return from a conventional investment is used to promote program, compared to the direct mission benefits returned on the program-related investment? Similar logic applies to investment in the internal needs of the organization versus external securities. In mission-related terms, will the return from a new computer system, or a staff training program, be greater than what might be accomplished with the financial returns from an external investment? For-profit businesses must make these calculations too, though the returns that matter to them are purely financial, whereas nonprofits sometimes need to assess the alternative impacts on their mission, which can be difficult to measure.

Finally, the concept of return on investment implies that the investing institution has a clear idea of the value of its assets. For a for-profit investor this is usually a straightforward calculation of market value—of securities, real estate, facilities and equipment, etc. As Fremont-Smith notes, the exercise of asset valuation can be much more challenging to nonprofits. Nonprofits maintain some unique assets, such as art collections, for which sale is constrained, and which in some ways contribute directly to mission just by being in place. Such assets have limited liquidity and cannot easily be deployed in alternative ways. Hence, the way they are valued and included in total return calculations represents a special challenge to nonprofits, worthy of further analysis.

Similarly, nonprofits and for-profits can both employ the logic of analysis at the margin to consider their investment decisions; how much one should allocate to one investment versus another can be a matter of equating returns at the margin. Given alternative investments of equal risk, it makes sense to continue to invest in the alternative with the higher marginal return, up to the point where the marginal return drops below that of the other investment. This logic seems especially relevant to decisions on whether to invest internally within the organization or to invest externally. If investments in staff training initially yield higher returns in terms of mission achievement, that may be a more sensible choice than external financial securities, up to the point where returns on training taper off.

The concepts of *cost-benefit analysis* also apply to both nonprofit and for-profit investing, but again with important differences. In particular, cost-benefit analysis requires that decision makers add up the costs and benefits of alternative investments over time, so that they can compare *present value*—i.e., the equivalent net value if all costs and benefits are projected back into the current time period. Such calculations require using an appropriate *discount rate* that reflects the decision maker's relative valuation of present and future benefits and costs. Just as for risk preference, this raises difficult questions for a nonprofit organization. Should a nonprofit be oriented to maintaining itself indefinitely into the future, or should it gauge its time preferences in terms of how long it might take to accomplish its mission? Some nonprofits might be better advised to invest for the short term so that they can concentrate their resources on solving an immediate problem, such as a cure for AIDS, even if that means going out of business in the relatively near future. Other organizations may have missions, such as maintaining the quality of life in a given community, that reflect the need for permanence.

Nowhere is the issue of time preference reflected more strongly in the nonprofit world than in the debate over payout policy for grant-making foundations. Fremont Smith points out that foundation payout policy is more likely to conform to the minimum five percent level required by law than reflect a serious evaluation of time preferences relative to mission. Here is a particular area where nonprofits could benefit from attention to the basic principles of cost-benefit analysis.

Finally, nonprofit investment and expenditure experience can also benefit from other applications of basic economic principles, but again with special considerations. For example, nonprofits can benefit from *gains from trade,* just as businesses do in dealing with one another, or as consumers do in making purchases in the market place. Fremont-Smith notes the particular application that results from nonprofits' special tax-exempt status: In some circumstances, such as public housing, nonprofits can trade—through leaseback arrangements—their rights to tax benefits, which are worthless to them as exempt entities, but which can be valuable to profit-making businesses. The idea of gains from trade is that both parties, though they probably value different things, are better off after the trade. This concept carries forward into the domain of institutional partnership arrangements.

New Strategic Directions

In recent years, nonprofit organizations have developed a variety of new initiatives in response to a changing economic environment in order to maintain and extend their resource capacities and more effectively address their missions. These initiatives often take the form of new programmatic ventures, often of a commercial character. While entrepreneurial activity, including commercial initiatives, has long been a part of the repertoire of nonprofit organizations in the United States, the last few decades have witnessed both a significant increase in the level of this activity and also changes in its forms (Young and Salamon 2002). For example, some funders have taken a new approach to this phenomenon in the form of "venture philanthropy," emulating venture capitalists in the business sector by emphasizing organizational development and capacity building, as well as social returns on their investments. Nonprofits themselves have begun to reach out in their venture activity, forming new partnerships and collaborations with other nonprofits and with business corporations as well as government. Nonprofits are also exploiting modern information and communications technologies by undertaking new initiatives in Internet commerce and fundraising.

All of these new approaches require the discipline of careful economic decision-making and the application of economic analysis principles to the special context of the nonprofit enterprise. For example, the assessment of new venture possibilities entails assessment of economic costs and benefits on the part of both the nonprofit organization itself and the philanthropic organizations that may choose to provide the seed money and start-up capital. Again, while there is a direct analogy between this context and undertaking new ventures in the business context, there are also important differences that can lead to very different choices and outcomes.

Consider the notion of return on investment, as suggested in Chapter 7 by Howard Tuckman. In the nonprofit context, the returns are not just financial profits, but a broader notion of social return that includes several other contributing benefits and costs. Ventures must be assessed directly in terms of what they contribute to the organization's mission and also what effects they produce that might detract from that mission. Moreover, several ventures can be considered in tandem, where cross-subsidization is possible and where the financial success of one activity can underwrite another activity that produces mission-related benefits at a financial loss. In addition, more subtle (opportunity) costs must be considered, such as losses in organizational morale and productivity that might result from cultural clashes between profit-oriented and mission-oriented people within the same organization. In all, the components of the social return of a nonprofit venture can be multiple and complex, and the costs more than just the dollar expenditures involved. The return on investment calculation for a nonprofit must be made on a broader basis than simple financial success, hence the kinds of ventures that nonprofits and their financial backers choose to undertake are likely to differ substantially from those that might be pursued in the business context.

Even on purely financial dimensions, nonprofit concerns differ from those of for-profit organizations. As Tuckman explains, nonprofits have to contemplate the possibilities of crowd-out and crowd-in if the generation of commercial revenues affects other revenue streams. For example, successful commercial ventures could undermine donor sympathies leading to reduced charitable contributions. Alternatively, foundation funders may view the financial success of commercial initiatives as a sign of a healthy organization, and be willing to maintain or increase their subsequent support. There is no direct analogy to crowding in and out in the for-profit sector. While businesses need to assess the impact on sales of existing products when they introduce a new one, they are solely concerned with sales revenues, not cross-effects of very different kinds of revenue streams.

Finally, the consideration of new ventures raises the issue of an organization's product mix and the differentiation of its product line. In the business sector, *product differentiation* often makes good sense—it allows a firm to take advantage of different consumer tastes and to move from a commodity orientation, in which the firm has little control over price, to more of a customized focus where the firm has some market power in the particular product niches that it establishes. This reasoning applies to nonprofit organizations as well. Moreover, it forces nonprofit organizations to think about what they do best, in relation to each other and to potential for-profit competitors. As usual, however, the nonprofit picture is more complex. Nonprofits do best what their for-profit counterparts cannot do very well—offer goods and services with a public goods character that often require subsidy. As noted, nonprofits often accomplish this by differentiating their services so that some of them are profitable and can underwrite other services that more directly reflect the mission. However, if a nonprofit cannot compete very well with business in its for-profit niche, this option is muted or even precluded. Nonprofit hospitals once produced a lot of charity care and emphasized public goods such as research and education of physicians. They now do much less of this kind of activity because for-profit hospitals have competed away the surpluses of various product lines that used to be profitable (Sloan 1998). In sum, it behooves nonprofits to differentiate their service lines with new ventures that are not only profitable in the short run, but can be maintained over the long term in the face of potential profit-making competitors. This is a very special challenge, and as Tuckman hints, it requires choices that take advantage of a nonprofit's unique assets. For-profit competitors cannot sell Museum of Art tee shirts or Girl Scout cookies. Nonprofits need to look close to home even to find mission-related ventures that can help them generate profits!

There is another, perhaps more fertile, tack in the pursuit of nonprofit ventures that can bring nonprofits and for-profits into greater harmony. The possibilities for institutional collaboration, particularly between nonprofits and businesses, are explored by Jim Austin in Chapter 8. In essence, business-nonprofit collaborations are intended to exploit the relative strengths of each partner, and to their mutual advantage. Nonprofits can bring great credibility, consumer trust, and often specific programmatic knowledge and skills to a partnership. Businesses can bring their commercial acumen, market visibility, and significant financial resources to bear. Businesses now recognize that partnering with nonprofits can often be a good business proposition, not just a charitable or public relations gesture. Nonprofits now recognize that they no longer have to approach corporations cup-in-hand through the corporate contributions window, but can bring serious business proposals through corporate departments of marketing, human resource development, strategic initiative, and other mainstream offices. Rather than competing head to head, collaborations can allow businesses and nonprofits to exploit their individual advantages in tandem with one another as they share the benefits.

The decision to partner with another institution should be scrutinized using many of the economic analysis concepts that we have reviewed for other aspects of nonprofit economic decision-making. The exercise would be similar for two businesses considering an alliance or a merger, though again, the details and the results differ for nonprofits. Various concepts apply. For example, partnerships can be viewed from the perspective of gains from trade. Austin refers to the creation of "win-win" situations, reflecting the fact that partnerships are voluntary arrangements that make no sense unless both partners come out ahead. For business partners, the potential benefits they seek are fairly clear. Marketing, human resource, community relations, and other benefits should lead to increases in the corporation's productivity and outreach, and ultimately its profitability. For the nonprofit partner, however, benefits can be both financial, enabling the nonprofit to support its mission more fully, and directly mission-related, such as a partnership that helps to project the nonprofit's social message to a wider audience. For example, when a corporation supports a running marathon devoted to raising funds for research on a particular disease, that event can achieve substantial media coverage for the cause as well as generate direct financial support for the charity. Both the business and the nonprofit partners must assess costs of the venture as well, to ensure that the net benefits are positive and that the proposition is indeed win-win. The nonprofit must concern itself with its reputation and image (including possible loss of credibility with its donors) as it becomes publicly associated with a particular corporation, while the corporation must concern itself with the expenditure outlays it commits to, as well as the consequences should the venture fail. Both partners must apply the concept of opportunity costs, particularly in connection with the time that partnership arrangements require from top leadership. Many of the examples that Austin cites work well because of the substantial commitment of top leadership of both the for-profit and nonprofit partners. Yet these commitments are also costly in terms of what those leaders could have accomplished had they devoted themselves to other activities.

The concept of gains from trade is also helpful in considering the symmetry of nonprofit partnerships. Partners to a voluntary deal do not like to feel exploited, even if the arrangement is technically "win-win." If the benefits are heavily one-sided, or if one partner seems to have received more than seems fair, partnerships may fall apart. This can be a particular issue for nonprofits partnering with large corporations. Dealing in the stratosphere of big business is a relatively new experience for nonprofits, even for large national charities. Hence, it is difficult for them to assess the value of what they bring to business deals and how much that is worth to their business partners. How much will a corporation's profitability increase if it can claim the confidence of a large, respected national charity? And do the benefits of the deal to the nonprofit fairly reflect a reasonable share of that increased profitability? In the world of business, answers to these kinds of questions can be estimated by projections of stock price changes. In the nonprofit domain, the issue remains much more of an art than a science.

Finally, the decision to partner again raises interesting questions of risk and diversification. As Austin indicates, it is not simply a matter of nonprofits spreading the risk of partnerships by diversifying their portfolio of partners. Indeed, there are substantial counter pressures to limit the number of partnerships and to develop them in depth. Business-nonprofit partnerships seem to work best when the two organizations really get to know one another and work together over a long period of time. Yet the development of more exclusive arrangements entails great risk if something goes sour. No doubt, similar considerations apply to business-to-business collaborations, but in that realm exclusionary arrangements are discouraged by the need to avoid the appearance of collusion. Both nonprofits and for-profits want to achieve desirable combinations of risk and return in their collaborations, but they need to pursue these portfolios in different ways.

The new domain of Internet commerce and fundraising reflects many of the considerations that apply to new ventures and collaborations. For example, as Dov Te'eni and Julie Kendall describe in Chapter 9, there are a variety of business models that nonprofits can consider in undertaking fundraising and the pursuit of new initiatives through the Internet, including: 1) corporate advertising on a nonprofit's Web site in exchange for payments or donations; 2) profit-sharing arrangements wherein statements on corporate Web sites signal to consumers that profits will be shared with particular charities; 3) referral portals wherein nonprofit or for-profit Web sites refer browsers to selected charities; and 4) for-profit businesses that raise money for charities on the Web. Sorting out what kind of arrangements may be best for a particular nonprofit organization entails applying many of the same concepts that we have alluded to throughout this chapter. For instance, options 1 and 2 require assessment of the gains from trade - whether the nonprofit will receive a positive return (when all relevant mission-related costs and benefits are considered) and a fair share of the benefits, as well as a review of all the other considerations that go into cultivation of successful collaborations.

Option 3 can be considered from either a sole venture or collaboration point of view. Nonprofits and businesses can mutually agree to use their own portals to refer browsers to each others' sites, or they can undertake individually to serve audiences of potential donors who wish to utilize a referral service to help with decisions to give or volunteer. In the first case, nonprofit and business partners will have to sort through the gains from trade, while in the second case the venturing organizations will have to compute the returns on the new venture—the overall social returns to the nonprofit, and the specific financial returns to the for-profit entering this market.

Option 4 raises the question of outsourcing for nonprofits—in what circumstances should a nonprofit attempt to raise its own funds on the Web versus using a commercial fundraising business? This question, of course, relates directly to the issues analyzed in Chapter 5 by Cordes and Rooney, including the chilling effect of potentially high fundraising cost ratios on the level of contributions offered by donors.

Running throughout Te'eni's and Kendall's discussion of nonprofit Internet initiatives is the question of nonprofits' comparative advantages and disadvantages in the virtual realm; central to this question is the issue of trust. Allowing a disreputable corporation to advertise on a nonprofit Web site (option 1) can erode trust. Profit-sharing arrangements on corporate Web sites (option 2) can exploit the trust that consumers have put in their designated charities, by association extending credibility to the participating corporation. But if promises of corporate support are not delivered or are meager in comparison with the magnitude of the corresponding commercial transactions, the trust and confidence of consumers/donors in both the corporation and the participating nonprofit will be undermined. If nonprofit referral services (option 3) point donors to questionable charities, then their comparative advantage with for-profit referral ventures will be eroded, because that advantage must be built on the special trust that the donating public is willing to put in a nonprofit service. By extension, trust will also be lost in meritorious nonprofits that are included in the mix of referrals with other, less desirable ones. And if nonprofits employ for-profit Internet businesses to raise money on the Web, trust in those charities may be at risk if the fundraisers are unethical or if they garner unconscionable shares of the take.

All of this raises an essential consideration that, in Te'eni's and Kendall's analysis differentiates nonprofit and for-profit ventures on the Web: the key to nonprofit success is building trust with donors and consumers. Indeed, it is this consideration that may bode well for nonprofit success on the Web over the long term. Donors and consumers are increasingly barraged with enormous quantities of sometimes confusing information. If nonprofits can exploit their special advantage as trusted intermediaries, to sort this information and make worthy recommendations and referrals in connection with charitable causes, they may be able to succeed where straightforward profit-making businesses cannot (see Te'eni and Young, 2003).

And We're Off

The following chapters cover a lot of ground, some of it new, and much of it considered from a different perspective than previous discussions of nonprofit organizational decision-making. While the scope of these chapters is very wide, it represents only a start in terms of the number of topics that could be considered and the depth in which each topic can ultimately be pursued. Together they sketch an ongoing agenda for the development of practical guidelines for wise economic decision-making by nonprofit organizations, and they suggest a research agenda to flesh out and test these guidelines in a variety of practical circumstances. As such, this book should be considered a beginning, with its subject matter to be revisited, revised, enhanced, and updated periodically.

Even at this stage, however, common themes and lessons run across the various chapters as they focus on alternative dimensions of nonprofit management decisions. In Chapter 10, we flesh out some of these threads, as touchstones for contemporary nonprofit decision makers and as building blocks for a more comprehensive body of practical knowledge for those making nonprofit economic and business decisions in the future. None of these themes is completely surprising, but they are remarkable in the pervasiveness with which they apply to a wide spectrum of nonprofit economic decisions. What are these themes?

- The primacy and centrality of mission in making economic choices

- The difficulties of codifying mission-related effects as a practical matter

- The acknowledgment of qualitative as well as quantitative benefits and costs

- The tensions between addressing mission and responding to market opportunities and incentives

- The importance of diversification in addressing risk among alternative choices

- The importance of external accountability as a driver in economic choices and the tension between focusing on core capabilities and responding to multiple stakeholders

- The impact of rapid change in the nonprofit environment and the capacity to adjust with new economic choices

Nonprofits have come to recognize that they are economic entities, with economic impacts and economic issues, as well as instruments of social purpose and social change. As they confront the scarcity of their resources, the importance of responsible economic decision-making has become all the more obvious. But nonprofits are also learning that they are not ordinary business enterprises and that in many ways their economic decisions entail complexities and subtleties with which businesses have little experience. Nonprofit managers cannot simply pick up business textbooks and apply the guidelines without modification. They need their own texts. This is a start.

References

Abramson, Alan J., Lester M. Salamon and C. Eugene Steuerle. 1999. "The Nonprofit Sector and the Federal Budget: Recent History and Future Directions." Chapter 2 in Elizabeth T. Boris and C. Eugene Steuerle (eds.). *Nonprofits & Government*. Washington, D.C.: The Urban Institute. 99–139.

De Vita, Carol J. 1999. "Nonprofits and Devolution: What Do We Know?" Chapter 6 in Elizabeth T. Boris and C. Eugene Steuerle (eds.). *Nonprofits & Government*. Washington, D.C.: The Urban Institute. 213–233.

Hammack, David C. (ed.) 1998. *Making the Nonprofit Sector in the United States: A Reader*. Bloomington: Indiana University Press.

Preston, Anne E. 1990. "Changing Labor Market Patterns in the Nonprofit and For-Profit Sectors: Implications for Nonprofit Management." *Nonprofit Management and Leadership*. 1(1):15 28.

Salamon, Lester M. 1999. *America's Nonprofit Sector: A Primer*. New York: The Foundation Center.

Salamon, Lester M. *Partners in Public Service*. 1995. Baltimore: The Johns Hopkins University Press.

Sloan, Frank A. 1998. "Commercialism in Nonprofit Hospitals." Chapter 8 in Burton A. Weisbrod (ed.). *To Profit or Not to Profit*. New York: Cambridge University Press. 151–168.

Smith, David H. *The Moral Responsibilities of Trusteeship*. 1995. Bloomington: Indiana University Press.

Smith, Steven Rathgeb. 1999. "Government Financing of Nonprofit Activity." Chapter 5 in Elizabeth T. Boris and C. Eugene Steuerle (eds.). *Nonprofits & Government*. Washington, D.C.: The Urban Institute. 177–210.

Te'eni, Dov and Dennis R. Young. 2003. " The Changing Role of Nonprofits in the Network Economy." *Nonprofit and Voluntary Sector Quarterly*. September 32(3). 397–414.

Weisbrod, Burton A. (ed.) 1998. *To Profit or Not to Profit*, New York: Cambridge University Press.

Weisbrod, Burton A. 1998. *The Nonprofit Economy*, Cambridge: Harvard University Press.

Weitzman, Murray S., Nadine T. Jaladoni, Linda Lampkin, and Thomas H. Pollak. 2002. *The New Nonprofit Almanac and Desk Reference*. San Francisco: Jossey-Bass.

Young, Dennis R. and Lester M. Salamon, "Commercialization, Social Ventures, and For-Profit Competition." Chapter 13 in Lester M. Salamon (ed.). 2002. *The State of Nonprofit America*. Washington, D.C.: Brookings Institution Press. 423–446.

Chapter 2

Pricing in the Nonprofit Sector

Sharon M. Oster
Charles M. Gray
Charles Weinberg

Abstract

This chapter explores the twin questions of whether nonprofits should price their services and how they should structure their prices. We begin by making an argument on the benefits of pricing, including reducing congestion, motivating both staff and clients, and providing better information. Problems in moving from zero or low prices to higher prices are also spotlighted. Then we explore pricing structures: What should be the relationship between prices and costs? Can organizations differentially price their services based on user or service characteristics? Should they? We rely on numerous examples from a range of nonprofits to make the case in favor of the judicious use of economics-based pricing.

Setting Up the Problem

Nonprofit organizations vary considerably in their reliance on earned income. Religious organizations, for example, on average earn less than 10 percent of their revenues from fees, while for many educational and health care institutions earned income is the dominant revenue source. Nevertheless, across the spectrum of nonprofits, we have seen growth in the reliance on fee-for-service activities. Some organizations have found new ways to generate revenues from their existing client base, while others, particularly those serving lower income clients, have found ways to use their skills and assets to create goods and services for sale to new populations. The Metropolitan Museum of New York, for example, generates over $75 million from merchandise sales, largely to existing museum-goers. A number of nonprofit schools offer fee-based after-school programs to their student bodies. For these organizations, already well versed in the use of fees, many questions emerge in trying to understand the relationship between fees in the core mission activities versus these ancillary services. NFTE, an organization that uses entrepreneurship to teach skills to inner-city youth, also markets their materials to more affluent populations. A number of community development organizations have begun selling technical assistance to small for-profits as a way to augment resources available for their community-based work. For these organizations, finding new markets for the expertise developed in core businesses and learning to price for those new markets is an exciting new challenge.

In this chapter, we explore some of the complicated issues associated with pricing in the third sector, with a particular focus on lessons for the nonprofit practitioner.

It is useful to think of pricing in the nonprofit sector as involving two somewhat distinct decision points. First is the decision about whether to price at all. In contrast to most of the for-profit sector, the nonprofit sector's access to alternative funding mechanisms means that for some organizations, for some periods, actually not charging for services may be a viable strategy. Our first set of issues has to do with this decision point: What tips organizations toward charging for services previously supplied for free, or to seek new fee-for-service activities to supplement their traditional offerings? Are there special mission- or business-related problems as organizations begin to cross this line?

Once the decision has been made to use pricing, a second set of issues arises: How should one set price levels? Should everyone be charged the same prices, or should we give discounts for certain types of clients? What form should prices take? Should we charge one price for a collection of services, or a menu of prices for narrowly defined services? Looking at many of these issues cuts to the heart of the complexities of the competing objectives of many nonprofits, and the struggle between commercial viability and mission preservation.

When to Charge Prices At All?

For many nonprofit managers, charging fees for services is an ugly necessity; ugly because fees tend to reduce the services demanded by clients, but necessary to provide the funds that allow that organization to provide services at all. In a world of unlimited resources, many would opt for offering their services for free. We will focus our discussion in this chapter by challenging this position, and by highlighting some of the benefits of charging fees beyond the revenue-generating properties.

But before we turn to the positives of pricing, it is helpful to acknowledge the downside. For most nonprofits, service provision is a key metric of success. Indeed, there is a wide range of academic literature that speaks to the ways in which nonprofits use service levels as an alternative to profits (Liu and Weinberg 2001, and Weisbrod 1998). Museums measure success in part by attendance levels; hospitals by occupancy or treatment levels; social service agencies by clients served. The way nonprofits build service levels under these circumstances is to increase quality on the one hand, and, given quality levels, lower prices on the other. In markets where there are good substitutes for the nonprofit's services, demand will be relatively responsive to prices, and the nonprofit will indeed find itself in the position we described earlier - torn between the need for revenue and the interest in maintaining service levels. Museums provide a cogent example. Evidence suggests that museum attendance is relatively *elastic*, and that moving from no price to a positive price may well have a disproportionately high impact. Attendance levels are considerably higher at the public museums that charge no fee than at the fee-charging nonprofits, even when holding size and quality of the collections constant (Goetzmann and Oster 2001). As we will see later in this chapter, one strategy to partially avoid the negative effect that setting fees has on reducing client use is to charge fees predominantly to the most able to pay clients through a process of *differential pricing*. Differential pricing can also serve the redistributional goals of some nonprofits.

> In 1999, under a new Director of Athletics, Yale University decided to eliminate charges for student tickets to most athletic events. In this case, the university decided to forego the ticket revenue in the hopes of building a fan base to reinforce college spirit.

In sum, one part of the "ugly necessity" of fees comes from the effect of those fees on reducing demand. Another piece comes from the ideological side. One could imagine circumstances in which an organization's mission is threatened by the imposition of a fee for service, even if the fees do not reduce the service demand. Although the American Red Cross could likely charge a fee for its disaster relief, doing so would fly in the face of the organization's mission.

How important it is to an organization that it may lose clients or patrons as a consequence of charging fees for service will depend a good deal on just what role that service plays in the organization's overall mission. Many organizations find it useful to characterize their different programs using the simple Program Matrix provided below in Figure 1. On the horizontal axis, the contribution of the program to an organization's core mission is measured. On the vertical axis, the program is rated in terms of revenue-generating ability. Clearly, one should avoid programs in the lower left-hand quadrant, which bring neither money nor mission benefits to the organization. The central fact of this perspective is to note that the stronger the service of a program is to an organization's mission, the more the organization should worry about any demand lost as a consequence of charging fees. Trying to move programs from the bottom right-hand corner in which they rate high on mission and low on revenue can sometimes result in a program that moves to the left in the matrix at least as fast as it moves up. An aim of this paper is to provide some guidance to avoid this scenario.

FIGURE 1: Program Matrix

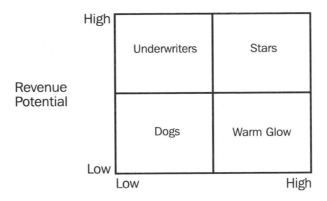

Contribution to the Mission

Of course, sometimes charging a fee makes no practical economic sense. For example, the cost of collecting fees may at times exceed the revenue raised from such fees. This is most common when the costs of monitoring usage are very high, for example in a recreational area with no natural fences or in an infrequently used facility. In addition, many nonprofits, such as Mothers Against Drunk Driving, advocate behavior patterns that are socially beneficial, and for which there is no direct service on which fees could be levied.

While acknowledging the dark side to pricing, however, we want to focus instead on the less-often discussed advantages of charging prices—advantages that transcend the power of fees to generate revenues. (Of course, we want also to acknowledge the power of revenue from users to help a nonprofit control its own destiny). We see possible advantages from charging fees for service coming from both the client side and the provider side.

Issues of congestion provide the first, simplest example. If we charge a zero price, anyone deriving even the smallest value from a service will enter the market. But in some circumstances, new clients create bottlenecks and congestion that reduce service quality for the rest of the service population. Waiting times in health care services, crowds at museum exhibitions, noise at recreational facilities are all familiar examples of what economists have called *externalities in consumption*. In these circumstances, the negative congestion effects may be so large that some clients stop wanting the service at all. Steinberg and Weisbrod (1998) refer to this case as one in which allocation occurs through quality dilution. In these cases, prices can be used to reduce congestion, and will result in an improvement in the quality of service for the remaining clients, even as the quantity of services declines. In this example, pricing is a vehicle for improving quality. Of course, prices are not the only solution to congestion, but they often can appear more even-handed than other selection techniques. (See Steinberg and Weisbrod 1998, for a discussion of waiting lists versus prices as rationing devices by nonprofits and for-profits in the same industry.)

Pricing can also help to change the timing of demand. By offering a lower fee for off-peak use of a service, an organization may be able to stretch its capacity to offer service to more people. Recreation centers, for example, may charge a lower fee during the day to encourage people to use the facilities at times other than morning or evening peaks when demand stretches capacity limits.

The issue of congestion highlights one of the curiosities of the times when a nonprofit may begin to think about charging a fee for its services. In some cases, it is the popularity of an organization's services, coupled with some economic or mission-driven limit on its capacity, that causes the organization to institute fees. This contrasts nicely with the circumstance in which a nonprofit is driven to charge fees when its market declines and it finds itself "pushed" into the act.

Instituting fees can further serve to change client behavior in ways that improve the nonprofit's ability to achieve the outcomes it desires. For many nonprofits, the goal of service provision is to effect a change in the client, not simply to satisfy the client. Of course, we see some of this interest in changing client behavior in the for-profit sector as well, particularly around issues of addiction services. But among nonprofits an interest in changing clients, rather than simply serving clients with existing preferences is more common. Museums, for example, take as a goal the education of the aesthetic sensibilities of viewers, not simply whether they enjoyed an exhibit and plan to return. Many social service agencies are devoted to changing client behavior and attitudes. Paying a modest fee may increase the likelihood that a patient will stick with a treatment program in physical or occupational rehabilitation. In the education sphere, we have struggled mightily against the view that students are "customers" in the for-profit sense, and attempt instead to mold young minds. (See Jane Smiley's *Moo* [1995] for a biting satire of this practice.) In this process, the attitude and cooperation of the client is often key in producing high-quality results. Numerous studies have suggested that in many circumstances, forcing clients to pay at least some fee, however modest in its revenue-generating properties, creates buy-in for those clients and can be mission-enhancing. In instituting a fee, we have fewer clients, but higher success rates with the clients we do have.

In an experimental study, Yoken and Berman (1984) demonstrate that before psychotherapy even began, clients who expected not to pay for treatment anticipated gaining significantly less from their sessions than those who were told they would be charged a fee. In a field setting, Kotler and Roberto (1989) reported that patients avoided a newly established free clinic in a South American hospital because, "they were not convinced of the quality and attention they would receive in the hospital" (p. 175). As a result, the hospital decided to charge a fee and the number of patients increased. However, it should be noted that when clients have a stronger basis for judging product or service quality, the role of price as a cue for high quality is more limited.

There are also times when charging some fee helps to preserve the dignity of clients served. The Cleveland Jewish Community Center, for example, recently introduced a transportation program for seniors, providing rides for doctor visits, shopping and other activities. Each senior paid "$1 per leg." Revenue raised in this manner is relatively modest, for there is no real congestion issue, and the service is not intended to change client behavior. The fee clearly does have a role to play, by signaling to seniors that they contribute to the program, that it is not strictly charity. For populations that are "newly needy" charging a modest fee may be much preferable to no fee at all.

In addition, charging a price may have an effect on the staff and management of the nonprofit itself. When a client is paying for a service—even at a highly reduced rate—providers may become more attentive to his or her needs. Even providers can find themselves lulled by the zero price of a service into thinking it is of zero or minimal value, particularly in our increasingly commercialized world. To the extent that prices are set with some eye towards costs, which we will discuss shortly, setting a price to the client may also encourage cost control. Controlling costs to help a favored client is much more motivational than controlling those same costs to please the agency's business manager.

Finally, charging a fee provides an opportunity for a nonprofit organization to set promotional prices to stimulate demand. The highly regarded Vancouver Public Aquarium, for example, charges a fee for attendance. It also offers an occasional free day, during which attendance often doubles. Giving something away free that normally carries a price can increase demand well beyond what one would find were the service always free. Here we have an example in which psychology clearly trumps economics.

Table 1 below summarizes the considerations associated with deciding whether or not to charge a price for a particular service. If we look at the table and consider the examples given earlier, they lead us to an interesting conclusion: Both the demand reduction and the ideological baggage that come with instituting fees for service in the nonprofit sector can, depending on the circumstances, either help the performance of a nonprofit or hurt it. Such fees can lower congestion and motivate clients to reinforce the objectives of the nonprofit, or they can reduce the effectiveness of the organization by reducing service levels, at some ideological cost. As with many features of management, the secret is in the application, and in matching the right sauce to the right main course.

TABLE 1: Pricing in Nonprofits

Charging Prices is most beneficial when:

- Demand is relatively inelastic, i.e., quantity demanded does not fall very much as price is increased

- Collecting fees is practical

- Charging fees does not violate organizational norms

- The nonprofit suffers congestion or peak problems

- Fees can motivate staff/client behavior

- Fees have positive behavioral effects

Transition Issues

Before we turn to look at pricing structure, it is worthwhile to consider some of the issues associated with the dynamics of pricing. In particular, we are interested in what happens to organizations as they price a good or service that previously was offered *gratis*, or alternatively, at dramatically high prices.

The recent experience in the dot-com business world is informative as we think about beginning to charge for previously free services. In a number of the e-commerce businesses, entrepreneurs worked with business plans that contemplated offering a product or service for free initially, whetting the audience's appetite for the service and then instituting a charge. *Slate*, an online magazine devoted to Internet technology and business issues, worked from this model. The major music companies, like Sony and EMI, are implementing programs to charge for online music, which has recently been freely available via technologies like Napster. As it turns out, the growing evidence from this field seems to suggest that once people are accustomed to receiving something for free, it is very difficult to get them to pay for it. Many nonprofits, as they move into an increasingly commercial age, may find themselves up against this same resistance. Introducing prices often requires the development of new financial controls, the setting up of mechanisms to process payments and the like. Moreover, for nonprofits, price resistance may be augmented by the kinds of ideological forces described earlier in discussing the Red Cross.

Are there ways to cushion the transition to price setting? One strategy is to introduce some quality or product change simultaneously with the price increase. A school that introduces a technology fee is well served to accompany that fee with some upgrade in technology. (Albeit, the upgrade must be well managed so that the full revenues generated by the pricing are not spent on new technology.) In some cases, one can continue to offer a version of the product free, while offering a preferred option at some price. Arts organizations that begin by offering free concerts will find it easier to introduce pricing if they maintain some free seats (or some free performances). The Kennedy Center coupled a substantial increase in admissions fees with increased attention to free performances. Health clinics that initiate co-pays for service might limit those co-pays for certain essential health services and/or vary them by patient characteristics.

How to Set Prices

Once a nonprofit has crossed the Rubicon and decided to begin charging a fee for a particular service, the question remains as to how that fee should be set. A description provided by Robert Cahen of the Cleveland Mandel Jewish Community Center provides what is likely a good approximation to the pricing practice at many of the more sophisticated nonprofits:

> Looking at my own agency's programs, we take into account: a) current price; b) demand; c) competition and its pricing; d) what

we need to bring in; e) ensuring ongoing product quality; and f)
the perceived need for incrementalism.

In fact, this process looks remarkably similar to what an economist might suggest. For most nonprofits, the right price takes into account costs (what we need to bring in), the value of the product (demand, and product quality), and the competition (Oster 1995). Overlaid on all of this is the recognition that sticker shock may hit if an organization tries to change prices too quickly. But even within this description, there are some subtleties that are worth pursuing.

Consider the role of costs. Most nonprofits distinguish between direct program costs and shared overhead costs. Shared overhead costs are sometimes called *fixed costs,* and as the name suggests do not change as the organization expands or contracts service offerings, at least within some reasonable range. Because these costs do not change as programs grow or ebb, and because they are often shared among a range of programs, shared overhead costs do not typically provide much guidance in setting fees for particular programs. When most organizations think about "breaking even" on an activity, they typically focus only on the direct costs, and in most cases this is quite appropriate. In some cases, foundation funding, government subsidies, and development funds support overhead costs. More importantly, since true organizational overhead is applicable to a range of programs, there is no meaningful economic way to apportion overhead to individual programs. The expenses of an executive director and his or her staff are rarely reduced as they make small to moderate changes in either program levels or variety. Since dropping a program is likely to have little effect on the overall overhead budget, executive directors can ignore those costs in making program decisions. Of course, overhead costs not covered by broad grants need to be covered one way or another. But the actual allocation of these costs is made in response to demand, not based on any arbitrary formulae. Programs support the overhead budget when there is enough demand for them to allow prices to be set at levels in excess of direct costs, and none of the mission-driven forces we described earlier militate against high price levels.

The issue of costs and how they enter into the fee-setting process is complicated and a simple example may be helpful. Consider a family service agency that provides job training classes to new immigrants and now decides to offer a second set of classes. At what fee level does it make sense, on strictly economic grounds, to offer such a new class? Most typically the class would require the hiring of a new instructor (or paying an old instructor for added hours). It might require the agency to print a new brochure describing the class. These costs, which could be avoided if the new class were not offered, are thought of as *semivariable;* alternatively, one could say they vary at the level of the class. Unless there are enough enrollees at fees sufficient to cover these costs, operating the new program will leave the agency worse off than it was before. There may also be costs, like instructional material for example, that vary by the number of students enrolled. These are *variable costs* at the level of the individual student and must also be covered by fees if the agency wants to "make money" on the new program. In this simple example, suppose the instructor fees are $1,000 per course, the brochure price is $200 and the maximum class size is 20. The semivariable costs are then $1,200 divided by the number of students in the class. If the class reaches its maximum enrollment, cost per student from these sources would be $60. Of course, if enrollments sink below that level, the costs per student rise. In contrast, the instructional materials costs are typically constant per student regardless of class size. Assume in this example that the instructional material, books and workbooks, cost $10 per student. At a class size of 20, individual fee levels of $70 would allow the agency to break even on the program, assuming that the class reaches maximum capacity. Note that if the class size turns out to be only 10, a fee of $130 will be required to break even. Decision-making is much more difficult when semivariable costs are high relative to variable costs, precisely because fee-setting then requires the nonprofit to be able to estimate enrollments more accurately.

In this example, one must consider rental on the room used by the new class. Here the economist is equivocal. If the room would otherwise be empty, with no alternative rental possibilities, it would be considered a fixed cost, with an *opportunity cost* of zero. Any rent at all generated by the new program is better than the current return of nothing. As a consequence, in calculating the minimum fee required to run the new program, these costs will be ignored. If it turns out—as one would hope—that there is enough demand to set fees high enough to allocate some rental portion to the program, then this is a welcome extra. In the same way, if the executive director of the agency can oversee the new program without compromising other ventures, her salary too will be seen as a fixed cost, and any contribution the new program makes to defray that salary will be a plus. We can then see that the first task in trying to determine fees in a new venture is to identify the fixed versus variable costs, and calculate the fee levels that will at least cover the variable costs.

Distinguishing among the cost categories allows for a more nuanced discussion of cross-subsidization among programs. In particular, one would like to distinguish between situations in which one program subsidizes another in the sense that it covers more of the agency overhead, or fixed costs, versus cases in which a program actually covers part of a second operation's direct, variable costs. It is only in the latter case that adding the second program actually "hurts" the first from an economic perspective, yet even this form of cross-subsidization may be socially beneficial.

Expanding on the diagram in Figure 1, nonprofits often distinguish among core or mission-driven activities, supplementary activities, and resource-attracting services. In the case of the latter two categories of activities, where mission content is relatively low, it is generally thought that programs should support not only their own direct costs, but make at least some contribution to overhead. Among core activities, however, for reasons described earlier, it is unwise or impossible to charge fees for service for some programs to support even their direct costs. These activities will need to find support either from other sources, or from the fees earned by other programs. It is the latter situation where issues of cross-program and cross-client equity become really sticky. A number of ballet companies, for example, perform the Nutcracker every Christmas season, not only because it has wide audience appeal, but also because the revenues generated help to support more avant-garde ballet, for which there is only a limited audience. In museums, revenues from blockbuster shows of Rembrandt support exhibitions of Delft ceramic ware. Executive education in universities supports the overhead of full-time student education and research.

An interesting example of some of the hard issues involved in allocating overhead across programs within an organization is provided by Washington's Kennedy Center. In 1991, when Lawrence Wilker took over the helm at the Kennedy Center, it was nine million dollars in debt. In addition to cutting staff costs, Wilker sought to spread some of the very large overhead costs of the Center by broadening its programs. By adding musical comedies to the more esoteric offerings of opera and classical music, Wilker hoped to open the Kennedy Center to a broader audience. Any broadening would both help in the economics of the Center and better serve one of its major stakeholders, the United States Congress. The question naturally arises in this example of how much overhead one should allocate to opera versus the musical comedy? Or, using our earlier language, in which direction should the cross-subsidy run? Pure economics suggests that opera-goers should bear most of the overhead. Opera has fewer substitutes than does musical comedy. Moreover, opera-goers are typically higher income individuals. Both of these features suggest that opera-goers will have a relatively *inelastic* demand. That is, these patrons will likely absorb price increases without cutting back too much on attendance. Another argument for loading overhead onto the opera is the Center's desire to broaden its appeal across the population. On the other hand, the Kennedy Center has a strong history and tradition of support for the high end of cultural events. This would suggest that opera is more "core" than musical comedy and should receive the subsidy, not provide it.

This issue of program subsidies brings us directly to one of the most interesting and potentially contentious pricing questions in nonprofits: To what extent can and should nonprofits engage in classic *price discrimination,* charging different people different prices for the same services? Many nonprofits struggle with the tension between setting high membership fees and offering generous discounts/scholarships to build client base among the less affluent, versus charging lower fees overall. For the high fee/big discount system to work, those discounts must be reasonably widespread. But advertising discounts runs the risk of alienating clients who pay full fare.

The language of price discrimination, common in for-profit economics literature, is rarely seen in the nonprofit literature, and even less seen in nonprofit management discussions. But the practice of charging different people different prices for the same good or service, the classic definition of price discrimination, is ubiquitous in the field. Sliding scale fees, based on the income or circumstances of families, are common in day care centers. Health facilities often vary charges by income. Some social service organizations charge on a "pay what you can" basis. In many of these cases, differential prices are designed at least in part to serve ideological goals, oftentimes involving some form of redistribution. In many circumstances, differential pricing can also have the effect of generating higher revenues than an organization would be able to achieve with a "one price for all" strategy. In the following sections, we will try to highlight both the revenue-generating advantages of differential prices and any mission-related issues.

The practice of differential pricing has been finely honed in the private educational market, and there are lessons from this market for nonprofits more generally. In private schools all over the United States, students at all levels are charged tuition that depends in complicated ways on their economic circumstances and academic ability. At the elite colleges, the price differential is staggering. Gordon Winston's recent work indicates that in the top decile of elite private colleges, an education whose list price is $31,000 is now sold for an average price of $8,400 (Winston and Zimmerman 2000). There is little doubt that the practice of differential pricing allows colleges to attract a stronger student body than they otherwise could. It also seems clear that price discrimination yields for these colleges greater revenue for a given student body size than would a one-price-for-all-students system. It is interesting to note in this case that the full costs of providing an education at these elite colleges is in fact considerably more than the tuition paid even by the full-pay students. Indeed, work in this area suggests that even the so-called full-pay students are paying only 44 percent of costs. As we will see shortly, highlighting this feature may make the price differentials more palatable. Nevertheless, it would be hard in the private sector to find similar differentials offered for identical products.

In other parts of the nonprofit sector, small product quality differences give rise to large price differentials in a kind of second-level price discrimination. For example, in the performing arts environment, price differentials across ticket categories are typically large relative to differences in seat quality, as perceived by the average customer. In the Cleveland Jewish Community Center, along with many YMCA's, health club memberships which come with higher level amenities help to support regular memberships.

In considering pricing at this level, organizations should be wary of the effect of product line pricing on the health of other services offered. One nonprofit serving blind people found that the price it charged for outpatient services was so low that as demand for these services surged, revenues were inadequate to maintain the residential program. Pricing imbalances may also direct clients into one program over another in ways that conflict with the ideal diagnostic matching.

For many nonprofits, the advantages to differential pricing are clear. There are dangers, however, particularly around client reactions. Here the way price discrimination works is often key. In the performing arts example, clients are choosing which seats to buy; museum-goers choose to become members at higher prices. Religious organizations provide the cleanest example of nonprofits operating with entirely voluntary pricing differentials. Recent analysis on the Mormon tithing practice indicates that church members self-impose quite strict tithing guidelines based on income definitions. A small preschool program in New Haven charges different day care prices on a sliding scale related to voluntary reporting of parental income and supported by an explicit ideology of inclusion. In these cases, there is a kind of voluntary or at least cooperative price discrimination and some attempt to promote buy-in of the principle of differentials. Some museums take an intermediate stance, treating admissions fees as voluntary donations, but listing a "suggested" fee. For modern day colleges, the picture is rather different. For many in the college world, differential pricing is a tool that improves institutional quality for all students, by allowing colleges to accept a student population without regard to ability to pay. Nevertheless, tuition differences are imposed, not chosen, and the ideological and practical importance of these price differentials, however clear they are to administrators, are not always widely embraced by parents. The result, in some colleges, is a growing resentment and gaming of the system.

For nonprofits that want to practice differential pricing, the lessons are clear: The more cooperative or voluntary such differentials appear, the less resistant clients will be to them. When differentials are imposed, rather than chosen, the nonprofit has a burden to convince clients of the value of the differentials in terms of product improvements for everyone. Winston and Zimmerman (2000), for example, suggest that colleges remind parents that even those students who pay the full $31,000 tuition are paying only a portion of the true total costs of an education. In this way, the point is made that in organizations supported in part by donative funds and/or endowments, each client is typically subsidized, and it is simply a question of how deep those subsidies are for different people. Again, in the college setting, making the case for the role of diversity in improving the college experience for all students is vitally important in reducing resistance to pricing differentials. For organizations like hospitals and arts organizations, with substantial infrastructure or fixed costs, differential pricing may help to expand the audience in ways that lower the overall average production costs.

In addition to considering how to set prices for different clients or customers, nonprofits often also grapple with pricing structures across their products. One way to think about this set of issues is to ask whether an organization should offer its clients a finely honed á la carte menu or a fixed price meal, or both? For arts organizations, this translates into a question of how much to stress series tickets, rather than single sales. For private schools, the question is often whether to charge one tuition price that covers everything, or to add on book fees, technology fees, athletic fees and the like. For community centers with summer camps, is the bus ride to camp "extra"? These are issues that confront nonprofits all the time.

As with most questions in this area, economics, psychology, ideology, and practicality all will play a role. One key issue for most organizations is how different are the demands of the service users. If everyone wants the same meal, then á la carte menus are not very important. When all students are essentially required to engage in athletics, use technology, and buy the same books, the practice of charging separate fees for each of these services serves no productive function. Sometimes schools divide costs this way in the hopes that parents don't "add up," or compare, alternative school choices, particularly when costs are paid at different times in the school year.

When clients differ in terms of their needs, the choice between fixed price and á la carte becomes more interesting. In this case, offering prices for each of the pieces lets clients pick and choose, and this has considerable advantages. As a consequence of this pricing strategy, there will likely be differences among clients in the way each uses services. On the other hand, the nonprofit may actually want to use the price structure to try to induce more homogeneity among clients. Sometimes more homogeneity is beneficial from a mission or values perspective. In a school serving a population from different socioeconomic backgrounds, charging differential fees for various after-school activities may be inconsistent with school integration goals. In other situations, an organization may find it economically cheaper to limit the choices their clients face. One nonprofit theater decided not to sell elaborate programs to play-goers rather than give them sample ones at no cost. This decision was not based on differences among patrons in how much they valued those playbills, but rather because audiences indicated that they did not want to make buying decisions just as they enter the theater. There may be other economic issues as well. If we return to the restaurant analogy, the chef may want to use the fact that most people want the roast beef to push them towards the soup of the day and away from the lower margin oysters. Judicious pricing can help an organization manage variety.

It is also worth thinking about the subtle messages an organization sends when it sets differential prices for different services. In recent years, the Chicago Symphony Orchestra has experimented with "demand to base pricing," in which concerts featuring somewhat more obscure composers are cheaper than those that are better known and traditionally crowd-pleasing. One danger in this system is that concert-goers will interpret the lower prices as connoting lower quality. In markets in which information about product quality is limited, lowering prices may actually discourage demand.

A last issue we want to consider in the area of pricing structure involves *product bundling*. Should an organization offer discounts to clients who buy in volume, or those who buy a range of the services offered? Such discounts are common in both the for-profit and nonprofit world. Theaters sell subscriptions to most or all of the plays produced in a season. In these subscriptions, theaters offer a series of plays for a price that is slightly lower than the price of the separate tickets, pushing patrons to attend a play they might otherwise eschew. Museums offer memberships, enabling patrons to pay a fixed up-front fee and then visit the museum whenever they want for no fee. These packages are especially useful in settings in which the incremental cost of adding client use is very small. When we offer a package, we are encouraging usage, because once the fee is paid, the added cost of attendance at the event is zero. For a museum with lots of open space, or a theater with empty seats, the demand expansion gained through product bundling can be very advantageous for both mission reasons and economics. Behavioral economists have found that these bundled subscription fees or memberships are especially attractive to customers when the products or services are meritorious goods. For high-end theater, opera, intellectual journals, and the like, customers buy subscriptions in part as a way to "force themselves" to use more of the product than they might episodically choose (Ryans and Weinberg 1979).

New York's Metropolitan Opera offers a wide range of bundled products. In addition to more than a dozen full-service subscription possibilities, each with 6–10 performances, the MET offers a 5-performance mini-series, and a 3-performance 'trio.'

Bundling can help organizations in the service of their missions in other ways as well. Judicious combinations of plays can help theaters to use the lure of popular plays to ensure attendance at more obscure choices. This bundling both fills empty seats at these plays, and educates audiences about new genres. For this reason, the components of series are usually carefully chosen to include some pieces that would have trouble standing on their own.

Bundled prices that promote homogeneity may serve an ideological function as well. Consider a community center in a diverse neighborhood that offers a range of weekend and after school activities. Pricing each activity differentially has certain appeal, particularly when some programs are likely to be oversubscribed and when those programs vary by costs. On the other hand, offering all, or at least most, of the programs for a fixed, single membership fee, promotes economic diversity in the program base. For many nonprofit organizations, this nonsorting effect may be the dominant consideration in choosing the á la carte or fixed-price scheme. However, as Aansari, Siddarth, and Weinberg (1996) demonstrate in a study of performing arts organizations, bundling often works somewhat differently in the nonprofit sector. The typical nonprofit arts organization prefers bundles with larger numbers of events, for example, than the for-profit. Bundling is thus used in part to expand volume, as well as to expand profits. As in the for-profit sector, most nonprofits employ strategies of mixed bundling, selling both single tickets and subscriptions, and subscriptions have added value to the nonprofit. This may well be in part because subscription sales often lead to charitable giving.

Future Challenges in the Pricing Area

The goal of this chapter has been to bring together practitioner and academic perspectives, focusing on issues of pricing. For organizations that face the challenge of meeting a mission while balancing a budget, in a world of diminished philanthropic dollars, this is an important challenge indeed. While we have made some progress in this area, there is considerable work to be done.

Managers in nonprofit organizations are often reluctant to confront pricing issues. At times, we see an ideological preference for charging a zero price or, at least, the lowest possible price. Of course, in some circumstances, this strategy is the right one. However, such cases are becoming rarer in times of diminished government support and increased demand for the socially beneficial services that nonprofits provide. In addition, as we have tried to show, pricing can provide real value, beyond revenues, to a nonprofit in validating the value of the organization's service, rationing or redirecting demand, and contributing to the dignity and control of clients.

Once an organization decides to impose prices, some of the broader lessons from both the business community and the academic community become salient. But there is a balance to be struck. As we have tried to suggest in this chapter, there are differences among nonprofits in the usefulness of prices and in the way in which prices can and should be used. Many nonprofits will be producing goods or services that have social as well as private content; in some cases, the way in which these goods and services are distributed may be at least as important as the prices charged. In a very interesting study of alternative methods to encourage condom use for public health reasons, Dahl, Gorn, and Weinberg (1998) found that the effectiveness of price discounting depended heavily on a range of distribution issues. What a nonprofit provides and how they provide it will often conflate the effect of any price changes on patronage. Finally, while economics and psychology have much to offer the manager in thinking about pricing issues, the practicalities of operating an organization with many different constituencies pose challenges for both academics and managers to overcome. We offer this chapter as a beginning in the task of marrying academic acumen and practical wisdom in the service of a social mission.

References

Ansari, Asin, S. Siddarth, and Charles Weinberg. 1996. "Pricing a Bundle of Products or Services: The Case of Nonprofits." *Journal of Marketing Research.* 2:86-93.

Dahl, Darren, Gerald Corn, and Charles Weinberg. 1998. "The impact of embarrassment on condom purchase behavior." *Canadian Journal of Public Health.* 89(6):368–370.

Goetzmann, William and Sharon Oster. 2003. "The Economics of Museums." In Edward Glaeser, *The Governance of Not for Profit Firms.* Cambridge: National Bureau of Economic Research volume on Nonprofit Organizations.

Kotler, Phillip and Eduardo Roberto. 1989. *Social Marketing.* New York: The Free Press.

Liu, Yong and Charles Weinberg. 2001 (working paper). "Rivalry beyond profits: An equilibrium analysis of price competition involving nonprofit organizations." University of British Columbia.

Oster, Sharon. 1995. *The Strategic Management of Nonprofit Organizations.* New York: Oxford University Press.

Smiley, Jane. 1995. *Moo.* New York: Knopf.

Steinberg, Richard and Burton Weisbrod. 1998. "Pricing and rationing by nonprofit organizations with distributional objectives." Burton Weisbrod (ed.). *To Profit or Not to Profit.* New York: Cambridge University Press. 65–82.

Weisbrod, Burton. 1974. "Toward a theory of the voluntary nonprofit sector." In Edmund Phelps' *Altruism, Morality and Economic Theory.* New York: Russell Sage. 171–95.

Weisbrod, Burton. 1998. "Modeling the Nonprofit Organization as a Multiproduct Firm." Burton Weisbrod (ed.) *To Profit or Not to Profit.* New York: Cambridge University Press. 47–64.

Winston, Gordon and David Zimmerman. 2000 (working paper). "Where is aggressive price competition taking higher education?" Williams College.

Yoken, C. and John Berman. 1984. "Does paying a fee for psychotherapy alter the effectiveness of treatment?" *Journal of Consulting and Clinical Psychology.* 52(2): 254–260.

Chapter 3

Compensation in Nonprofit Organizations

Anne E. Preston

Abstract

When crafting nonprofit compensation packages, managers need an understanding of the labor markets in which they operate, plus a strong awareness of the defining characteristics of their organizations. Salary levels must be in the ballpark of offers from competing institutions; therefore, managers must accept that there will be natural market-driven disparities across employees of different professions. However, carefully crafted nonpecuniary benefits should be added to the package with the goal of attracting, retaining, and motivating employees who buy into the mission of the organization, and possibly increasing equality in the overall distribution of compensation.

Introduction

The nonprofit sector is a varied set of organizations that are distinctive in both the specialized corporate and tax laws under which they operate and, perhaps more importantly, in their overwhelming diversity of purpose. While for-profit organizations are linked in their shared goal of profit-making, nonprofits seem especially scattered in their adherence to heterogeneous goals that are "other than profit-making." But when it comes to hiring and compensating all but the very specialized professional employees, these diverse nonprofit organizations are often competing in a common labor market. The variation in compensation across workers and organizations in the nonprofit sector reflects the competitive pressures that nonprofit organizations face as they operate in labor markets where changing demand and supply forces constantly impact the "going wage." Nonprofit organizations are not competing for talent simply among themselves, but often they are trying to attract and retain employees who are also being wooed by government agencies and for-profit firms. While some labor markets in which they compete are local, others are national and international. Regardless of whether the organization is competing with nationally renowned finance firms for a chief financial officer or with other local nonprofits for a recently graduated social worker, each organization must create a compensation package that is competitive. The degree and nature of competition in the particular labor market is likely to have a big impact on the overall level of compensation which will ensure employment of a high-quality employee. But a compensation package is not one-dimensional; it is a combination of both pecuniary and non-pecuniary benefits. In crafting the compensation package, the organization needs to identify its own defining characteristics, the constraints that these characteristics impose, and the advantages that they offer.

As a first cut, the distinction between the nonprofit and for-profit firm is an important one in defining constraints and opportunities in compensation. The most frequently noted defining characteristic is that the nonprofit organization may not distribute profits to those in charge of the organization. Fiduciary care responsibilities also require nonprofits to keep costs, including salaries, at reasonable levels. Together, these requirements have historically limited the level and flexibility of employee compensation. However, the resulting salary regulations were somewhat vague and subject to changing interpretations. In addition, the sole penalty the IRS could impose for violations was revocation of the organization's tax-exempt status. New regulations on salary in the form of the Taxpayer Bill of Rights were enacted in 1996, and after a series of amendments and interpretations, final regulations were issued in January 2002. The IRS has used the Taxpayer Bill of Rights to prosecute organizations that are overpaying persons with substantial control over organizational affairs. Often called "intermediate sanctions," this bill defines more clearly what constitutes excess compensation in nonprofit organizations, and proposes a set of penalty excise taxes imposed potentially on both the overpaid individual and the board members responsible for the overpayment. Therefore, different from for-profits, nonprofit organizations are operating with a ceiling on compensation, and violation of the ceiling can be extremely costly.

The nonprofit organization also sets itself apart from for-profits in that it has no owners; rather, a voluntary board oversees the operations of the organization. Without owners, the nonprofit organization does not have certain instruments—such as stock options and employee ownership—in its compensation repertoire that publicly owned for-profits use to great advantage. Furthermore, characteristics of the voluntary board are likely to impact general compensation strategies and particular compensation decisions of high-level staff. In particular, voluntary board members with strong ties to the financial sector may steer compensation levels and strategies toward income-enhancing initiatives more common in the for-profit sector. Similarly, board member opinions on equality and fairness are likely to affect the distribution of salaries within an organization.

Finally, the for-profit and nonprofit products are inherently different. If we constrain the analysis to 501(c)(3) and 501(c)(4) organizations, by state law these charitable organizations provide a product with some social benefit. While these organizations still cover a wide range of services, from medical research to preparation of food for shut-ins to community theater, they all work explicitly to contribute to the social good. The mission of the specific organization and its public identity, which make each organization unique among nonprofits, may impinge on the flexibility of the compensation scheme. In particular, organizations with a "helping" orientation may be reluctant to pay high salaries, and organizations with egalitarian "values" may resist large variations in salaries. In return for providing a social benefit, 501(c)(3) nonprofits can raise tax-deductible revenue from donors. Similar to stockholders, these donors may exercise some degree of control over the workings of the organization, either through explicit intervention or by altering access to their pocketbooks. Compensation, especially at the highest ranks of the organization, is observable and easy to monitor, and at very high levels it may be a signal to donors that the organization does not need their money.

While the mission and identity may be constraining, they also may present advantages that organizations should exploit. By identifying the characteristics that make it special, each organization can start to leverage its compensation packages towards nonpecuniary benefits that stress these defining characteristics. Stressing the social value of the nature of the work and the collegiality of the workplace will likely attract workers who value these attributes and who are willing to accept a slightly lower monetary compensation for the opportunity to experience these defining attributes. By offering a *labor donation,* the employees are easing the cost pressures on the organization and signaling a commitment to the mission of the organization. Incorporating nonpecuniary characteristics that stress the mission and character of the organization into the compensation package may also give these organizations a leg up on for-profit organizations in designing motivational tools. Psychological theories of motivation generally do not point to money as an important motivator of human effort, even in for-profit organizations. Maslow's (1943) hierarchy of needs theory and Herzberg's motivation-hygiene theory of job satisfaction (1993) both consider adequate salary levels prerequisites for a satisfied work force, but imply that motivation is only elicited through psychological rewards that build self-esteem.

The Labor Force.   The nonprofit work force is distinct from the economy-wide labor force. Roughly 70 percent of the nonprofit work force is female, compared to 44 percent of the for-profit workforce. The nonprofit worker is highly educated, with 48 percent of nonprofit employees having at least a college degree, a percentage twice that of the for-profit sector. Almost two-thirds of nonprofit employees are professionals, again roughly twice the percentage of for-profit employees. Furthermore, because of state laws, which, although diverse in wording, always specify the types of organizations that can apply for and earn 501(c)(3) or 501(c)(4) status and the areas in which they are legally allowed to operate, nonprofit employees are predominantly housed in a small number of industries. Eighty-eight percent of nonprofit employees are employed in religious organizations, social services, hospitals, higher education, elementary and secondary education, nursing and personal care facilities, or other professional services. Finally, in the 1990s, nonprofit employees were paid salaries approximately 11 percent below salaries of for-profit employees with similar characteristics (Ruhm and Boroski 2000).

New research has shown that this salary differential falls significantly, possibly to zero, when analyzing differences in salary between nonprofit and for-profit employees within the same industry (Ruhm and Boroski 2000, and Leete 2000). Nonprofit employees are low paid because they are employed in low-paying industries, not necessarily because their employing institutions are non-profit. But to divorce the two is somewhat counterproductive since, by virtue of what they are designed to produce, nonprofits do not generally locate in high-paying industries. Furthermore, the question remains as to why highly educated professionals are attracted to work in industries where wages and salaries are on average below salaries of individuals with similar attributes and training in other industries. Answers to this question may help to determine the kind of compensation structure that can retain and motivate these employees.

Compensation. A compensation system has three main goals. First, it must attract competent employees who can perform the work required. Second, it must retain those employees, ensuring that they do not leave for better opportunities. Finally, it must motivate those employees to perform in ways and at levels that will help the employing organization meet its own goals (Caruth and Handlogten, 2001). In general, in creating compensation packages that achieve these goals, nonprofit managers first must understand the labor market in which they are operating. Then they need to pinpoint the defining characteristics that make their organization different from their competitors. Armed with an understanding of these differences, nonprofit managers can evaluate the constraints these differences impose and the opportunities they create.

The rest of this chapter is divided into sections on attraction, retention, and motivation of nonprofit employees followed by a section devoted to the compensation structure of top-level executives in nonprofit organizations. The chapter concludes with a set of guidelines for crafting nonprofit compensation packages.

Compensation and Attracting the Nonprofit Worker

Historically, attracting desired workers was not as critical an objective of the nonprofit organization because the professional staff was made up predominantly of women with few other professional alternatives, and the managerial staff was made up of professionals who had climbed their way up the hierarchy of the organization. Before civil rights legislation of the 1960s, women looking for professional positions rarely strayed from nursing, teaching, and social work. But since the 1960s, there has been a surge of women entering the higher paying male professions, including medicine, law, and engineering. No longer able to rely on a captive labor force, nonprofits have had to focus on creating workplace opportunities that attracted the desired type and number of employees. However, and especially in the professional occupations where expertise often requires several years of specific educational investment, any deterioration of nonprofit opportunities in the present will not have immediate effects because the current set of new professionals made their occupational choices years earlier at the beginning of the educational process. But there can be serious consequences down the road as students today decide to forego the nonprofit professions. In fact, the hospital sector is now trying to deal with a severe shortage of nursing staff that was set in motion several years ago with nurses' complaints about salary and working conditions. In addition, in recent years nonprofits have attempted to improve management techniques and expand into money-making endeavors. A number of graduate programs focusing on managerial training of the nonprofit employee have developed during the last twenty years. For example, Case Western's Mandel Center for Nonprofit Organizations, as well as the Center for Philanthropy at Indiana University/Purdue University, train employees for nonprofit work exclusively. Programs have grown in other prominent institutions with traditionally business or government foci, including the Columbia Business School, the Wharton School, the Kennedy School of Government, and the Yale School of Management. As a result, nonprofits are increasingly hiring management and administrative employees whose skills are valued in profit-making institutions. While salary may not be the attracting characteristic, it has to be sufficiently high to keep the employee from turning away from the opportunity altogether. Furthermore, well-balanced compensation schemes with attractive nonpecuniary compensation may tip the scales as employees are deciding between job offers.

In attempting to attract workers, the nonprofit firm has to identify its competitors, or the *demand side* of the relevant labor market. The more competitors looking to hire from a fixed number of potential applicants, the higher the average wages will be bid up. Therefore, one would expect that employees whose only options are nonprofit or government work would earn salaries below those earned by employees who are also qualified for work in industries dominated by for-profit institutions. Skills that are transferable across sectors and industries will be rewarded with higher average salaries. As a first cut, nonprofit professionals, like social workers, are probably going to experience lower salaries than nonprofit managers, relative to their economywide professional counterparts, because social work skills are not easily transferable across industries while management skills are. Similarly, the nonprofit firm has to understand its applicant pool, or the *supply side* of the relevant market. All else equal, the smaller and more specialized the applicant pool, the higher that wages will be bid up as competing institutions vie for the applicants. Thus average salaries for a group of workers will increase with education, experience, and other relevant and rare qualifications. Economic pressures resulting from supply and demand forces dictate average salary levels for relatively homogeneous groups of workers, but these averages are likely to vary considerably across groups of workers with different professions and skills. Since nonprofits generally hire a diverse group of workers, substantial within-organization wage dispersion, often not welcome in egalitarian-minded nonprofits, is inevitable. The challenge to the nonprofit manager is to find ways to temper these disparities with nonpecuniary characteristics of compensation that are relatively consistent across employees.

While market considerations (demand for and supply of workers), may dictate average salary levels for a group of employees with a given set of skills, the characteristics of the institution, its mission, and its management are all likely to determine where the individual nonprofit's salary offer falls relative to the market average. One important characteristic of the institution is its ability to pay—institutions with higher budgets or endowments can afford to attract employees with higher than average salaries. On the other hand, the degree of donor involvement in the organization may limit salaries if donors respond to increased salaries with a reduction in funding. The mission of the organization may have important implications for salary. Organizations whose mission is to give out funds, such as foundations and umbrella social service organizations, may be more likely to offer higher salaries than organizations that provide a direct service to the poor.

Management style is also a relevant determinant. Nonprofits have no owners, and by law earned profits are put back into the organization. When profits arise, they need not be used to produce more services, but can serve a variety of purposes including boosting employee salaries. Managers and board members will use their judgment about how best to use these funds.

The employment relationship is the result of a matching process. Not only are organizations looking for appropriate workers, but potential employees are looking for employment opportunities where they will find satisfaction and growth. Potential employees who have invested in a professional degree predominantly employed in nonprofit work or who are investigating a nonprofit opportunity, are probably not attracted to the work because of pay, because pay is higher in other industries. Professional employees have picked a nonprofit profession presumably with knowledge of the low wages relative to other professions with similar educational requirements and greater prominence in the for-profit sector. And managerial employees seeking work are probably aware of salary dispersion across organizations and sectors. Rather, employees may be attracted to nonprofit organizations because they favor the service produced, or buy into the mission of the organization, or feel comfortable with the management style. While the salary may not be the attracting characteristic, it is part of the package and must be set at levels to make the package sufficiently attractive. In addition, many nonprofits have added attractive forms of nonpecuniary compensation to the package. In higher education, colleges often attract professionals and administrators with tuition credit for family members and subsidized housing on or near the campus. In the nursing professions, examples include elementary schools attracting nurses with the promise of school holidays, and plastic surgery offices promising free procedures for members of the nursing staff. These types of compensation serve multiple purposes. First, they attract the types of employees the organization desires. In the case of higher education, the organizations are attracting employees who value education and community. Elementary schools are likely to attract teachers who enjoy children, and plastic surgery offices attract nurses who value the types of procedures offered. Second, by attracting desirable employees, the nonpecuniary compensation may be furthering the mission of the institution—for colleges and universities, it is the development of an intellectual community where members learn and teach, and, for elementary education, it is the development of a nurturing educational environment in which children can grow. Finally, the cost of the nonmonetary characteristics to the organization may be well below the value the employee places on those characteristics, making this kind of compensation particularly attractive for organizations with tight budgets.

The public good aspects of the workplace are also likely to attract workers who place a positive value on their environment. For example, organizational culture is likely to be different in nonprofit organizations than for-profit organizations because of the stress on democratic or even consensus decision-making. Employees who thrive in cooperative rather than competitive work environments may find nonprofit work especially attractive. However, other employees, especially those accustomed to the pace of the for-profit sector, may be frustrated by seemingly low levels of accountability, risk taking, and flexibility. Stressing the qualities of the work environment as a potential benefit to employment is a good strategy to ensure that mismatches are avoided as much as possible.

Compensation and Retaining the Nonprofit Employee

Retention of employees became increasingly difficult in the late 1990s, as the unemployment rate fell to historically low levels. Salaries of the highly educated increased rapidly as they trailed the seemingly meteoric climb of salaries in the information technology industries. Turnover of managerial and professional employees was high as workers shopped for better opportunities. How nonprofit organizations fared in the retention wars is difficult to say. On the one hand, The Taxpayer Bill of Rights seemed to allow more flexible and generous compensation packages. Furthermore, during the 1990s, the rapid increase of hours worked by Americans was making many professionals long for a more manageable schedule, and many for-profit workers, by mistake or not, often equate nonprofit work with greater flexibility. On the other hand, economywide forces may have restricted nonprofits' abilities to raise salaries. Because the high salaries of the late 1990s did not trickle down to blue collar and service worker salaries, the United States income distribution became increasingly unequal, a phenomenon well documented in the press. With many nonprofit institutions committed to serving the poor and needy, boards of directors may have felt uncomfortable responding to pressures to increase salaries in an environment where inequality was increasing.

Compensation schemes designed to encourage retention offer deferred benefits so that the value of the compensation package increases with seniority. Labor economists have long shown that upward-sloping salary profiles are often used in institutions to discourage separations. Nonsalary benefits, such as health insurance or pension contributions often do not kick in until the employee has been through a probationary period, but benefits that truly encourage retention must increase with seniority. Nonprofit organizations may be at a disadvantage in building retention devices into compensation packages since stock options that increase with years at the firm are not a possibility. However, many nonprofits have been creative in crafting seniority based nonpecuniary benefits. For example, in institutions whose employees live in subsidized housing, basing housing choice on seniority ensures that the value of the housing benefit will increase with years on the job. Institutions that promise tuition benefits to employees' children ensure the delayed benefit when hiring young workers, and when hiring older workers they can attach an eligibility requirement tied to years of service. Because nonpecuniary benefits may be the compensation characteristics attracting employees to nonprofit opportunities, managers may want to focus on how the value of these benefits can be manipulated to increase with seniority so that the compensation package has a built-in retention device. Furthermore, seniority-based benefits are egalitarian in nature and may help to appease concerns over disparate salary distributions. However, because extensive use of deferred compensation hinders hiring of older workers who have less time to accrue the deferred benefit, managers must determine the appropriate balance of current and deferred compensation to meet all the employment needs of the organization.

Compensation and Motivating the Nonprofit Employee

Incentive contracts, on one level, seem to be an ideal compensation device in nonprofit organizations where motives of the different constituencies vary and behavior of employees is difficult to monitor. In addition, the 1996 Taxpayer Bill of Rights seems to give the green light on incentive contracts as long as there is a provision to ensure that employees are not given excessive compensation. But pay for performance is at best a problematic motivating tool for two important reasons. First, by nature of their occupational choices, pay is not the major motivating force of nonprofit employees, and therefore may not be the ideal carrot to hold out for these people. Second, identifying and measuring desired performance is especially hard in organizations that do not usually measure their success with the bottom line.

Current legal regulations do not prohibit pay for performance in nonprofit organizations (see Livingston 2002 for a good summary of current interpretation of the 'Intermediate Sanctions'). Generally, salaries of employees with pay below $80,000, who do not have substantial influence over the affairs of the organization, who are not related to persons who do have substantial control, and who are not major donors to the organization, are not regulated by the Taxpayer Bill of Rights. For these employees incentive contracts are viable options. In the case of executive directors, or other high-level personnel, according to the bill, revenue sharing and bonuses are not illegal per se, but should be accompanied by some limit on the amount of compensation resulting from the revenue-sharing arrangement, or the bonus, to ensure that compensation remains at reasonable levels. Therefore, with a little care to ensure no possibility of overpayment, incentive contracts can be used to motivate employees at all levels.

As noted earlier, Maslow's hierarchy of needs theory and Herzberg's motivation-hygiene theory of job satisfaction both consider adequate salary levels necessary for a satisfied work force, but find that increased salary is not a good motivator for high levels of performance. Vroom's expectancy theory of human motivation also questions the validity of pay for performance in nonprofit organizations. (For a good discussion of psychological theories of motivation, see Caruth and Handgloten 2001.) The theory states that three links must be present in any motivating scheme, and the stronger the links, the more effective the motivating scheme. One of the links is the individual's valuation of the promised reward. If nonprofit employees are being paid adequate salaries, money is probably not the reward that will elicit the strongest motivational response. Furthermore, offering pay for performance may attract employees who are motivated by money, rather than individuals attracted to the organization because of its mission. Nonpecuniary benefits tied to the mission of the organization are potentially a good alternative choice for a compensation-for-performance scheme. Educational institutions might give star teachers funding to take a sabbatical to conduct a project related to their teaching interests. Cultural institutions might give out tickets to opening performances or invite rewarded employees to gatherings with featured artists. While such rewards are quite public and could cause concerns about fairness, the recognition of the rewarded employee is probably as important a motivational tool as the reward itself.

Vroom's expectancy theory also posits that the stronger the link between the individual's effort and his or her performance, and the stronger the link between the performance of the individual and the desired outcome in the organization, the more effective the motivational scheme. For several reasons these links may not be strong in nonprofit organizations. First, measuring the desired outcome is difficult. Services provided by nonprofit organizations are often intangible, and the desired outcome often has a long-term component. Because the recipient of the service does not always pay for the service, revenue measures of service provision are often not even available. In fields such as day care and elderly care, where the buyer is different from the recipient of the care, the revenue paid by the buyer may not accurately reflect quality of care. In response to the difficulty of fully measuring outputs, organizations may use in their incentive schemes only those characteristics of outcomes that are easily measurable. Employees then are likely to distort behavior to achieve these outcomes at the expense of other important outcomes. For example, when teachers are rewarded for how well their students fare on a test, the concern is that teachers will teach exclusively to the test and possibly try to ensure that only the smartest children enroll in their classes. Neither activity fits in comfortably with the educational mission of most private schools. Alternatively, when no characteristics of the outcome are easily measurable, the organization may instead reward inputs, such as teacher longevity. In this latter case, the purpose of the incentive scheme has been compromised. Second, even if appropriate outcome measures can be identified, they may not be clear indicators of performance or employee effort because other factors, such as the characteristics of the clients, the available technology, and environmental factors.

Even with all the difficulties associated with incentive schemes, anecdotal evidence seems to point to increased reliance on organizationwide compensation-for-performance schemes in organizations as diverse as higher and secondary education, nursing, and social service institutions. The extent of these schemes is difficult to assess since there is little comprehensive empirical research on compensation in the nonprofit sector. Practitioners universally acknowledge that such a scheme requires large time commitments from upper level staff as they define and articulate the goals of the organization and then educate each employee about how employee performance helps to achieve those goals. In addition, each employee of the organization has to buy into the system in order for it to work.

> The William Penn Foundation, a 57 year-old foundation designed to improve the quality of life in the Philadelphia region, offers a creative compensation package for members of its board of directors. Each board member is given $35,000, which he or she must donate to one or more charities of choice. The only limitation on the recipients is that they have 501(c)(3) status in the United States. In addition, the foundation matches each board member's personal contributions to charitable organizations, up to a limit of $15,000, with two dollars for every one donated by the board member.

Compensation of Executive Directors

Examining compensation of executive directors is an instructive exercise for a number of reasons. First, there are extensive data on salaries and benefits of executive directors from tax returns and several annual surveys. Second, there have been a number of studies on the factors determining salaries of executive directors. Third, the link between boards of directors' decisions and employee salaries is potentially strongest for salaries of executive directors. Finally, because executive director salaries are the most public, the impact of organizational characteristics and donor preferences on salary levels will be strongest.

Changing Legal Regulations. As noted earlier, the Taxpayer Bill of Rights regulates compensation of persons with substantial influence over the affairs of the organization, and executive directors, except for those newly hired, fall into this category. The Bill of Rights requires that nonprofits release executive compensation figures to the public, and the board of directors must be able to justify and outline the compensation determination process. The first tier requires the overpaid executive to pay a tax of 25 percent of the "excess benefit." If this first tax is not paid promptly, the executive must pay a second-level tax, which is 200 percent of the excess benefit. Organization managers, or members of the board of directors, must also pay a tax of 10 percent of the excess payment if the board members willfully and knowingly engage in the transaction. However, this organizational tax is limited to $10,000 per excess benefit transaction. These new regulations are called "intermediate sanctions" since they do not go so far as to revoke the organization's tax-exempt status. Revenue sharing and performance-related bonuses are allowed, but limits on compensation from these plans are recommended to ensure that compensation does not get too high. The 1999 amendments to the bill, which allow salary comparisons to comparable for-profit employees when justifying the salary determination process, lift the ceiling on compensation of nonprofit executive directors considerably.

Magnitude of Pay. Executive compensation in nonprofit organizations is much lower than in for-profits. Twombly and Gantz (2001) analyzed data from the National Center for Charitable Statistics on reported wages and benefits of executive directors of 55,000 nonprofits. The sample included all nonprofit organizations that complied with IRS regulations in reporting compensation information on Form 990 and that compensated their chief executive officers. It is notable that of the 166,000 reporting nonprofits, only a third, or 55,000, reported paying their directors. Furthermore, roughly 40 percent of the 55,000 organizations were human service organizations, which pay relatively low salaries. As a result, the median salary of executive directors of nonprofits was only $42,000, a mere fraction of the salaries earned by their for-profit counterparts. However, that median falls to $37,400 when one subtracts out hospitals, whose median pay to executive directors is $169,000, and even further to $35,500, after subtracting out higher education, where median pay is $114,000. Religious organizations pay the lowest executive salaries, with a median salary of $24,000. Within the sample, only 38 percent of nonprofits provided supplemental benefits such as pension plans to executive directors and this type of compensation was highest among hospitals and institutes of higher education. The low executive salaries in the sector are especially significant given the high degree of job complexity—executive directors must balance the competing agendas of a number of diverse constituencies, while managing a board of directors—complexity that surely contributes to the high rate of turnover in these jobs.

Since the 1999 amendments to the Taxpayer Bill of Rights that allow salary comparisons between nonprofit and for-profit employees, compensation of executive directors at large, well-funded organizations has been rising rapidly. According to results from a salary survey conducted by the *Chronicle of Philanthropy* and sent to the 400 nonprofits that raised the largest amount of donations in fiscal year 1999, the median salary increase for nonprofit executives between 1999 and 2000 was 6.7 percent, well above the 4.8 percent median salary rise for executives of private companies. Percentage salary increases of nonprofit executive directors were higher than increases of for-profit CEOs for the two preceding years as well. However, it is safe to assume that the value of bonuses and stock options awarded to for-profit executives was increasing at a much more rapid rate during this period. These increasingly valuable bonuses, as well as the low unemployment and rising salaries of the late 1990s, helped to fuel nonprofit salary increases as organizations were increasingly competing with for-profits for qualified personnel. Experts also believe that businessmen sitting on nonprofit boards are increasingly using for-profit standards when setting salaries. The largest increases occurred in the areas of the arts, followed by the United Way, and then by private foundations. Although hospitals did not show large increases in pay over the period, 17 of the 18 individuals with compensation above $1 million were employed in hospitals or medical centers (Anft 2001). However, the structure of the sample included organizations that relied heavily on donations for funding, which applies to only a handful of hospitals. Except for the most prestigious, hospitals rarely rely on donations for a sizable portion of revenue. Interestingly, operating foundations, education groups, and Jewish organizations reported compensation increases of less than one percent. In these organizations, missions that advocate equality or service provision to the less advantaged may have limited compensation increases during a time when income inequality was increasing.

The largest increases in compensation accrued to new hires, implying that the increased compensation was used for attracting new employees rather than retaining or rewarding existing personnel. Furthermore, the intermediate sanctions do not pertain to compensation of new hires, so boards may feel more comfortable offering high salaries at this stage of the employment relationship. Eight percent of the organizations reported offering deferred compensation and twelve percent reported some type of performance bonuses. For example, the editor of MIT's *Technology Review*, who earned $872,585 in total compensation, apparently earned a large portion of that sum through bonuses based on advertising revenue.

Determinants of Pay. Studies on executive compensation almost universally find that the compensation of the executive director increases with size, as measured either by budget or by employees. In addition, compensation varies by industry. Hallock (2000a) finds that salaries are highest in medical research and general and rehabilitative health industries, and lowest in religious and housing/shelter industries. Oster (1998), using a 1995 *Chronicle of Philanthropy* survey similar to the 2001 survey discussed above, finds that hospitals give their executive directors the greatest compensation packages while social services give the smallest. Twombly and Gantz (2001), using the most complete sample, find that hospitals pay the highest salaries, followed by higher education. The third highest paying set of organizations is health (excluding hospitals), but the median executive salary for these organizations is half of the median executive salary for higher education organizations and a third of the median executive salary for hospitals. Employee benefit plans are also most common in hospitals and higher education, which also tend to be the largest organizations. Religion-related organizations paid the lowest executive director salaries, but also were most likely to augment base pay with expense accounts. In addition to size, market considerations predict these differentials, which are consistent across organizations, because nonprofit hospitals, health-related institutions, and increasingly business offices in higher education engage in substantial competition for employees with for-profit institutions, while social service and religious organizations do not. Separating out the influences of size and competition with for-profit firms for workers may be difficult since the larger the organization, the greater the need for well-trained managerial and financial personnel, which have historically been employed in the for-profit sector.

Executive compensation differs by gender as well. In "The Gender Pay Gap for Managers in Nonprofits," Kevin Hallock (2000b) finds that women are executive directors in only 19 percent of nonprofit organizations, a striking statistic given that women make up close to three-quarters of the nonprofit workforce. Furthermore, compensation of female executive directors is at least 20 percent below compensation of male executive directors. Guidestar, using the more complete national database on nonprofits, which includes numerous smaller nonprofits, finds a much higher disparity, on the order of a 50 percent gender differential for chief executives (Lewin 2001). The likelihood of having a female executive director varies inversely with size of organization and also varies with the industry of the organization. When Hallock divides the organizations into ten groups according to value of assets, women make up 39 percent of executive directors in the smallest organizations and between 8 and 15 percent of executive directors in each of the five groups with the largest assets. Once Hallock controls for the characteristics of the organization, the differential in pay between men and women becomes insignificant. Women are employed as executive directors in low-paying organizations.

The strong relationship between size of organization and compensation implies, albeit indirectly, a tie between executive compensation and performance. Twombly and Gantz (2001) show that, within organizational type, the correlation coefficient between size and salary of executive director is over 0.79 for all organizations except hospitals and religion-related organizations. While the correlation coefficient is still over 0.50 for these two types of organizations, it is notable that they represent the highest paying and lowest paying organizations. Hallock, however, measures a direct tie between size and compensation using longitudinal analysis by showing that higher growth rates of an organization lead to higher salary increases for its executive director. In a study of hospitals, Brickley and Van Horn (2002) document a strong relationship between CEO turnover and return on assets and between CEO compensation and return on assets, for nonprofit hospitals. CEOs running hospitals with the highest return on assets earned salaries 8 percent higher than CEOs running hospitals with the poorest return on assets. Furthermore, the relationship between turnover and return on assets is stronger for nonprofit than for-profit hospitals, implying that because of legal and donor-imposed salary constraints, nonprofits are more likely than for-profits to use threat of separation as a disciplinary device for executive directors whose hospitals are performing poorly.

The pay-for-performance link seems strongest for nonprofits operating in highly competitive markets. In a study on hospitals, Arnould et al (2000c) find that, as competition in the health care market increases, executives' compensation is more tightly tied to profitability. Oster (1998) documents a positive relationship between compensation and size of organization that varies by industry, and the relationship is strongest for foundations and hospitals, organizations that most closely compete with for-profit institutions for employees.

Both Oster and Hallock find that characteristics of the organization may affect salaries. Oster finds that increased reliance on donations limits executive compensation; for every percentage point increase in reliance on private donations, average compensation falls by $1,000. Arnould et al (2000) find that donors seem to steer away from nonprofit hospitals that are competing with for-profit hospitals. In hospitals with increasing competitive pressures and compensation tightly linked to performance, donor contributions are lower. Alternatively, this correlation may be due to the fact that highly competitive hospitals spend less time catering to donors and fundraising. Oster finds that ideology affects salary; organizations with a religious affiliation pay their executives about $100,000 less than similar organizations without a religious affiliation. There is also some evidence that characteristics of boards of directors also matter. Foundations with a family member of the original founder on the board pay lower executive director salaries than foundations without a family member (Oster 1998). Hallock (2000a) finds some evidence that larger boards pay lower nonprofit salaries, possibly because board members take on more of the duties of the executive director.

Guidelines for Setting Compensation

Do the research

Salaries need to be in the ballpark of salaries that other institutions pay to similar employees. If salaries are too low, the quality of potential applicants will suffer. Institutions should have access to regional and national salary studies on a number of different types of workers. When establishing salary guidelines for a professional, e.g., a social worker, attention should paid to average salaries of social workers in the nonprofit sector, average salaries of social workers in the for-profit or government sector, and average salaries of professionals with similar training. In addition, salary surveys can give information about how salaries differ with experience.

Think hard about what kind of employee is desired and try to develop a compensation package that will attract such a worker

While salary offers have to be competitive, the compensation package that will attract a given worker to the organization has to be superior to all other compensation packages that he or she may be offered. Nonpecuniary compensation is a great way to attract specific types of employees. If the institution wants individuals who value education, give tuition reimbursements. If the institution wants individuals who value family, offer a set of family-friendly policies. Often nonpecuniary compensation may be less expensive for the organization than pecuniary compensation of the same value to the employee.

Offer benefits that increase with seniority

Deferred benefits that increase with seniority encourage retention of employees, which cuts down on hiring and training costs, increases institutional human capital, and often results in higher institutional loyalty. Furthermore, seniority-based benefits are egalitarian in nature and may help to balance other market-driven salary disparities.

Exercise care when establishing compensation-for-performance systems

The desired performance and organizational outcome must be in line with the mission of the organization and must be well defined, well articulated, and measurable. Try offering nonpecuniary rewards to elicit performance. Think through whether behavioral outcomes represent desired behaviors, since these schemes have the effect of distorting behavior toward rewarded characteristics.

References

Anft, Michael. 2001. "Compensation Rises by 6.7% for Nonprofit Executives," *Chronicle of Philanthropy.* October 4. http://philanthropy.com/premium/articles/v13/i24/24004601.htm.

Arnould, Richard, Marianne Bertrand, and Kevin Hallock. 2000 (working paper). "Does Managed Care Change the Mission of Nonprofit Hospitals? Evidence from the Managerial Labor Market." University of Illinois.

Brickley, James A. and R. Lawrence Van Horn. 2002. "Managerial Incentives in Nonprofit Organizations: Evidence from Hospitals." *The Journal of Law and Economics.* April. 45(1) 227–250.

Caruth, Donald L. and Gail D. Handgloten. 2001. *Managing Compensation.* Westport, CT: Quorum Books.

Hallock, Kevin. 2000a (working paper). "Managerial Pay and Governance in American Nonprofits." University of Illinois.

Hallock, Kevin. 2000b (working paper). "The Gender Pay Gap for Managers in Nonprofits." University of Illinois.

Herzberg, Frederick, Bernard Mausner, and Barbara Block Snyderman. 1993. *The Motivation to Work*. Somerset, NJ: Transaction Publishers.

Leete, Laura. 2000. "Whither the Nonprofit Wage Differential, Estimates from the 1990 Census." *Journal of Labor Economics.* 19(1). 136–170.

Lewin, Tamar. 2001. "Women Profit Less than Men in the Nonprofit World, Too." *New York Times.* June 23. 23.

Livingston, Catherine E. 2002. "Intermediate Sanctions: A Detailed Overview and Current Developments." Prepared by Caplin and Drysdale.

Maslow, Abraham H. 1943. "A Theory of Human Motivation." *Psychology Review.* Reprinted in Ott, Stephen J., Sandra J. Parker, and Richard B. Simpson (eds). 2003. *Readings in Organizational Behavior,* 3rd edition. Chicago: Dorsey Press. 152–163.

Oster, Sharon. 1998. "Executive Compensation in the Nonprofit Sector." *Nonprofit Management and Leadership.* 8(3). 207–21.

Ruhm, Christopher J. and Carey Boroski. 2000. "Compensation in the Nonprofit Sector." Cambridge: National Bureau of Economic Research.

Twombly, Eric C. and Marie G. Gantz. 2001. "Executive Compensation in the Nonprofit Sector: New Findings and Policy Implications." *Charting Civil Society.* Washington D.C.: The Urban Institute.

CHAPTER 4

Outsourcing by Nonprofit Organizations

Avner Ben-Ner

Abstract

This chapter examines the issue of when nonprofits should choose to employ their own staff or house their own operations, versus contracting out tasks and activities to other suppliers. Various examples are offered of nonprofit decisions that may be outsourced or retained in-house. The concepts of *specialization, comparative advantage,* and *transaction costs* are used to explain the logic of outsourcing, how it applies to various circumstances encountered by nonprofit organizations, and the desirability of this strategy in each case.

Introduction

Outsourcing or contracting-out is the organizational practice of purchasing some services or products from other organizations, rather than producing or generating them within the organization itself. From the early 1980s until the late 1990s, a trend of increased reliance on outsourcing took place in the United States, resulting in the downsizing, breakup, and divestiture of companies. Several factors contributed to the rise in the importance of outsourcing, including improvements in information technology and communication, developments in transportation, deregulation, and legal decisions in favor of competition. This trend started in the for-profit sector, but it soon also affected government operations and many nonprofit organizations.

Outsourcing has generated substantial savings for many firms, government agencies, and nonprofit organizations by allowing them to shed operations that are done more effectively and economically by specialized firms that have better expertise and a larger scale of operations in a narrow activity, and that can pay undivided attention to that activity. There are also many examples of outsourcing gone awry: IT services being too expensive as well as unreliable when the contractor takes advantage of an organization's ignorance of the area, government agencies spending a lot of resources on monitoring and enforcing contracts with private contractors for a total cost that exceeds the cost of running the contracted function in-house, nonprofit organizations outsourcing activities to companies with connections to board members resulting in dubious savings and appearances of conflict of interest, and so on.

While outsourcing may clearly generate better services and savings, it can also cause decline in services and escalation of costs. But where does the line between useful and counterproductive lie? As parents know, or should know, one can outsource some of the care for children, but one cannot outsource loving while also remaining a responsible and functional parent. This chapter examines the issue of outsourcing from a theoretical and practical perspective, seeking to provide a solid understanding of what are the fundamental drivers behind the decision to outsource a certain activity versus keeping it in-house.

The chapter first identifies general principles that should guide outsourcing decisions, juxtaposing the principles of *specialization, economies of scale,* and *division of labor* with the problems of managing activities and people within an organization and across organizations. It is clear that some activities, particularly those concentrated in narrow niches that require a lot of expertise to produce but can be readily evaluated, can be more efficiently and economically executed by contracting companies that specialize in those activities rather than generated within organizations that have other primary products. Such activities often include complex computer programming, routine cleaning, infrequent filing activities, temporary need to satisfy peak demand, and so on. However, there are some activities that can be more effectively managed and controlled when they are subject to managerial authority rather than to the terms of an agreement or contract between two organizations. This even includes some of the types of activities listed above: routine cleaning of areas that contain sensitive information may be subject to security breaches, doing routine paperwork on behalf of a government agency such as processing visa requests may tilt the trade-off too heavily in favor of savings at the expense of accuracy, and so on.

The balance between these two considerations (and a few others) may tip in favor of outsourcing or of in-house production, depending on the nature of the activity, its centrality to the organization, the ability of executives in the organization to write and enforce contracts with other organizations, availability of competing suppliers, and so on. It is impossible to come up with a list of activities that should be outsourced. Clearly, activities that are central to the operations of an organization should not be outsourced; everything else is a candidate for outsourcing, but the decision has to be weighed carefully against various contingencies. The chapter develops these ideas, and the idea that nonprofit organizations should not outsource anything that is central to their being not-for-profit.

What to outsource? Principles underlying the make-or-buy decision

Production requires many inputs. These inputs may be produced, owned, or directly controlled in the organization, or they may be purchased or hired from other organizations or individuals. Examples of the two alternatives abound. A car manufacturer can produce its own engine, car bodies, and several thousand other parts, or it can purchase them from other firms; it can sell the cars through its own dealerships, or it can use independent dealers; it can even buy fully assembled cars from another company and only attach its brand name before selling them to customers. Parts may be purchased from suppliers who are steady partners, or from occasional suppliers that are chosen as needed from a list of potential suppliers. A nonprofit hospital can employ staff physicians, or contract with physicians for their services; it can own its own laboratories, or it may purchase laboratory services from other firms; it can operate its own laundry services, or it may purchase them from other companies; it can sterilize its medical instruments, or it may purchase these services from others; it can use its own staff to transcribe physician dictations, or it may contract with another firm. Some software companies outsource help-line services; many clothes retailers use suppliers that manufacture clothes according to the retailers' design, or buy clothes designed and manufactured by other companies; some counties and states have contracted out to private firms the operation of their prisons; and some nonprofit organizations pay for-profit firms to raise funds for them. Most organizations have the option to do their own payroll, operate their mailroom, perform public relations functions, and so on, or buy the relevant services from other companies.

What kind of services should an organization purchase from outside suppliers: common, nonspecialized, standard services, or rare, unusual, specialized services? What are the criteria for choosing which activities to outsource? What are the contingencies that make outsourcing desirable in one situation but not in another? Do the principles of outsourcing decisions differ between nonprofit organizations and for-profit firms? Should nonprofit organizations outsource to for-profit firms or to nonprofit organizations?

Consider an input used by an organization in the production of its own final product. The input in question can be mail services, fundraising, laboratory tests, car engines, payroll services, marketing, and so on, whereas the organization's final product may be health care services provided by a hospital, cars delivered to consumers, services for the elderly, museum services, and so on. The production, ownership, or control of the input can be kept in house, a decision referred to as 'make,' or else it can be outsourced to another company, the option often termed 'buy.'

Under the in-house alternative, responsibility for input-related activities rests with the same authority (management) that is in charge of production of the final product. Management's responsibility also extends of course to oversight over additional activities, as well as for their integration with the input in question in the production of the final product. For example, a nursing home may hire its own nurses, and make sure that their work is coordinated with other activities necessary to provide adequate care for patients. Clearly, for effective patient care, the nursing home's management must be proficient at hiring and managing nurses and other groups of employees, as well as integrating the activities of these groups.

An organization may outsource inputs to other organizations, that is, to enter into a purchaser-supplier relationship. In this event, some decisions about the outsourced input are made in the supplying organization, and other decisions are made in the purchasing organization. In the nursing home example, nurses would be hired by an employment agency ('temps agency' or 'contract house') that decides, perhaps in consultation with nursing home representatives, what kind of nurses, and sometimes which specific nurses, will be deployed. But the ultimate decision on hiring of nurses, including what their qualifications and experience should be, is in the hands of the employment agency; whereas the decision regarding the deployment of the nurses rests with the management of the nursing home, as does the responsibility for their integration with other employees and their activities in the care of nursing home patients. It is also the employment agency that collects information about the behavior and performance of its nurses and then chooses what information to share with the management of the nursing home.

Is 'making' (e.g., hiring and employing nurses directly) more economical than 'buying' (using the services of the employment agency), or is it the other way around? The answer depends on: 1) the magnitude of the benefits of specialization and economies of scale; 2) which organization can better control *agency problems* that arise within it (obtaining employees' cooperation); 3) how easy it is to control agency-type problems between the purchaser and the supplier; and 4) the centrality of the input in question to the production of the organization's final product and its mission. For example, adding a specialized computer engineer or programmer to a nursing home's staff in order to maintain the agency's Web site, create forms, maintain patients' records and link them with hospital records, and so on, requires that the manager spend time understanding the alternative software solutions on the market, benchmark the programmer's work for purposes of supervision and compensation, and so on. This entails sacrificing time that otherwise could be spent on managing the organization and developing staff tied to the core activities of the nursing home.

Specialization, comparative advantage, and economies of scale.

An effective production process requires skills of employees, knowledge of production techniques, awareness of innovation in product and process, and management practices that may be specific to the product. The more specialized a production process is, the greater the specific investment that it requires. This means that if the production or control of the input entails a different set of management skills than the production and control of other inputs used in the organization, then the organization will have to invest in different tracks of specialization for the various inputs. If the scale of operation is sufficiently large, this will allow the organization to reap the benefits of investment in the specialized production or control of the input. However, in the absence of economies of scale, the investment will not pay off as compared to investment by an organization with a larger scale production or operation of the input in question. For example, an organization that makes little use of audiovisual presentations should not invest in either a specialist who is specially trained in such presentations, nor in expensive equipment. All other things equal, organizations benefit from specialization. This consideration favors outsourcing.

The concept of comparative advantage emphasizes that specialization is the consequence of one firm having lower *opportunity costs* in the production of certain goods than other firms. The notion of lower opportunity cost implies not that a firm should produce all the goods that it can produce more effectively than other firms, but that it should specialize in the production of the goods that entail a relatively lower sacrifice of inputs than for other firms. This consideration is particularly apt when there are important constraining inputs, such as management's time, span of control, and expertise. Thus even a very talented manager of a small organization should be wary of adding many activities that he or she could manage well because such additions may reduce the manager's opportunities to devote time to the organization's mission. In other words, the organization could produce more of its main product by buying some services from other organizations rather than overseeing them in the organization itself. The comparative advantage consideration militates in favor of outsourcing many activities, and focusing in-house on what is often termed 'core competencies.' We return to this issue later.

The production of different products may be *complementary* in that some skills, equipment, management, or other factors may be utilized in common, preventing duplication of effort and other investments and therefore generating savings. For example, selling season tickets for a theater and soliciting donations from certain groups of theater-goers may be complementary, as are information technology services for maintenance of donor databases and for Internet registration to events. This consideration suggests that products benefiting from complementarity should be produced together.

Comparative agency costs in organizations.   Every organization has the obvious need to obtain the cooperation of its employees towards the attainment of organizational goals, and every organization faces difficulties in accomplishing this task. Whereas some individuals may always do what their supervisors request, most people will seek opportunities to pursue their personal objectives when they can do so within constraints of legality and their personal values. This means that employees may work less hard than their employers would like them to, or that they may pursue projects that are of interest to them, but are not considered to be optimal from the point of view of the organization. Problems of this sort are called *principal-agent* or *agency* problems. Owners and the board of directors are usually thought of as principals, whereas managers and employees are thought of as agents. However, for the purpose of examining the relationship between management and employees it is useful to think of management as principals (while they are agents for the board of directors), and employees as their agents.

Nonprofit organizations typically pursue multiple objectives, whereas for-profits pursue primarily one objective, profit. The existence of multiple objectives that are not easily weighted by relative importance and the fact that some objectives are not quantitative makes it difficult to offer executives and many managers a simple financial incentive scheme that ties pay to desirable outcomes. In for-profit firms, the compensation of upper management and even line employees may be linked to the one overreaching goal of the firm, profit.

To obtain maximum cooperation, organizations institute incentive schemes that align the interests of the agents with those of the principals, monitor and supervise agents, use the threat of dismissal, and engage in other means aimed at getting agents to act in ways that promote principals' interests. Generally, the larger an organization the more severe are the agency problems it faces because of the greater distance between principals and their agents and the difficulties in exercising effective discipline associated with such distance. As a result, larger organizations have to spend disproportionately more resources for coping with agency problems than smaller organizations; that is, the costs of agency per unit of the final product are greater the larger the organization. And the more an organization produces internally (rather than outsources) the larger it will be, and therefore it will face more severe agency problems. Hence, all things equal, outsourcing is desirable from an agency perspective.

Of course, all things are rarely equal. Large organizations can often reap benefits of scale that smaller organizations cannot enjoy, and these additional benefits may in some cases outweigh the greater agency costs associated with larger size. Some organizations have a better ability to deal with agency problems than other organizations, perhaps because they have more skilled management, or because their operations are such that agency problems can be dealt with more easily. This is the case, for example, when there are few possible hidden actions employees can take to benefit themselves at the expense of the organization without being detected by supervisors.

Employees in many nonprofit organizations support the organizational mission and are loyal to their organizations more than employees in for-profit firms, hence agency problems in such organizations may be less severe. However, nonprofit organizations may rely less on financial incentives than for-profit firms to alleviate the difference between personal goals and organizational objectives, suggesting that agency problems may be more difficult to manage in these organizations.

The discussion of agency problems suggests that outsourcing is an important option to consider, particularly for nonprofit organizations that have difficulty in controlling such problems internally. However, outsourcing creates agency-like problems too, as the relationships between two organizations (purchaser and supplier) are not free of issues of alignment of different objectives. In order to decide which solution is better—make or buy—we must compare the agency costs incurred in executing a certain function within the organization with the agency-like costs born in purchasing on the market services from another organization.

Agency costs across organizations: costs of transactions in markets.
The relationship between a purchaser and a supplier can be regarded as an agency relationship, although neither is formally the principal or the agent of the other. An organization that contracts out a service to a supplier wants to make sure that its objectives are being met, just like a manager seeks to have employees act in accordance with the organization's objectives. However, the arms-length relationship between two organizations gives rise to opportunities for one organization to seek to advance its interests at the expense of the other, generally more so than in the tighter relationship between a manager and employees within the confines of the same organization.

Several factors influence the magnitude of the costs of transacting with other organizations for the purposes of selling and buying a service. These factors include: the complexity of the service, whether the service is a 'private' or 'public' good, the reliability of the supplier, trust between the supplier and purchaser, the competitiveness of the market for the service, the dependence of the purchaser on a particular supplier, the state of contract law, and the enforceability of agreements. We shall explore each of these factors in some detail.

Some services may be quite complex, with many dimensions that are difficult to assess, and with performance that is difficult to observe in the short term. In such cases it may be quite difficult and expensive to write and enforce contracts. Furthermore, in the case of such contracts the parties have incentives to attempt to take advantage of each other in order to make additional gains. For example, a software developer may seek to extend a contract by claiming unexpected difficulties in implementing a Web-based reservations system, or a search firm may want to convince a nonprofit organization that the candidates it has brought for a certain position are the best qualified people available in the market in order to obtain its fees quickly. As a result, complex services are more difficult to outsource than simpler services.

The service may be a *private good* or a *public good* (and everything in between). Publicness and privateness are measured on two dimensions: *rivalry* and *excludability*. Rivalry means that the use by one organization eliminates (or at least reduces) the possibility of use of the same service by another organization. Nonrivalry means just the opposite, so that no matter how many organizations use a certain service, there is still room for more users without degrading the value of the service to other users. Advertising a product (but not a brand) or a cause is nonrival because all those who make the product or support the cause benefit from the advertising. Protection by a national military is also nonrival because it benefits all citizens. The treatment received by a patient in a nursing home is a rival good for the patient, but from the perspective of a community that cares about its elderly citizens, the treatment is nonrival. A theatrical production of *Hamlet* is rival because it displaces in any given point in time a production of *Twelfth Night,* but once the production is mounted, it is nonrival because many people can simultaneously enjoy the same performance.

The second dimension is excludability, which refers to control over access. Excludable products are those to which access can be denied or conditioned upon payment. Examples include land, property rights, copyrights, and patents, which typically involve payment for access or use. Nonexcludable products, such as advertising for a product or a cause as well as expired copyrights or patents, are in the public domain and require no payment. The treatment received by a patient in a nursing home is excludable, for nonpayers can be prevented from receiving it. But from the perspective of a community that cares about its elderly citizens, the treatment in nonexcludable for all who care about treatment for the elderly, whether they pay or not. Where nonrivalry and nonexcludability are prominent, the costs of transaction in the market are very high because it takes a lot of resources to deny nonpayers access, and it requires much effort to identify the kinds of products that will satisfy different groups of customers of nonrival goods. Consequently, there will be strong incentives for making nonrival and nonexcludable services in-house rather than outsourcing them.

The services of a purchasing agent or buying group provide an example of a nonrival and nonexcludable input, as all clients of the group receive the same service. The clients are interested in achieving lower prices associated with a larger purchasing pool. The purchasing group, if it is a loyal agent on behalf of its clients or if it is overseen well by the clients and held accountable to them, will do its best to negotiate the lowest prices and keep its own costs low. However, the purchasing agent may have enough latitude to pursue its own interests at the expense of clients. For example, numerous hospitals have combined resources to own a purchasing company in order to achieve savings in the cost of various supplies they purchase. However, despite their ownership, the purchasing group's management may succeed in pursuing its own welfare at the expense of the hospitals' objectives.

> In order to take advantage of economies of scale in negotiating prices of hospital supplies, nearly 1,500 nonprofit hospitals have partnered to combine their purchasing through a buying group, Premier Inc., which they own. However, the buying group has failed to provide the expected savings and hospital executives have expressed irritation at the high cost of Premier's executive compensation and perquisites. (Mary Williams Walsh, "A Mission to Save Money, A Record of Otherwise," *The New York Times*, June 7, 2002, page C1). The buying group represents an outsourcing solution with considerable agency problems between the purchasing organizations (individual hospitals) and the provider (Premier, Inc.). Controls by the hospitals over Premier seem to have been weak, despite the fact that the hospitals jointly owned the company, allowing the provider to take financial advantage of the situation. As a result, the savings enjoyed by the hospitals were lower than expected and less than what was possible with stricter controls. The controls might have been too weak because of the *free-rider problem* each hospital executive faces: engaging in oversight of Premier is rather complicated and costly for the individual hospital whereas the benefits would be spread over the nearly 1,500 hospitals.

Reliability of the supplier has several facets. One is the ability to evaluate the service directly at the time of purchase; when purchasers cannot examine or certify the quality of a service before purchasing it, they will be wary of purchasing it from unknown or untrustworthy suppliers. Trust in the supplier can be grounded in the supplier's reputation for prompt delivery of promised services and the credibility of its warranty. Reputation and trust are weak in the case of new firms and in markets with many firms and a high turnover where it is hard to keep track of reputations. These circumstances militate in favor of make rather than buy. In contrast, the more competitive a market is, the easier it is to find alternative suppliers, which makes outsourcing safer (if one supplier does not work out, it can be replaced with another) and therefore reduces the incentives for in-house production.

Purchaser and supplier depend on each other to various degrees. Frequently a purchaser wants assurance that the service will be available in the future, and the supplier wants to count on the purchaser's future business. Whereas the purchaser needs reliable delivery, the supplier needs reliable payment. Specificity of the service or customization can bind the parties, particularly if the purchaser invests in staff knowledge and skills, facilities, and equipment or technology designed for use of the supplier's product, and the supplier makes investments tied specifically to the purchaser's needs. Specificity of the relationship can affect the relative bargaining power of the two parties, and either can hold the other captive, generating a fear of exploitation when investments connected to the particular relationship are high. For example, a supplier can raise prices or delay shipment to a dependent purchaser in order to engage in another lucrative activity. A purchaser can defend itself preemptively against opportunistic behavior by diversifying suppliers or, if diversification is not feasible or is too costly, making the product in-house. Contracts can be a fairly good substitute for trust because they provide remedies in the event of breach of the terms of the contract, and therefore allow the contracting parties to take the risk of depending on one another. Thus the existence of a legal framework that supports complicated contracts that regulate relations between purchasers and sellers, and the enforcement of contracts, are additional factors that influence the make-or-buy decision.

In the United States during the late 1800s and early 1900s, for example, in-house production was extensive because levels of both interorganizational trust and legal enforcement of contracts were low. In contrast, Japanese firms outsourced a lot because the culture of dependability reduced the need to make rather than buy (and risk depending on others). Low levels of dependability in post-Soviet Russia due to lack of appropriate laws, weak enforcement mechanisms, and the absence of long-standing reputations have led companies to make a lot and buy little.

Enforceability of contracts depends not only on external factors, but also on the ability of a purchasing organization to write, evaluate, and enforce contracts in which it engages. To be effective in relying on a contract with a supplier, an organization must acquire familiarity with the market in order to evaluate alternatives, and acquire legal knowledge—or the ability to purchase it—in order to write and enforce contracts and monitor the details of the fulfillment of the supplier's responsibility arising from the contract. Thus outsourcing may require engaging lawyers, having a representative of the purchaser spend a lot of time monitoring the supplier's work—sometimes on the supplier's premises, engaging at times in legal action, and more. The execution of many of these functions may be quite expensive, to the effect that effective outsourcing may be more expensive than in-house production, particularly for small organizations.

The centrality of an activity to the organization's main product.

Core activities are directly related to the organization's product, mission, and identity. The skills and knowledge that support these activities are the organization's core competencies. The central function of coordination of activities required for production of the organization's final product is at the core of organizational activities. Thus, in a nonprofit health care organization, management services should be carried out by those who are under the nonprofit umbrella rather than by a for-profit management company.

The coordination of production by outsourcers may be the only activity that is carried out in-house, as the examples of clothes retailers and others at the beginning of this chapter suggest. Thus an organization should not necessarily produce the final product in-house. However, activities that define the identity of the organization, activities that are critical to the maintenance of the organization's reputation, and activities that are difficult to observe, should not be considered for outsourcing. For example, the selection of key staff in the organization, which requires detailed knowledge of the organization and which is open to problems after the hiring, should not be outsourced. (Search firms can be used to identify candidates.) In the same vein, activities that entail great vulnerability for the organization (such as sterilizing medical instruments), but are subject to substantial problems of monitoring because of difficulty obtaining information about the quality of the service (how well sterilization was done) and which are crucial to the performance of the organization should be kept in-house.

There are additional considerations specific to nonprofit organizations. A particular core competency of any nonprofit organization is its ability to solve problems that for-profit firms cannot solve. This is the special advantage that the nonprofit form of organization enjoys. Nonprofit organizations exist because they can deal with problems that arise from the publicness of some goods and services, and the *asymmetric information* between providers and customers, or suppliers and purchasers. The problem with asymmetric information is that in the case of some goods and services, the purchaser cannot evaluate the full value of the product and the provider is tempted to take advantage of this fact. As a result, some purchasers will buy less than they would buy otherwise, they will be willing to pay less than otherwise, and therefore the market for the product in question may suffer. A nonprofit provider, particularly one that is controlled by purchasers, provides assurances to purchasers that the asymmetric information between them and the provider will not be used against their interests. This will entice purchasers to engage in transactions with the provider. The interesting thing about the nonprofit form of organization as a superior solution to problems associated with public (nonrival and nonexcludable) goods and asymmetric information is that, in a certain sense, the nonprofit form is a rejection of pure market outsourcing of some products. This is so because some purchasers band together by organizing a nonprofit to supply themselves with the product rather than buying it on the market.

For a nonprofit organization to maintain its credibility, it must ensure that it remains a solution to the problems which it is uniquely suited to solve. It cannot therefore usefully outsource activities where there are opportunities to exploit customers' informational weakness, or other activities that define the organization's special relationship with its stakeholders. For example, a nonprofit hospital that facilitates the provision of services of contracted medical personnel but has few staff physicians and nurses; a charity that uses for-profit fundraisers; a nonprofit health care facility that is run by a for-profit management company; a nonprofit research organization that distributes its net income to contract researchers; and a public radio station that raises revenue primarily from the sale of advertising—all risk the loss of their special advantage derived from their nonprofit status. Such core activities are best kept in-house; the same applies to the competencies that support these activities.

Outsource to nonprofit organizations or to for-profit firms?

Should a nonprofit organization care whether it purchases services from another nonprofit organization or should it prefer a for-profit trading partner? As noted in the previous section, nonprofit organizations occupy special market niches that are related to the nature of their final product. However, the problems that affect the final product often relate to the production process and the inputs that were used in it. That was the basis for the recommendation that nonprofit organizations should not outsource activities that relate to their special advantages. But if trustworthy suppliers are available to provide some inputs, outsourcing becomes more attractive. Nonprofit organizations may be exactly such suppliers, particularly in a local context where nonprofit organizations may be linked through overlapping directorates, enjoy overlapping customer bases, or have other bonds that foster trust. For example, some organizations may avail themselves to fundraising administrative services sold by nonprofit organizations.

However, a severely limiting factor is the fact that there are few nonprofit organizations operating in many areas in which outsourcing may be useful.

Nonprofit organizations providing services to persons with disabilities in the Rochester, NY area are individually too small to provide themselves with efficient, high-quality administrative services. In 1999, the nonprofit Al Sigl Center for Rehabilitation Agencies, Inc. formed Business Services, a unit that provides services in human resources, telecommunications, risk management, purchasing, management information systems, legal, public relations/communications, accounting and finance, pension/403(b), fundraising, and facilities management. These services are provided to the eight partner agencies of the Al Sigl Center (The Arc of Monroe County, Epilepsy Foundation of Rochester & Syracuse Regions, Mary Cariola Children's Center, Medical Motor Service, National Multiple Sclerosis Society/Upstate NY Chapter, Rochester Hearing and Speech Center, Rochester Rehabilitation Center, and United Cerebral Palsy Association). According to the The Peter F. Drucker Foundation for Nonprofit Management (now the Leader to Leader Institute, Web site viewed on July 20, 2002), "Business Services effected a 1999 cost savings of $143,348 for the partner agencies. By mid-2000 savings were projected to be $250,000 for a total of $393,350 over two years. The telecommunication service alone has reduced collective local/long distance rates by 40% from $140,000 to $84,000 annually, and has centralized the multitude of vendor solicitations that once filtered through agency directors."

Conclusions

The decision of whether to make or buy is, according to Ronald Coase (1937), winner of the Nobel Prize in economics, a matter determined by a comparison of the cost of carrying out transactions across external markets versus the cost of executing those transactions within the organization. From the perspective of an organization that considers how to best obtain a service, there are costs and benefits associated with outsourcing. Outsourcing allows for specialization, and permits clear evaluation of the costs of various inputs by comparing prices on the market. It also allows for flexibility in adjusting the size of the organization and its production without hiring and laying off employees. However, outsourcing entails search and selection of suppliers, which can be costly. Also, the relationship with suppliers has to be managed through contracts, which entails costs of writing and enforcement of contractual agreements, including the monitoring of performance by suppliers.

The relative costs and benefits of outsourcing have to be juxtaposed with keeping production in-house. But the more an organization produces internally, the greater is the agency problem due to increased span of control. On the other hand, in-house production provides access to information, monitoring, and other beneficial activities that reduce agency problems and are available only through direct control.

Outsourcing clearly has a place in nonprofit organizations, but it has to be done in a way that does not harm the trust that its customers and other stakeholders place in it. To put it in an extreme form, a nonprofit organization should not outsource so many activities that it becomes a for-profit firm in disguise.

Nonprofit organizations can safely outsource many information services and most business services, including payroll, but this should be subject to a careful analysis of the organization's ability to deal with the complex transactions that are often entailed by outsourcing. Small nonprofit organizations should outsource only simple-to-manage activities, where no complicated controls or contracts are required and where the opportunities for being taken advantage of by suppliers are minimal. In particular, nonprofit organizations should consider not just the price of an outsourced activity, but also the cost of managing the relationship with the supplier.

References

Barthelemy, Jerome. Spring 2001. "The Hidden Costs of IT Outsourcing." *Sloan Management Review*. 60–69.

Ben-Ner, Avner. 2002. "The Shifting Boundaries of the Mixed Economy and the Future of the Nonprofit Sector." *Annals of Public and Cooperative Economics*. 73(1). April, 5–40.

Ben-Ner, Avner, and Theresa Van Hoomissen. 1991. "Nonprofit Organizations in the Mixed Economy: A Demand and Supply Analysis." *Annals of Public and Cooperative Economics*. 62 (4):519–550. Reprinted in *The Nonprofit Sector in the Mixed Economy*. (Avner Ben-Ner and Benedetto Gui, eds.). 1993. Ann Arbor: University of Michigan Press. 27–58.

Coase, Ronald H. 1937. "The Nature of the Firm." *Economica*. 4:386–405.

Domberger, Simon. 1998. *The Contracting Organization: A Strategic Guide to Outsourcing*. New York: Oxford University Press.

Handy, Charles. 1995. "Trust and the Virtual Organisation" *Harvard Business Review*. May-June: 40–50.

KPMG Peat Marwick LLP & G2R, Inc. 1998. *A Case Study Guide to Business Process Outsourcing*. Financial Executives Research Foundation.

Powell, Walter W. 1990. "Neither Market nor Hierarchy: Network Forms of Organization." *Research in Organizational Behavior*. Stamford, CT: JAI Press. 12:295–336.

Putterman, Louis. 1995. "Markets, Hierarchies, and Information: On a Paradox in the Economics of Organization" *Journal of Economic Behavior and Organization*. 26:375–90.

Rothery, Brian and Ian Robertson. 1995. *The Truth About Outsourcing*. Aldershot, Hampshire, England: Gower Publishing Limited.

Surpin, Jo and Geri Weideman. 1999. *Outsourcing in Health Care: The Administrator's Guide*. Chicago: AHA Press.

Williamson, Oliver E. 1975. *Markets and Hierarchies: Analysis and Antitrust Implications, A Study in the Economics of Internal Organization*. New York: The Free Press.

CHAPTER 5

Fundraising Costs

Joseph J. Cordes
Patrick M. Rooney

Abstract

Gifts from individuals and business continue to be an important source of non-profit revenue. Although it is widely recognized that some expenditure of resources on fundraising is necessary, individual nonprofit organizations are often criticized for spending too much on fundraising compared to delivery of services, or for mounting fundraising campaigns that are seen as dissipating too large a percentage of contributions received in the form of fundraising expenses. Indeed, donors are encouraged to scrutinize reported fundraising expenses; and some private watchdog agencies strongly suggest that "good practice" by nonprofits requires limiting the percentage of total expense attributable to fundraising.

Much of the attention paid to fundraising activities both inside and outside the nonprofit community has to do with *fundraising efficiency*—the extent to which fundraising activities succeed in increasing net resources that are available for the delivery of nonprofit services. The broad notion of fundraising efficiency has both a private and social dimension.

Evaluating the fundraising efficiency of individual nonprofits, or the non-profit sector, raises challenging issues both of measurement, and of public over-sight and accountability. Measurement issues include properly accounting for the full costs of fundraising activities and developing appropriate indexes for comparing the full costs of fundraising activities with their financial returns. Issues of oversight and accountability hinge on the feasibility of developing meaningful standards for evaluating a nonprofit's fundraising performance.

Introduction

Although nonprofit organizations have become more and more reliant on income sources other than charitable contributions, gifts from individuals and business nonetheless remain an important source of nonprofit revenue for many nonprofits.

In a typical year, about four out of five nonprofits report receiving at least some revenue from individual and/or corporate gifts. Aside from hospitals, and other health-related nonprofits that are distinguished by their heavy reliance on fees for services provided, one of every two nonprofits receives at least 20 per-cent of total revenue from contributions, and one out of four receives at least 66 percent. Even among nonprofits that depend heavily on fees and earned income, charitable contributions often provide a "critical margin" to cover expenses, and the presence of income from gifts can permit fees to be structured differently than if such income were not available (see Chapter 2).

Perhaps just as important, fundraising programs that are intended to elicit charitable contributions are often a visible activity of nonprofits, and are seen by the public to be a defining feature of nonprofit organizations just like their tax-exempt status is.

Nonprofit practitioners, scholars, and government and private monitors of nonprofit organizations have a mixed view of fundraising. Everyone recognizes that some expenditure of resources on fundraising is necessary. Some nonprofits may be able to rely entirely on unpaid volunteers for their fundraising efforts, but it is the rare nonprofit that can count on receiving substantial contributions on a sustained basis without spending financial resources on fundraising. Indi-vidual nonprofits also feel that organized fundraising efforts are necessary in what they see as an increasingly competitive environment for contributed dollars.

At the same time, some organizations are criticized for spending too much on fundraising compared to delivery of services, or for mounting fundraising campaigns that are seen as dissipating too large a percentage of contributions received in the form of fundraising expenses. Indeed, donors are encouraged to scrutinize reported fundraising expenses; and some private watchdog agencies strongly suggest that "good practice" by nonprofits requires limiting the percentage of total expense attributable to fundraising.

It also appears that individual donors would like to believe that all or most of their contributions go toward increasing the ability of the organization to provide its primary services, rather than to defray the costs of fundraising. For example, the Better Business Bureau's Wise Giving Alliance found that 79 percent of Americans surveyed say that the cost of fundraising is important or very important to them in deciding whether to contribute to a charity; and the BBB is currently revising its fundraising costs standards based on these survey results and on input from experts in the nonprofit sector.

This chapter focuses on fundraising efficiency from two theoretical perspectives: *private* and *social* concepts of *efficiency*. We start the chapter with a brief discussion of what these concepts are, and then proceed to discuss each in more detail. Private fundraising efficiency is complicated by the different ways in which it has been measured historically, by the difficulty of accounting for joint costs and volunteers, as well as measuring the impact of professional fundraisers, and by traditional problems like accounting for differences in timing of costs and benefits. Each of these concepts is addressed before we focus on the tension between fundraising as a revenue strategy versus fundraising efficiency as a cost-minimizing strategy. The social efficiency of fundraising is a topic that has received little or no formal scholarly treatment, but we think it bears mentioning (and further research). We raise questions about competition for gifts and coordination among nonprofits in evaluating the social return to fundraising. These issues are becoming more important as standards and public disclosure—as well as accountability and assessment—become the norm. We touch briefly on such issues before concluding with some recommendations and suggestions for further research.

Fundraising Efficiency

Much of the attention paid to fundraising activities both inside and outside the nonprofit community has to do with fundraising efficiency—the extent to which fundraising activities succeed in increasing net resources that are available for the delivery of nonprofit services. The broad notion of fundraising efficiency has both a private and social dimension.

The private efficiency of fundraising has to do with the overall payoff or return to fundraising by individual nonprofit organizations. Here the kinds of questions that one might pose about fundraising activities are similar to those that any private enterprise would pose about its operating and revenue strategies. What criteria should an individual nonprofit use to guide internal decisions about whether to engage in particular fundraising activities? How can fundraising efficiency be measured, both internally for planning purposes, and externally for purposes of informing the giving public? How can fundraising activities be structured to maximize their efficiency? What should be the roles of internal staff and outside professional fundraisers in the process of eliciting charitable gifts? What is the payoff to pursuing fundraising as a broad revenue-raising strategy, compared with alternatives, such as running nonprofit operations more efficiently and/or pursuing other streams of revenue?

Unlike private businesses, which are mainly accountable to their owners and shareholders, nonprofit organizations are seen as being accountable to the broader public. As a result, there is a social as well as a private dimension to fundraising efficiency.

The concept of social efficiency in fundraising has several aspects. One has to do with the social productivity of decentralized fundraising among individual nonprofits. Individual nonprofits may have no choice but to invest more resources in fundraising if they wish to compete with other nonprofits for contributions. From society's perspective, however, one wonders whether more spending on fundraising by all nonprofits taken together increases the total financial resources of the sector.

Because nonprofit organizations receive a range of public benefits, one can also ask whether there should be public oversight of fundraising activities, and if so, what form should oversight take—by both government and private bodies—to ensure that fundraising activities are not only legitimate but also efficient. A related question is whether norms for gauging fundraising behavior and performance should be sectorwide—i.e., comparing the fundraising performance of all nonprofits relative to some common benchmarks, or whether separate norms should be established for different nonprofit groups—e.g., comparing the fundraising performance of new nonprofits versus other new nonprofits, research universities versus other research universities, nonprofit advocacy groups with one another, and so on.

Private Fundraising Efficiency

At the level of the individual nonprofit organization, if the main objective of fundraising is to increase the net financial resources of the organization, then fundraising efficiency should measure the extent to which spending on fundraising increases the net resources that are available to support nonprofit activities. Using this definition, a fundraising campaign that costs $100,000 to raise $100,000 of contributions would be seen as inefficient because the net increase in resources available for programs is $0.

Unfortunately, measuring the contribution that fundraising makes to increasing net financial resources is much more complex than is suggested by the simple example. To make sure measurements, an organization needs to be able to: 1) accurately measure the resources that are devoted to fundraising activities, and 2) track the relationship between increased (or decreased) expenditures of these resources and contributions.

Organizations are required to separately report expenses allocated to fundraising, including both the value of internal staff time, and amounts paid to professional fundraisers. These reported expenses, in turn, are often used to calculate two financial ratios. The *fundraising-expense ratio,* which is the percent of total expense attributable to spending on fundraising, is meant to describe how much of an organization's resources are devoted to fundraising as distinct from its core mission-related activities. *The fundraising-contribution ratio,* which is the ratio of fundraising expense to total private contributions received, is intended to describe the financial payoff or return to fundraising expenditures.

If these ratios are accepted as measurements for fundraising efficiency, they indicate that, by and large, fundraising activities among a wide range of nonprofits are fairly efficient (Cordes, Pollak, and Wilson 1999):

- Over half of all nonprofits report being able to receive contributions while having no reported fundraising expense.

- Among nonprofits that have positive fundraising expenses, spending on fundraising accounts for a fifth or less of total expenses for nine out of ten nonprofit organizations; and half of all organizations report spending 4 percent or less of total outlays on fundraising.

- Among nonprofits that have positive fundraising expenses, three out of four organizations have ratios of fundraising expense to contributions of 0.3 or less.

There is, however, some question about whether these commonly reported financial ratios truly measure fundraising efficiency.

Ratio of Fundraising Expense to Total Expense. The first question is whether reported fundraising expenses accurately measure actual fundraising expenses. A number of issues arise having to do with: 1) apportioning joint costs between fundraising and other activities; 2) accounting for volunteer time; and 3) the role of professional fundraisers.

Accounting for Joint Costs. It is widely recognized that there are many complexities involved in allocating the time of nonprofit staff who have multiple responsibilities, including participation in fundraising activities. Some practitioners and scholars believe that organizations are able to use these complexities to their advantage by allocating joint costs between fundraising and program activities in ways that understate the true cost of fundraising while overstating program spending. Research on how joint cost allocation might affect reported fundraising expenses includes comparisons of fundraising expenses reported in "public disclosure documents," such as the IRS 990 return, with those reported on organizations' audited financial reports (Froehlich and Knoepfle 1996); an in-depth case study of expense allocation at a major Midwestern university (Rooney 1999); and surveys of fundraising and administrative expenses reported by higher education and health care organizations (CASE 1990).

The practice of commingling fundraising appeals with the educational activities of nonprofit organizations has also received greater scrutiny in recent years. Beginning in 1992, nonprofit organizations have been required to identify on the IRS 990 return whether they reported as program service expenses any joint costs from a combined educational campaign and fundraising solicitation; and joint cost allocations for all nonprofits are supposed to be guided by SOP 98-2 from the American Institute of Certified Public Accountants (AICPA).

A preliminary analysis of joint costs for education and fundraising activities reported on 990 tax returns suggests that the practice of allocating joint costs in this manner is not yet widespread, with less than 1 percent of organizations reporting that they allocated joint costs from a combined educational fundraising campaign to fundraising and program services. On the other hand, the list of organizations that report doing so includes some of the more visible nonprofit organizations: over 50 percent of the joint costs reported in the sample are incurred by just twenty organizations, which reported an average of $13,000,000 per organization in joint costs that were allocated. In addition, when joint costs are allocated between education and fundraising, on average about 60 percent of such joint costs were allocated to program services and 40 percent to fundraising (Cordes, Pollak, and Wilson. 1999).

Accurately attributing overhead costs to fundraising expense is further complicated by the fact that some components of overhead costs that arguably could be allocated to fundraising activities are overlooked in many cost studies. One such category is the overhead related to fundraising itself: gift processing, thank-you letters, donor recognition, and prospect research (James Greenfield, personal correspondence. December 8, 2001). Another is the *opportunity cost* associated with fundraising activities that place demands on (scarce) organizational infrastructure that is provided for the nonprofit and its mission (e.g., Rooney. 1999). For example, development offices commonly share space with the main office of the nonprofit, but the pro rata share of rent (or depreciation if the space is owned) and utilities are often not included in the estimated cost of fundraising, which might substantially alter these cost ratios.

Accounting for Volunteers. In principle, the value of time spent by volunteers in fundraising also is part of the cost of fundraising. Yet, even if one could track volunteer time, which itself can be difficult, serious questions arise about how to value that time. Is it the value of the time to the volunteer (e.g., based on the volunteer's income or wage)? Or is the value of the volunteer time to the nonprofit organization (e.g., the value of staff time saved by volunteers)?

Professional Fundraisers. Lastly, issues arise about how to account for the use of professional fundraisers. Presumably it is relatively easy to measure the costs of professional fundraising staff, who are paid by the nonprofit on a salary basis. But, some nonprofits make use of either fundraising consultants, who are paid to advise nonprofits on how to conduct their annual fund or capital campaign, etc., but who do not actually solicit gifts, or fundraising solicitors, who are hired by nonprofits to raise funds on behalf of the nonprofit (James Greenfield, personal correspondence. December 8, 2001). Fundraising solicitors might be paid a flat rate, a commission (percentage), or some combination of both. It should be noted that commission-based payments are in violation of the ethical guidelines developed by the Association of Fundraising Professionals.

The best available evidence suggests that no more than one in every ten nonprofits reports making direct payment to professional solicitors, and although there is some variation in this fraction among different types of nonprofit organizations, the range of variation is fairly small. As in the case of reported total fundraising expenses, there is a degree of skepticism about the reliability of these figures. Some people believe that nonprofits tend to understate the use of professional fundraisers by reporting contributions received net of commissions taken off the top by professional fundraisers. Some evidence suggests that this concern may be somewhat misplaced, but it is frequently voiced, nonetheless (Greenlee and Gordon 1998).

Among organizations that report using professional fundraisers, however, relying on those fundraisers increases the reported costs of fundraising. At the same time, these higher expenses seem to be productive in the sense that nonprofits that use professional fundraisers also garner more contributions.

Fundraising-to-Contribution Ratio.   Properly measuring fundraising expenses is challenging enough, but an additional challenge is posed by how to evaluate the productivity of these expenses. A number of private watchdogs of nonprofit organizations have called for wide public disclosure of the reported ratio of fundraising cost to contributions received. Others counter that focusing on fundraising cost ratios may be a form of "functional fixation" (fixating on something that does not matter) in many nonprofits.

Economists who study the behavior of nonprofit organizations support the concept of measuring the efficiency of fundraising expenses, but question whether donors and/or regulators should view the commonly reported fundraising-to-contribution ratio as providing information on fundraising productivity (Steinberg 1986 and Young and Steinberg 1995). These economists point out that the most useful cost measure in gauging whether additional fundraising is likely to increase net resources is the additional or *marginal cost* of raising an additional $1 of contributions. Simply put, as along as spending an additional $1 on fundraising increases contributions by more than $1, the dollar spent on fundraising would be efficient, because it raises the net resources available to the organization.

The fundraising-to-contribution ratio as commonly reported, however, does not measure the marginal cost of raising a dollar, but rather the *average cost.* Some scholars have suggested that such average cost ratios may serve as a rough proxy for the marginal cost of fundraising, but it is quite easy to create plausible examples of cases in which information on the average cost of fundraising provides little guidance about the actual marginal costs. In such cases, relying on the average fundraising-to-contribution ratio to gauge fundraising efficiency can be misleading: seemingly efficient nonprofit organizations, based on their average fundraising-to-contribution ratio, may in fact be operating in a very inefficient range of investing additional dollars in fundraising.

The basic point is illustrated in Table 1, which for purposes of illustration assumes that the organization would be able to raise $50,000 in contributions without any fundraising expense (e.g., the proverbial "over the transom" gifts without active fundraising efforts). Column 2 of Table 1 shows the different amounts of contributions that would be received at different levels of total spending on fundraising shown in Column 1. Column 6 shows the average fundraising cost ratio that corresponds to the fundraising-to-contribution ratio commonly calculated for nonprofits, and Column 7 shows the corresponding incremental (marginal) cost ratio.

As may be seen from Table 1, the mere fact that the organization's average fundraising cost is less than $1 provides little information about the marginal fundraising cost. For example, in the illustration, an organization could report that fundraising expense was 23.8 percent, while at the same time effectively spending an incremental $5.00 in order to raise an additional dollar.

An implication of the simple example is that donors should exercise great caution in using fundraising ratios to judge organizational fundraising effectiveness. But aside from what donors may believe, the example also points to the desirability of having organizations develop internal measures of fundraising effectiveness that at least roughly track the incremental costs and benefits of fundraising activities.

An important and unsettled issue is whether donors care enough about reported fundraising expenses to act on the kind of information that would typically be provided in fundraising ratios calculated from financial data. Some research suggests that there may be little or no direct link between reported fundraising expenses and private contributions (Rose-Ackerman 1982 and Steinberg 1986); or that donors seem to respond to additional fundraising efforts while not paying much attention to the reported efficiency of the organization (Frumkin and Kim 2001). Other studies, however, find that (donor perceptions of) the price of giving, which is affected by fundraising costs, does affect the amounts that people give (Okten and Weisbrod 2000).

TABLE 1. Illustrative Fundraising Cost Calculations						
Fundraising Cost	Contributions	Incremental Cost	Incremental Contribution	Net Revenue	Avg. Cost Ratio	Incremental Cost Ratio
[1]	[2]	[3]	[4]	[2]-[1]	Col. 1/ Col. 2	Col. 3/ Col. 4
$0	$50,000	N.A.	N.A.	N.A.	N.A.	N.A.
$1,000	$50,500	$1,000	$500	$49,500	2.0%	$2.00
$2,000	$54,000	$1,000	$3,500	$52,000	3.7%	$0.29
$3,000	$58,000	$1,000	$4,000	$55,000	5.2%	$0.25
$4,000	$62,000	$1,000	$4,000	$58,000	6.5%	$0.25
$5,000	$66,000	$1,000	$4,000	$61,000	7.6%	$0.25
$6,000	$69,000	$1,000	$3,000	$63,000	8.7%	$0.33
$7,000	$72,000	$1,000	$3,000	$65,000	9.7%	$0.33
$8,000	$74,000	$1,000	$2,000	$66,000	10.8%	$0.50
$9,000	$76,000	$1,000	$2,000	$67,000	11.8%	$0.50
$10,000	$78,000	$1,000	$2,000	$68,000	12.8%	$0.50
$11,000	$79,500	$1,000	$1,500	$68,500	13.8%	$0.67
$12,000	$81,000	$1,000	$1,500	$69,000	14.8%	$0.67
$13,000	$82,000	$1,000	$1,000	$69,000	15.9%	$1.00
$14,000	$82,500	$1,000	$500	$68,500	17.0%	$2.00
$15,000	$82,900	$1,000	$400	$67,900	18.1%	$2.50
$16,000	$83,200	$1,000	$300	$67,200	19.2%	$3.33
$17,000	$83,400	$1,000	$200	$66,400	20.4%	$5.00
$18,000	$83,600	$1,000	$200	$65,600	21.5%	$5.00
$19,000	$83,800	$1,000	$200	$64,800	22.7%	$5.00
$20,000	$84,000	$1,000	$200	$64,000	23.8%	$5.00

Timing Issues. The tracking and measurement of the costs of and returns to fundraising are further complicated by the fact that fundraising campaigns are undertaken over different periods of time. For example, investments in annual giving may be able to track costs and returns, but even this is complicated by the desire of annual funds to create and cultivate major and planned gifts in the long run. Major and planned gift fundraising may have significant fundraising costs for several years before any gift is realized (if ever), yet once it is realized, the cumulative cost of fundraising (if it could be tracked) might be substantially lower than the average cost of fundraising would be, absent major and planned gifts. This suggests that part of the investment in fundraising be "capitalized" or amortized over a longer period of time than is typically done today. This corresponds to the "matching principle," which is the need to match revenues with costs in any given year. To the extent that such matching is not feasible, a nonprofit may produce numbers that lack validity and comparability.

Other Issues. Practitioners also point to a number of other factors relevant to evaluating fundraising activities that may be obscured by focusing too much on simple financial reporting ratios. For example, the move to planned and major gifts as a strategy of lowering fundraising costs can have the unintended consequence of giving the wealthy more input and influence into "ownership" of nonprofits and their programmatic aspects. Turnover among development professionals within organizations and across the sector can also affect the amount and the distribution of "fundraising human capital." As professional fundraisers enter and exit from nonprofit organizations and from the sector, such turnover may affect the ability of organizations to raise funds and the sector's ability to build support (Duronio and Tempel 1997).

Fundraising as a Revenue Strategy

Our discussion thus far has focused on the efficiency of fundraising as a generator of gifts and contributions. But to focus exclusively on fundraising efficiency begs a broader question of how fundraising should be regarded as a general operating strategy. Much of the new literature on nonprofit management, for example, contends that nonprofit managers should devote more time and effort to streamlining their operations and less to traditional fundraising efforts (Frumkin and Kim 2001). To date, scholarly research that has examined the link between expenditure of resources and contributions received by organizations suggests that investments in fundraising do pay off. For example, Weisbrod and

Dominguez (1986) find evidence that fundraising expenditures by nonprofit organizations succeed in encouraging donors to overcome the incentive to "free-ride" (e.g., make little or no financial contributions to a nonprofit even though valuing its services). As noted above, there is also evidence that increased expenditures on professional fundraising raises average contributions received (Greenlee and Gordon 1998).

Fundraising may also have potentially offsetting effects on donors. On one hand, fundraising stimulates giving by advertising the needs and accomplishments of nonprofits. On the other hand, resources spent on fundraising may be seen by donors as raising the cost of giving. A recent study attempted to quantify these offsetting tendencies and found that, on balance, the positive effect of fundraising expenditures outweighs the negative effect of fundraising expenditures (Okten and Weisbrod 2000).

By itself, this evidence merely demonstrates that spending time and effort on fundraising is productive. It does not address whether spending less time on fundraising in order to devote more to efficient management of operations would perhaps provide an even greater return, either in the form of additional revenue from other income streams, or through greater giving from contributors who value more organizational efficiency. Yet, as noted above, some recent research finds that devoting greater resources to fundraising has a positive effect on contributions, but that greater (reported) organizational efficiency (as measured by the ratio of management and overhead expense to total expense) does not (Frumkin and Kim 2001).

Future research on the importance of fundraising as a revenue strategy will need to be sensitive to the fact that the role of fundraising in nonprofits may vary by the mission (e.g., private contributions typically make up a small share of hospitals' total revenue) and size of the organization. Despite such variation among organizations, however, in many organizations, regardless of mission or size, private philanthropy will continue to play a critical role in providing access to services by lower and middle income groups (e.g., educational and health services), in creating excellence and stimulating diversity (e.g., research, education, the arts, etc.), and in fostering pluralism in a democratic society.

Social Fundraising Efficiency

Regardless of whether one believes that reported fundraising expenses provide a complete picture of the resources that are devoted to fundraising by individual organizations, there is general agreement that it would be in the public interest to limit certain forms of "wasteful" expenditures on fundraising. Does increased competition among nonprofits for donations cause more resources to be invested in fundraising, resources that could instead be used to meet the needs of service recipients? What role, if any, should the government play in regulating the fundraising practices of individual nonprofits?

Competition, Coordination, and the Social Return to Fundraising.

From the perspective of the community, the question is not only whether fundraising activities are productive for individual nonprofits, but also whether total giving increases by more than the extra resources devoted to seeking donations. If it does, then increased spending on fundraising prompted by competition can actually have the beneficial effect of increasing the net amount of resources available for meeting social needs.

It is an open question, however, whether greater competition for donations among nonprofits significantly increases the amount of total giving or instead causes a largely fixed pool of charitable dollars to be redistributed among existing organizations. In the latter case, competition for dollars may create strong incentives for nonprofits to make expenditures for fundraising that, while rational for any individual organization, are wasteful in the aggregate.

Umbrella campaigns, such as the United Way, have traditionally been one means of reducing wasteful competition among nonprofits. But in many large urban areas, pressures to allow greater donor choice have had the effect of reviving such competition. Although it may be desirable in principle to reduce incentives for organizations to engage in socially wasteful competition, it is more challenging in practice to develop either new social institutions, or policies that limit such spending.

The social welfare aspects of fundraising are ultimately an empirical question, but one that has not received adequate attention. *Giving USA 2001,* the recent iteration of the AAFRC Trust for Philanthropy's annual compendium of giving in the United States, estimates that giving in the United States totaled over $200 billion in 2000—more than doubling since 1990.

Yet, by several measures, relative giving has not increased in a meaningful way. First, total giving as a percentage of Gross Domestic Product (GDP) has hovered around two percent, but it has not exceeded 2.1 percent since 1970. Second, personal giving as a percentage of personal income has ranged between 1.6 percent and 1.9 percent since 1970. Third, corporate giving as a percentage of corporate pretax income has gone from as a low as 0.7 percent to as high as 2.1

percent since 1970, but it has been more than 1.6 percent only three times in the last thirty years.

The observed growth in absolute, but not in relative giving has taken place in the context of a rapidly growing number of nonprofits (67 percent increase in the past decade, according to *Giving USA 2001*) and the growth in the development field as a profession (there are currently more than 25,000 members in AFP). Future research should address some possible explanations for these trends.

Perhaps increases in (relative) giving lag behind increases in investments in fundraising (see Schervish and Haven 2000). It may also be that part of the observed growth in professional fundraising staffs reflects a shift from unpaid volunteers to paid fundraising staff, as more women (who in the past formed the core of unpaid fundraising efforts) entered into the paid labor force (Duronio and Tempel 1997). Similarly, examining simple time trends does not tell much about what would have happened to relative giving if nonprofits had failed to increase investment in paid professionals.

The Role of Standards and Disclosure. Increasing the public accountability of nonprofit organizations for their fundraising practices might be seen as one way of limiting certain forms of socially inefficient fundraising activity. Both government regulators and private nonprofit watchdogs have called for greater disclosure, both of fundraising costs and fundraising practices. In the context of nonprofit organization management, the quest to improve uniformity of reporting by nonprofit organizations dates back to work conducted by Levis and New (1981), Greenfield (1996 and 1998), and Rooney (1999).

Within the accounting profession, new guidelines have been gradually adopted for nonprofit organization reporting (Financial Accounting Standards Board 1993). The allocation of joint costs for activities, such as mailings, that include both fundraising and program components have been addressed in several official publications (AICPA SOP 87-2 and SOP 98-2). However, the Form 990 instructions do not specifically require compliance with these standards. A useful question to consider is whether these guidelines result in consistent reporting on both financial statements and on the Form 990.

Another contentious issue is whether or not there should be one number for fundraising efficiency that is used as a benchmark nationally, or benchmarks that differ by subsector or by even more gradations (e.g., by subsector and size). Practitioners and scholars disagree on this point.

Some point out that such comparisons are difficult to make even among similar nonprofit organizations. It may be difficult, for example, to compare fundraising expenses among different types of theaters, not to mention the arts more generally, or the nonprofit sector as a whole. Other skeptics maintain that the cost of fundraising is a number without much meaning, and suggest that organizations be evaluated based on mission fulfillment.

Those who support making reasonable efforts to measure and report indexes of fundraising efficiency counter that the public and policy-makers, especially corporation leaders, expect items to be quantified. Thus, it is in the interest of the nonprofit sector to devise measures of fundraising expense and fundraising efficiency that use consistent methodology, and that make an effort to address at least some of the main criticisms levied against reported financial ratios.

Accountability and Outcome Measurement. Research on accountability and outcome measurement is also important to consider in the context of assessing fundraising effectiveness. This work often attempts to measure organizational effectiveness through comparison. However, it is extremely difficult to fairly and objectively compare the efficacy of programs across different types of nonprofits. In addition, evaluations are often based on a vague and varied interpretation of productivity. Nonetheless, research has shown that various nonprofit stakeholders not only make, but also act on their judgments of effectiveness. Therefore, as Herman and Renz (1998) have noted, it is clearly "in the interest of the NPO and its leadership to facilitate a dialogue with key stakeholders to surface and overtly identify the various performance criteria, outcome measures, and other constructions of effectiveness that sooner or later will become the basis for stakeholder judgments of organizational effectiveness." CASE (1994, 1996, and 1998) has made strides in this arena, but there is great need for more work and more widespread implementation of standardized methodologies for understanding and reporting costs.

Recommendations for the Nonprofit Sector and for Future Research

Despite the complexities and problems of measuring fundraising efficiency, the concept is clearly of interest to a variety of stakeholders, including the giving public, those who manage nonprofit organizations, and those charged with monitoring their performance.

There are several real allocation and cost-accounting issues that need to be better understood and better implemented across the sector. For example, attention should be given to the treatment of the cost and revenue from special events, the difference between the gross and the net when using external consultants, and the allocation of joint costs.

Another avenue for research is following up on a suggestion that Richard Steinberg made in 1991, which he calls the "differencing technique." If we think about fundraising efficiency as a marginal benefit concept (i.e., the net between marginal revenues and marginal costs), but if we cannot identify all of the needed information about the marginal benefit and/or the marginal costs at any given slice in time, perhaps we could analyze the dynamic efficiency of nonprofits (in the sense that the implementation of this technique will move nonprofits closer and closer to their ideal investment in fundraising over time). Steinberg's idea, while it has been tried by a few nonprofits, has been conspicuously underutilized and merits serious consideration. For example, we could track total fundraising costs and benefits over time and compare the differences at some regular time interval (e.g., annually). If the marginal benefits of a given nonprofit are growing faster than the marginal costs, then the efficient nonprofit would invest additional efforts in fundraising to reap the potential benefits of greater returns. Conversely, if the change in the marginal benefits of fundraising investments between any two years is less than the change in the marginal costs, then the nonprofit should reduce its investment in fundraising. (See Steinberg 1991, for more discussion of the advantages and limitations of this technique.)

References

AAFRC Trust for Philanthropy. 2001. "Giving USA 2001." Indianapolis: AAFRC Trust.

American Institute of Certified Public Accountants. Statement of Position. 1987. 87–2.

American Institute of Certified Public Accountants. Statement of Position. 1998. 98–2.

Cordes, Joseph J., Thomas Pollak, and Sarah Wilson. November1999. "Patterns of Fund Raising and Administrative Costs: What are the Data Telling Us? A Preliminary Analysis of Digitized Data from Scanned Images of IRS Form 990." ARNOVA conference paper.

Council for Advancement and Support of Education. 1990. "Expenditures in Fund Raising, Alumni Relations, and Other Constituent (Public) Relations." Washington DC: CASE (Council for Advancement and Support Education).

——. "Case Campaign Standards: Management and Reporting Standards for Educational Fund-Raising Campaigns." 1994.

——. "Case Management Reporting Standards: Standards for Annual Giving and Campaigns in Educational Fund Raising." 1996.

——. "Fund-Raising Standards for Annual Giving and Campaign Reports for Not-for-Profit Organizations Other than Colleges, Universities, and Schools. 1998.

Duronio, Margaret, and Eugene Tempel. 1997. *Fund Raisers: Their Careers, Stories, Concerns, and Accomplishments*. San Francisco: Jossey-Bass.

Financial Accounting Standards Board. 1993. *Statement of Financial Accounting Standards No. 117: Financial Statements of Not-for-Profit Organizations*. Norwalk, CT.

Froelich, Karen A. and Terry W. Knoepfle. 1996. "Internal Revenue Service 990 Data: Fact or Fiction?" *Nonprofit and Voluntary Sector Quarterly* 25(1): 40–52.

Frumkin, Peter and Mark T. Kim. 2001. "Strategic Positioning and the Financing of Nonprofit Organizations: Is Efficiency Rewarded in the Contributions Marketplace?" *Public Administration Review*. 61(3): 266–276.

Greenfield, James M. 1996. *Fundraising Fundamentals: A Guide to Annual Giving for Professionals and Volunteers*. New York: John Wiley and Sons.

——. 2001. The Nonprofit Handbook: Fundraising. New York: John Wiley & Sons.

Greenlee, Janet S. and Teresa P. Gordon. 1998. "The Impact of Professional Solicitors on Fund-Raising in Charitable Organizations." *Nonprofit and Voluntary Sector Quarterly*. 27(2): 277–299.

Gronbjerg, Kirsten A. 1993. *Understanding Nonprofit Funding*. San Francisco: Jossey-Bass.

Levis, Wilson C. and Anne New. 1981. The Average Gift Size Factor. *Philanthropy Monthly*, July/Aug. 5–14.

Okten, Kagla and BurtonWeisbrod. 2000. "Determinants of Donations in Private Nonprofit Markets. *Journal of Public Economics*. 75:255–272.

Rooney, Patrick. 1999. "A Better Method for Analyzing the Costs and Benefits of Fund Raising at Universities." *Nonprofit Management and Leadership*, 10(1): 39–56.

Rose-Ackerman, Susan. 1997. "Charitable Giving and Excessive Fundraising," *Quarterly Journal of Economics*. May. 193–212.

Schervish, Paul G. and John J. Havens. October 31, 2000 (working paper). "The New Physics of Philanthropy: The Supply-Side Vectors of Charitable Giving." Boston: Social Welfare Research Institute.

Steinberg, Richard. 1991. "The Economics of Fundraising." In *Taking Fund Raising Seriously*. Dwight Burlingame and Monty Hulse (eds.). San Francisco: Jossey-Bass. 239–256.

Steinberg, Richard. 1986. "Should Donors Care About Fundraising?" in Susan Rose-Ackerman (ed.), *The Economics of Nonprofit Institutions*. New York: Oxford University Press. 347–364.

Tuckman, Howard and Cyril Chang. "How Pervasive Are Abuses in Fundraising Among Nonprofits?" *Nonprofit Management & Leadership*. 9(2): 211–221.

Weisbrod, Burton and Nestor Dominguez. 1986. "Demand for Collective Goods in Private Nonprofit Markets: Can Fundraising Expenditures Overcome Free Rider Behavior." *Journal of Public Economics*. 30: 83-95.

Young, Dennis and Richard Steinberg. 1995. *Economics for Nonprofit Managers*. New York: Foundation Center.

CHAPTER 6

Investment and Expenditure Strategies

Marion R. Fremont-Smith

Abstract

The investment and expenditure decisions of nonprofit organizations should adhere to the concept of "modern prudent investing" as embodied in current law. This requires that nonprofits follow principles of modern finance and economic analysis. This chapter identifies these principles and applies them to the circumstances of contemporary nonprofit organizations. The principles include investing for *total return, portfolio diversification* to accommodate risk, appropriate valuation of "alternative investments" in new ventures, tangible personal property and other unique assets, evaluating the benefits and costs of all expenditures *at the margin,* broader consideration of investment alternatives that themselves contribute to the mission of the organization, and integrating investment and expenditure decisions for maximum impact on mission.

Introduction

Like for-profit investors and fund managers, nonprofits are concerned with financial returns, risk, and liquidity. In addition, however, nonprofits must consider other factors, including social returns on their investments, handling their unique sources of funding from contributions, "expenditures" of volunteer labor, and the appropriate amount they should expend from their permanent funds. Nonprofits also face unique constraints associated with special fund-accounting requirements.

The environment in which nonprofit directors and trustees make decisions relating to investment of their organizations' funds has changed drastically in the last twenty years. Nonprofits are freer now and obligated to apply basic principles of modern finance and economic analysis to their investment and expenditure decisions. These include investing for total return, portfolio diversification to accommodate risk, and appropriate valuation and use of alternative investments that may include new ventures, tangible personal property and other unique assets. Use of common trust funds, mutual funds, and other vehicles for pooled investment is encouraged as a means for facilitating diversification and providing specific management skills and facilities not otherwise available to the organization. Delegation to professional managers is permitted, and in fact may be the most prudent course of action in situations where the board and the staff lack sufficient expertise to carry out a prudent investment program.

New freedom often brings with it new constraints, and in the case of new investment strategies, it has become imperative that nonprofits integrate their investment and expenditure decisions to assure that they are carrying out their missions most effectively. They must evaluate the benefits and costs of all expenditures not on an average basis, but in regard to each additional dollar of expenditure at the margin, giving broader consideration to investment alternatives that contribute to the mission of the organization. Above all, they must integrate investment and expenditure decisions in order to provide maximum impact on the mission of the organization.

Comparison of Nonprofits and For-profits

One gains insight into the investment and expenditure policies of nonprofit organizations by comparing the ways in which these organizations are similar to their for-profit counterparts, as well as the ways in which they differ. Both types of organizations are subject to an injunction to act reasonably, and the liability of their managers is measured by that standard. They are under a mandate to adopt good accounting systems that permit accurate and thorough internal as well as external review. They are constrained to formulate their expenditure policies in a manner consistent with their missions. They are also under a mandate to use their funds efficiently, a mandate requiring in practice that each expenditure be subjected to a *benefit/cost analysis.*

The concept of total return, which is itself a rule of reasonableness, applies equally to nonprofits and for-profits. It is, in fact, a new practice for nonprofits. Traditional trust law required that the principal of endowment funds, which included all realized and unrealized gains, be preserved and only the dividend and interest income expended. This meant that trustees were forced to make a choice between investing a large percentage of their funds in assets with high expected dividends and few capital gains, thereby in many instances failing to keep up with inflation, or choosing assets with few expected dividends and high capital gains, severely limiting the funds available to meet current needs. Such a narrow definition of income seldom applies to for-profit organizations seeking to maximize total profit; accordingly, modern investing has created a new area of similarity between the two types of organizations.

The most basic difference between nonprofit and for-profit organizations is that nonprofits do not have as their primary goal the maximizing of profits. Rather, society assumes their goal to be the enhancement of social welfare—a far more difficult goal to measure and one that in the past was often assumed merely by virtue of the fact that their purposes were charitable. Today, we require nonprofits to measure their performance in terms of their mission: it is not sufficient for staff to merely accrue gains to their organization without demonstrating how those gains further the organization's ability to carry out its purposes.

A second difference arises from the fact that nonprofit organizations are almost always formed with the assumption that they will last in perpetuity in their same form. In the for-profit sector, economic forces encourage mergers, acquisitions, and dissolutions. There are no precisely similar forces operating in the nonprofit sector—nonprofits by their very nature are prohibited from distributing their profits through the sale of equity, so that there is no ordinary market for control through trading activities. It is true that in the last decade a number of health care organizations have sold their assets to for-profit corporations, with the proceeds of sale forming the capital for grant-making foundations, but there is little evidence that this trend will spread to other types of nonprofits

(Fremont-Smith 1999). The consequence of their permanent status is that, all too often, nonprofit organizations assume that unlimited life is an entitlement, and they sometimes fail to achieve the efficiencies that can be attained by various forms of combination.

A third difference arises from the fact that nonprofits hold themselves out as providing social benefit, looking to the public for support in the form of contributions, and to the government for tax and other benefits. The public and government, in turn, demand from nonprofits a different, often far higher, level of accountability than that expected from the for-profit sector.

There are other differences between for-profits and nonprofits that translate into different sets of policy considerations in regard to investments and spending practices. Nonprofits have a different mix of multiple and uncertain revenue streams, including contributions, grants from foundations and government, income from mixed portfolios, and receipts for services. These revenue streams are interdependent, and investment decisions made without considering the contribution of each source to the whole produce misleading results. In addition, unlike for-profit organizations, the risk-bearers for the financial and real assets in a nonprofit organization are not the same as the suppliers of its funds. In a for-profit entity, the investors/shareholders are the risk-takers. They are the ones who lose if the organization fails. In a nonprofit organization, the risk-takers are not the donors—whether private or governmental. Rather, it is the potential beneficiaries (and thus ultimately society at large) who stand to lose if organizations are unable to carry out their missions. At the same time nonprofits do give some heed to donor choice. Hence, every nonprofit is faced with a decision, even if unarticulated, as to whose risk preference should prevail: donors, clients, or management, or some combination of these.

A final set of differences that influence investment and expenditure decisions relates to the ability of nonprofits to take advantage of special benefits that arise from their tax-favored status. For example, a donor can usually gain by giving money away early for a future cause since money will grow at a before-tax rate if kept in the nonprofit; the nonprofit might in turn invest to accommodate this goal. Nonprofits might accept a lower return (even if financed from borrowings) from rental property if they do not owe property tax. Sometimes nonprofits and profit-making institutions engage in trades, such as implicit or explicit sales-lease-backs, to take advantage of one another's tax position (for example, the profit-making institution can make better use of depreciation allowances). Some of these are quite controversial and also affect public perception. Furthermore, in response to the controversies generated by these activities, there are increasingly arcane anti-arbitrage rules, such as those affecting nonprofit use of tax-exempt bonds, and those affecting passive property investments and the application of the tax on unrelated business income.

At the same time, nonprofits are subject to limitations on their freedom of choice by virtue of the ability of donors to restrict the use of assets—constraints not imposed on their for-profit counterparts. For example, donors may require that donated stock or real property be retained in perpetuity or may place restrictions on the categories in which the nonprofit may invest.

A New Legal Framework for Investment Decisions

Legal rules governing the investment of funds held by nonprofits traditionally were thought to be conservative, mandating avoidance of risk and, in many states, limiting the ability of fiduciaries to invest in securities other than those appearing on a mandatory "legal list." Major changes in investment strategies were adopted in the latter half of the twentieth century in response to changes in the mix of available investments and in the surplus distribution policies of business corporations. The most important development was a shift from high yield to growth, which in turn led to the adoption of a total return concept by business and individual investors. One reason for this development was that bonds, in a world of accelerating inflation, ended up being very high risk from a long-term perspective—and, hence, not so conservative.

The Modern Prudent Investor Rule. These economic changes, and the responses to them by investment managers, were explicitly recognized in the late 1980s and embodied in a "Modern Prudent Investor Rule," adopted by the American Law Institute in 1992 as the Restatement (Third) of the Law of Trusts. These changes were subsequently codified by the Commissioners of Uniform State Laws as the Modern Prudent Investor Act, which is now in force in 36 states and applies to nonprofits whether they have been formed as trusts or nonprofit corporations. The Rule was also codified by the Commissioners as part of the Uniform Trust Act so that its liberal approach is also applicable in measuring administrative decisions, as well as those affecting investment of assets.

Modern prudent investing does not rule out any investment category, but rather directs fiduciaries to consider and balance safety of capital with obtaining a reasonable return, considering both capital growth and income. It measures both administrative and investment performance in terms of three elements: care, skill, and caution. Decisions must be made in light of all of the circumstances, including the purposes, terms, and distribution requirements of the organization. It requires that the use of reasonable care, skill, and caution in managing investments, applied in the context of the entire portfolio, be considered as part of an overall investment strategy that incorporates risk and return objectives reasonably suited to the organization. It implies a duty to diversify investments unless under the circumstances it is prudent not to do so.

The Uniform Management of Institutional Funds Act. The change in standards for trust investing embodied in the new Prudent Investor Rule had been preceded by a significant change in the law governing investment and expenditure of endowment funds that was formulated in the 1970s. Under trust law, endowment funds are funds donated to a charitable organization subject to a restriction that the principal be permanently invested and only the income— interest and dividends—be used by the charity either for its general purposes or for limited purposes encompassed within its general purposes specified by the donor, such as scholarships, or purchase of medicines or works of art. As noted, under modern interpretation, a rule prohibiting expenditure of capital gains, whether realized or unrealized, imposed a severe restriction on investors, requiring them to invest for yield and thereby forgo growth of capital, or to invest for growth and severely limit the amount available for current distributions to carry out the charitable purposes of the organization. Moreover, the yield/growth division in the old preservation of capital approach was fairly arbitrary and easy to manipulate, for example, by switching utility stock for high growth stock.

Now in force in 46 states, the Uniform Management of Institutional Funds Act (UMIFA), permits the use of a reasonable amount of capital appreciation on investments in addition to interest and dividends, the traditional sources of income. The act contains a standard for investment of institutional funds not dissimilar to the new prudent investor rule, as well as a provision explicitly permitting delegation of investment management. A major drawback to the statute was the fact that it applied only to endowment funds, and not to an organization's general funds, which were subject to the more restrictive provisions of general law. The adoption of the Modern Prudent Investor Rule has, of course, remedied this defect.

The Elements of Modern Prudent Investing

The essential components of Modern Prudent Investing may be summarized as follows:

Total Return. The overall approach to investing is to look to total return in order to make prudent investment decisions, as well as to determine the appropriate amount of expenditures. Unlike traditional trust principles that limited expenditures to interest and dividends, the concept of total return involves measuring growth in the fund by adding together appreciation on assets during a fixed period and the interest and dividends realized during that period. The appropriate amount of current expenditures are then determined by a formula designed so that a portion of the appreciation will be retained while some of it will be expended currently—or in the case of investment in high-yield securities, the retention of some of the dividends or interest. Trustees often accomplish this by setting an annual payout rate relative to endowment or assets held for investment, as well as a time frame in which it is to be applied. Private foundations, of course, are subject to a legally mandated minimum payout equal to 5 percent of the average value of the foundation's assets (including interest and dividends earned during that period) in the preceding year, although some use a higher rate. For other charities, the payout rate applied to endowment appears most commonly to range from 4 to 6 percent, but with exceptions on either side.

Generally, a fixed payout is applied retroactively to an average of asset value over a fixed period of years, often three years. However, critics point out that this has the effect of reducing expenditures following periods of recession when they may be most needed. At a minimum, it may follow a stock market cycle that is unrelated to societal needs (Steuerle 1999). Some advocate a counter-cyclical policy, or at least the avoidance of any set formula that will lead to diminution of programs during times of recession, regardless of the effect such a policy would have on the long-term life of the organization. As a result of the economic downturn that started in 2001, some nonprofits modified their payout formula to what was described as a "decaying" payout rate, which gave greater weight to the more recent prior years, or they added an estimate of the forthcoming year to a three-prior-year formula.

Diversification. Diversification has always been a component of prudent investment. Modern prudent investment theory recognizes the benefits of diversification, both in regard to the types of investments that comprise the portfolio, as well as the specific investments within each of its categories. It also recognizes that there may be situations in which it would be imprudent to diversify and, in fact, situations in which, due to donor restrictions, it may not be possible to do so. Within these constraints, nonprofits are under a duty to diversify their portfolios to reflect appropriate attitudes toward risk.

In considering prudent diversification, it is important to distinguish between diversifiable risk and market risk. The former, also referred to as "uncompensated" or unique risk, refers to the cyclical risks that are inherent in any single investment. Market risk is risk that is not affected by business cycles. The price of individual securities reflects their inherent risk and thus is compensated through the pricing mechanism. In contrast, market risk is not compensated in the marketplace. The distinction is useful in setting risk-level objectives, with diversification being the tool for reducing uncompensated risk. "No one compensates the investor for having a portfolio that neglects to hold securities in enough industries and firms to achieve effective diversification" (Langbein 1996). Diversification is thus the tool for reducing uncompensated risk, and can be achieved with a small number of well-selected securities representing different industries and having other differences in their qualities. Broader diversification, however, is usually to be preferred in order to achieve the ultimate goal of a portfolio with only the "rewarded" or "market" element of risk. In constructing such a portfolio, an investor must balance the amount of risk he is willing to accept in order to obtain a higher or lower level of expected return. This, in turn, will depend on the nature of the organization, its long- and short-term needs, anticipation of additions to its capital and, unique to almost all charities, the expectation that it will last in perpetuity.

Alternative Investments.   There are several special considerations for non-profit organizations that choose to expand the range of their investments beyond a portfolio comprised of equities and fixed-income instruments. Pricing techniques for so called "alternative investments" vary greatly and it is often difficult to find reliable appraisers. Equally important, the fact that almost all alternative investments are illiquid makes it imperative for an organization to consider the likelihood that it will need the funds within a specific time frame before making the investment. To this must be added the additional costs for specialized investment advice or appraisals that are often entailed in evaluating specific investments.

Fixed and Special Assets.   Nonprofits often fail to take into consideration the nature and value of their fixed assets, and the place of these assets in their portfolios. The same is true of unique assets such as art collections or specialized facilities. It is not uncommon for nonprofits to record assets of this nature at book rather than market value and they are often disregarded when a portfolio is under review. In many instances, because of their unique nature or the legal constraints surrounding them, they cannot be considered fungible in the same way that other assets may be. For example, a museum may be prohibited from de-accessioning certain donated objects or, if they can legally be sold, the organization may be required to purchase items of a similar nature.

Maintenance of special assets may also entail additional expenditures not anticipated at the time of acquisition, whether acquired by gift or purchase. This is particularly true in the case of real estate, historical artifacts and works of art, but can also occur in connection with ownership of other forms of property, such as insurance.

Recent Changes Attributable to the Application of Basic Principles of Modern Finance and Economic Analysis to Investment Decisions

There is little doubt that the reformulations of the law governing investments have led to changes in the actual investments nonprofits are making, as well as to the manner in which they are managing their investments. The change in investment choices was amply substantiated in a survey of private foundation investments released by the Council on Foundations in 2001. Based on a survey of 720 foundations with total assets of $130.7 billion in 1999, 64 percent of these assets were invested in domestic and foreign stock at the end of that year, in contrast to 55 percent in 1996. In addition, the proportion of assets invested in venture capital funds increased to nearly 2 percent during that period, a four-fold rise (Council on Foundations 2001).

Other evidence of change came from reports of the National Association of College and University Business Officers, who described a striking increase in the amount of college and university endowment funds that were invested in hedge funds between 1993 and 2001. Although small in terms of the totality of endowment assets, the percent of endowment assets invested in hedge funds rose from 0.5 percent in 1993 to 2.9 percent in 2001 (Klinger 2002).

A second area of change has affected the role of board members in the investment process. Instead of looking to volunteers to make investments, as was common in the past, there appears to be far greater reliance on paid professionals—banks, investment managers, and fund consultants—with the role of the board becoming one of oversight, limited to choosing the professionals and monitoring their performance. In the Council on Foundations Survey described above, 77 percent of the responding foundations reported that they rely on outside investment managers to handle all trades; the percentage of larger foundations in the survey (those with $500 million or more) was even higher—82 percent reported delegating investment decisions to outside managers.

The investment policy of the Museum of Fine Arts Boston reflects the nature of an institution with perpetual life. According to its deputy director of operations, John Stanley, as reported in the Boston Globe on November 18, 2001, "Unlike individuals who might invest differently in different parts of their lives, our investment horizon is infinity, or at least we'd like to think so. We have to take the long-term view" (Syre, 2001). Thus, in Stanley's view, one bear market can't make much of a dent in the organization's investment philosophy. The museum's $408 million endowment is invested at the direction of a blue-chip committee of trustees and overseers that is headed by Peter Lynch of Fidelity Investments and which included MFS Investment Management's president, John Ballen, and Scott Black, president of Delphi Management. In 2001, 65% to 75% of the endowment was invested in stocks, up from an equal split a decade before, thus bringing it in line with modern investment portfolio strategy with successful results that appeared to be holding even with market downturns of 2001–2. As of the first quarter of 2003, there had been no change in investment philosophy, the investment mix remained as it had been and performance of the endowment funds mirrored, but was no worse than, that of the market.

Duties of the Prudent Board Member in Regard to Investments

Every trustee/director of a nonprofit organization is under an affirmative legal duty to exercise care in the management and direction of the organization, and in so doing, to apply the skills that an ordinary prudent person would exercise in similar circumstances. If an individual fiduciary has additional skills in a particular area, he is expected to exercise them. The discussion of modern investment theory emphasizes the broad degree of discretion given to fiduciaries in their choice of investments.

An important adjunct to the new rules governing proper investments has been expansion of the power to delegate the management of investments in two ways, in the first instance, to a finance or investment committee, and in the second, to professional advisors. In either case, the duty of the board and of its individual members is modified; it is not, however, discharged. Furthermore, in making decisions in regard to delegation, the duty of care mandates avoiding excessive administrative expenses. In regard to investment policy this means balancing the costs of obtaining expert advice against the risks entailed in foregoing professional counsel and, as among advisors, weighing the costs and benefits of investing in pooled or mutual funds against using individual portfolio managers, and further determining their nature and number.

In all of these decisions, the first rule for individual board members is to become fully informed, and the second is to act affirmatively on the basis of the information obtained. It is not sufficient to avoid liability by claiming ignorance, if requisite information was available on proper inquiry. The modern rule is that board members may rely on information provided by properly constituted committees. Thus, in the first instance, a board must adopt policies defining the scope of delegation, the powers conferred on its committees, and the outside agents it chooses. Whether it is the board or a committee of the board that is assigned the responsibility of overseeing the choice and scope of duties of an independent agent, individual members are required to use reasonable care and skill in choosing the advisors, setting the policies they are to carry out, directing them as to scope of their duties, and assuring that they receive timely and complete reports that will be reviewed at regular intervals.

In most nonprofits, adoption of an investment policy is a basic step, regardless of whether it is to be carried out internally or externally. It will normally comprise a statement of objectives, a direction as to categories of assets, diversification requirements (including any within specific asset categories), the quality of the assets, the cash needs of the organization and their timing, any legal restrictions on investment such as the prohibition against jeopardy investments applicable to private foundations, or those imposed by donors or under state law, and any other criteria that the board wishes to establish that may be tied to the organization's mission or a policy of social responsibility.

The duty to develop and articulate a proper reporting structure is considered by Fry, in his essay *Creating and Using Investment Policies*, as being almost as important as the investment policies themselves (Fry 1997). Further, he considers a written monthly report that reflects all of an organization's investments at month end, including the unrealized gains and losses on all investments, as the most critical reporting component. Second in importance is providing information to the board, or its finance committee, with which it can track portfolio performance, using appropriate standard indices and benchmarks. With appropriate attention to these basic requirements, board members will be carrying out their responsibilities as required by law, thereby fulfilling their duty to the organization they serve as well as acting responsibly so as to protect themselves from liability.

The ability to delegate investment management does not mean abdication of responsibility in the choice of managers nor excuse for failure to monitor their performance. And even the most knowledgeable board members are not immune from mistakes. Here are two examples from the mid 1990's and the start of the twenty-first century: In 1997, the board of directors of the Art Institute of Chicago acting on the advice of one of its long-term investment consultants, approved investment of $43 million, representing 6.4% of its $667 million endowment, in hedge funds that subsequently proved entirely worthless. Newspaper reports pointed out that among the board members approving the transaction were some of the best-known business people in Chicago, including the former chairman of the Sara Lee Corporation who served as chairman of the Museum's board, the chairman of Hyatt Hotels Corporation who was the board's vice chairman and the president and chief executive of the Chicago Board of Trade who was the board treasurer. In December 2001 the Institute filed a suit against the former investment managers charging misrepresentation (Corfman, 2001).

In the mid 1990's, the New Era Foundation persuaded 250 charities and donors, including donors Laurence E. Rockefeller and William E. Simon and charities such as the University of Pennsylvania, the Nature Conservancy and many religious organizations, to loan funds to the foundation for three years on a representation that they would be matched by anonymous donors, thereby enabling the charities to double their "investment" in six months (Allen & Romney, 1998). When the scheme collapsed and the foundation declared bankruptcy, New Era had $31,000 in assets and more than $350,000 in liabilities. The originator of the scheme was sentenced to 12 years in jail. In settlement of the civil fraud, Prudential Securities, which handled the foundation's funds, agreed to pay $18 million to settle fraud charges. The first charitable participants that had received profits on their investments returned $39 million to help repay those charities that had lost funds, with the result that charities received approximately 65% of the amounts originally deposited with the foundation (Associated Press, 1997).

Integrating Investment and Expenditure Decisions with Mission and Social Benefit

Although there is evidence that nonprofits are changing their investment policies and practices to reflect changes in investment theory and law, there does not appear to be similar changes in the way that investment decisions are coordinated with spending decisions. Instead, investment decisions are made in isolation from programmatic considerations. All too often, trustees with investment or banking expertise are assigned to an investment or finance committee that focuses exclusively on management of the portfolio, or they retain and supervise management counsel and report to the full board and staff the amounts available for current expenditure from which a budget will be prepared. Staff, meanwhile, working within the limits of the budget, will present programmatic proposals to the board and report progress. Rather than having the mission of the organization at the forefront in every investment and program decision, boards tend to get lost in the minutiae of budget compliance. It is only rarely that they consider issues in light of all the circumstances surrounding the organization, its sources of revenue, and reasonable ways in which it can carry out its mission. In short, it is rare that investment choices are coordinated with mission impact. For example, nonprofits need to think through the time profile of their decisions. Will their impact be greater if they give precedence to considerations of perpetuity, or will it be better to expend for the short term?

One way in which investments can be used to enhance the ability of an organization to achieve its mission is by making what are commonly referred to as "program-related investments." The term refers to investments that may carry greater risk than would normally be prudent, but which are permissible by virtue of the fact that they combine the possibility of gain with support of activities that further the mission of the organization. Examples include investment in minority-owned businesses or in companies located in inner cities, which might not attract traditional investors because of the risks involved in operating in those localities.

In Section 4944 of the Internal Revenue Code, which prohibits private foundations from making investments that will jeopardize the carrying out of their exempt purposes, there is a special exception for program-related investments, which are defined as investments, the primary purpose of which is to accomplish one or more tax-exempt charitable purposes. However, they are largely avoided as being either too difficult to carry out wisely, or too risky. Furthermore, Section 53.4944-3(a)(2) of the Treasury Regulations requires that "no significant purpose" of the investment may be the production of income or the appreciation in value of the property, a requirement that is difficult to substantiate and that limits the possibilities for creative investing. There is interest among attorneys who specialize in tax-exempt nonprofit organizations in modifying the regulations so as to encourage greater use of this vehicle (Exempt Organizations Committee 2002). Meanwhile, for nonprofits that are not private foundations, there are myriad opportunities for making investments with social impact. Loans to exempt organizations for working capital, or to support a charter school, are but two examples of dual-purpose investments.

In recent years, there has been a great deal of interest among nonprofits in expanding their sources of revenue by conducting profit-making ventures (see Chapters 7, 8, and 9 in this volume). A decision to undertake such activities requires at the outset consideration of the interdependencies of the organization's revenue and benefit streams. To what extent will an organization's investment in a profit-making venture negatively affect the level of charitable contributions it receives, or detract from its mission-related activities in other ways? Questions of this nature are too often not addressed until after the venture is in place—when it may be too late to mitigate its negative effects.

For operating nonprofits or those administering large profit-making ventures on the side, yet another troublesome area has arisen when returns on investment are shifted from nonprofit purposes into the pockets of a few select managers. Thus, the strategies of profit-making institutions looking to purchase the assets of nonprofits include offering, as one condition, large payments or salary increases to senior managers who recommend or decide in favor of the merger/sell-out/joint venture, not on its merits for the organization but on personal considerations.

Expenditures Practices

As noted at the outset, nonprofit spending practices often diverge from those of for-profit organizations in their failure to apply appropriate cost/benefit analyses to their expenditure decisions. Modern business practice requires that this analysis be applied at the margin, while it is common for nonprofits to look only to average costs when measuring benefits. The fact that nonprofits have notoriously failed to look at the benefit from each extra dollar of expenditure does not mean that it is not applicable to them. Rather, it is imperative that they recognize the importance of *marginal analysis* and adopt procedures to conform to this guideline.

Nonprofits must also consider expenditures, which are more in the nature of internal investments, along with their external investments in terms of the mission-related benefits they produce. Market value may not always be the appropriate or sole determinant of a given choice. For example, a university may decide that its overriding educational mission requires that it devote more funds to scholarships instead of spending them for salary increases to its lowest paid workers or investing them externally. Or a nonprofit hospital may determine that it receives a greater return by expanding its pediatric care even though it could raise more revenue if it expanded psychiatric treatment. Another problem relates to internal investing, where the social rate of return may be higher than the market rate. Specifically, by investing internally, an organization may obtain a stream of future benefits to its mission that exceed the benefits to mission that could have been secured through future purchases made with assets realized from external investment returns. For example, by building a laboratory with current funds, a university may accomplish more for its students over time than would have been accomplished if it had invested the funds so that it could build a larger, or better equipped, laboratory in the future. Another example of internal investing is providing funds for the continuing education of faculty and staff.

Aids to Improve Investment Policies

There are a number of consulting organizations, both for-profit and nonprofit, that provide comparative information regarding investment policies and practices. Banks and accounting firms are excellent sources for comparative data. It would be useful to have organizations that can provide benchmarking services to groups of nonprofits with similar missions or similar methods of operation, such as museums and educational organizations. Models for this type of organization are to be found in the pension area. A potential source of information on the practices in the nonprofit sector may be provided by Guidestar and the National Center on Charitable Statistics (NCCS) at the Urban Institute, nonprofit organizations that have been engaged in posting information from Form 990, the federal information return, on the Internet. If the reporting forms were revised to include more specific information on investment practices, comparative analysis of this data could be useful for nonprofit organizations interested in making changes and looking for new directions for programs and investment activities.

There is great variation in the amount of comparative information on investment strategies and practices available to different parts of the nonprofit sector. Much is known and shared regarding the operations and policies of foundations and of schools and colleges. Relatively little is known about museums, research facilities, or cultural organizations, to name a few. The antitrust laws can be a barrier to some types of information sharing, but they are not a total hindrance.

Some of the most effective information sharing is done by nonprofit organizations themselves, although valuable insights can also be provided by outsiders.

As to specific areas for investment, although there is a good deal of professional, unbiased information available about "traditional assets," meaning stocks and bonds, there is little regarding investments in real estate or tangible personal property, such as works of art.

The nonprofit sector would benefit greatly if there were more organizations such as The Investment Fund for Foundations (TIFF), a nonprofit organization that permits small organizations to pool their assets for common management (Investment Fund for Foundations 2002), or The Commonfund, which manages the endowment funds of some 1,500 colleges and universities with assets valued at approximately $29.9 billion (The Commonfund 2002). It would also benefit from organizations that provide information regarding investment strategies and critiques of investment vehicles.

Examples of troublesome policies and practices that warrant attention include maintaining a high proportion of fixed-income securities in periods where stock market values are within normal ranges relative to earnings or gross domestic product (such as occurred with the reported substantial investment in bonds by Temple University that led to a drastic reduction in the value of its endowment funds); investing in start-up companies and continuing to fund them despite poor results (exemplified by Boston University's investment in a biomedical start-up company, which resulted in losses in excess of $1,000,000, or the losses incurred by the New York Public Theater, the producer of Shakespeare in the Park, which invested in an unsuccessful commercial theater production); and boards of directors who fail to adopt meaningful conflict of interest policies (exemplified by the practices at Adelphi University, which led to the imposition of substantial fines and removal of all but one of its trustees for breaches of the duties of care and loyalty).

Conclusion

The widespread changes in the laws governing investments have provided nonprofit organizations with the opportunity to improve their investment practices, and it is apparent that many of them have done so, enhancing the performance of their portfolios and thereby improving their ability to carry out their missions. The sector will benefit from better information on good investment practices and investment vehicles, particularly non-traditional investments, as well as comparative analyses of data on performance. It will also benefit from the creation of organizations that permit pooling of investments so that smaller organizations can obtain professional advice at reasonable cost, together with opportunities to make alternative investments. Finally, organizations must be encouraged to seek creative ways in which they may combine their investment strategy with their mission-oriented programs, thereby enhancing their ability to fulfill their public purposes.

The overriding challenge for nonprofits as they frame their investment and spending policies is to adopt procedures to assure that investment decisions will be coordinated with programmatic considerations, looking to short- and long-term societal needs, and to adopt spending policies commensurate with all of their resources. Each investment decision and each spending decision must be made in light of its relation to the mission of the organization and whether the chosen course of action will enhance the organization's ability to carry out its mission.

References

American Law Institute. 1992. *Restatement (Third) of the Law of Trusts (Prudent Investor Rule)*. St. Paul, MN: American Law Institute Publishers.

Associated Press. 1997. "Charity Pyramid Schemer Sentenced to 12 Years." *Chicago Tribune*. September 23. N6.

The Commonfund. "*About Commonfund*." 2002. Retrieved April 15 from http://www.commonfund.org.

Corfman, Thomas A. 2001. "Art Institute Alleges Fraud: Sues Trading Firm Over Investments." *Chicago Tribune*. December 11. N1.

The Council on Foundations. 2001. "Finances, Portfolio Composition, Investment Management and Administrative Expenses in Private Foundations.*" Foundation Management Series*. 10th ed. 1: 1–12. New York: Council on Foundations.

Exempt Organizations Committee, American Bar Association. 2002. "Report of the Program-Related Investments Task Force." *Exempt Organization Tax Review*. 35: 357–360.

Fremont-Smith, Marion R. 1999. "The Role of Government Regulation in the Creation and Operation of Conversion Foundations." *Exempt Organization Tax Review*. 23: 37–54.

Fry, Robert P., Jr. 1997. *Creating and Using Investment Policies*. Washington, D.C.: BoardSource.

Internal Revenue Code. §4944.

Internal Revenue Code. Treasury Regulations. §53.4944-3(a)(2).

The Investment Fund for Foundations. 2002. *TIFF Mission*. Retrieved April 15, from http://www.tiff.org.

Klinger, Donna. 2002. "Outpacing the Economy." *Business Officer.* January. 19–22.

Langbein, John H. 1996. "The Uniform Prudent Investor Act and the Future of Trust Investing." *Iowa Law Review.* 81: 641–669.

Steuerle, Eugene. 1999. "Foundation Giving: Will It Follow the Bubble Economy?" *Tax Notes*. June 21. 83: 1797.

Uniform Laws Annotated: Uniform Management of Institutional Funds Act. 1972. St. Paul, MN: West Publishers.

Uniform Laws Annotated: Uniform Prudent Investor Act. 1994. St. Paul, MN: West Publishers.

Uniform Laws Annotated: Uniform Trust Act. 1937. St. Paul, MN: West Publishers.

Additional Reading

Barboza, David. 1998. "Loving a Stock, Not Wisely But Too Well." *New York Times*. September 20. C1.

Bendremer, Frederic J. 2001. "Modern Portfolio Theory and International Investments Under the Uniform Prudent Investor Act." *Real Property, Probate & Trust Journal*. 35: 791–809.

Blum, Debra E. 2001. "Charities Seek Ways to Offset Financial-Investment Losses." *Chronicle of Philanthropy.* November 1. 56.

Borkus, Randall H. 2001. "A Trust Fiduciary's Duty to Implement Capital Preservation Strategies Using Financial Derivative Techniques." *Real Property, Probate & Trust Journal*. 36: 127–166.

Corfman, Thomas A. and Barbara Rose. 2001. "Art Institute Investment Strategy Raises Questions." *Chicago Tribune*. December 16. C1.

Cary, William L. and Craig B. Bright. 1969. *The Law and the Lore of Endowment Funds*. New York: Ford Foundation Press.

Dobris, Joel C. 1993. "Real Return, Modern Portfolio Theory, and College, University, and Foundation Decisions on Annual Spending from Endowments: A Visit to the World of Spending Rules." *Real Property, Probate & Trust Journal*. 28: 49-81.

Gordon, Jeffrey. 1987. "The Puzzling Persistence of the Constrained Prudent Man Rule." *New York University Law Review*. 62. 52–114.

Halbach, Edward. 1992. "Trust Investment Law in the Third Restatement." *Iowa Law Review.* 77: 1151–1185.

Hechinger, John. 2000. "Emory U Gets a Lesson in Subtraction as Coke's Stock Fails to Make the Grade." *Wall Street Journal.* January 28. C1.

Internal Revenue Service. 1998. "A 20-Year Review of the Nonprofit Sector." *Statistics of Income Bulletin.* Fall. 149.

Internal Revenue Service. 2001. "Large Nonoperating Private Foundations Panel Study." *Statistics of Income Bulletin.* Summer. 142.

Nicholas, Lynn. 1988. [Review of the book *Modern Investment Management and the Prudent Man Rule*]. *Business Lawyer.* 43: 779–786.

Poon, Percy S., & Aalberts, Robert J. 1996. "The New Prudent Investor Rule and the Modern Portfolio Theory: A New Direction for Fiduciaries." *American Business Law Journal.* 34: 39–71.

Pulley, John L. 2002. "Betting the Endowment on Risky Investments." *Chronicle of Higher Education.* January 18. 28.

Sommerfeld, Meg. 2000. A Royal Call to Action for Foundations. *Chronicle of Philanthropy.* May 18. 7

Stehle, Vince. 1998. "Falling Price of Reader's Digest Stock is Big Blow to Wallace Funds." *Chronicle of Philanthropy.* February 26. 21.

Syre, Steven. 2001. "Stock Markets Don't Reward Good Intentions: Slump's Proving to be a Tough Test for Endowment Managers." *Boston Globe.* November 18. F4.

Train, John. 2000. *The New Prudent Investor Rule, Yesterday, Today and Tomorrow: The Harvard Class of 1950 Reflects on the Past and Looks to the Future.* Arlington, MA: Travers Press.

CHAPTER 7

Nonprofit Commercial Ventures and Their Funding Agents' Responses

Howard P. Tuckman

Abstract

This chapter presents a framework for exploring the benefits and costs for nonprofits to engage in commercial ventures and the response of funders to these activities. We begin by examining the question of why nonprofits might want to add commercial activities to the portfolio of goods and services they deliver. This is followed by an analysis of the challenges facing nonprofits that undertake new business ventures. We then discuss the concerns of funding organizations of supporting entities that produce both for-profit and nonprofit activities. Several actions are suggested to make it easier for nonprofits and their funding agents to evaluate the viability of a commercial activity. We conclude that the time is ripe for nonprofits, government, and private funders to establish a dialogue leading to guidelines as to how best to develop the blended services that society seems to be asking for.

Introduction

This chapter presents a framework for exploring the motivation that nonprofits have for engaging in commercial ventures and the response that those who fund them have to these activities. Its goal is to assist those interested in commercial ventures to understand the benefits and costs of undertaking these ventures and to aid funding agents in grasping the issues that arise in dealing with nonprofits that have undertaken them. Nonprofit commercial ventures include activities undertaken solely by nonprofits, those undertaken in conjunction with for-profit partners, those involving licensing of the nonprofit's name or its endorsement of commercial products, and engaging in other activities that produce revenues in return for nonprofit participation in the marketplace for commercial goods and services.

The chapter is organized as follows. We begin by examining the question of why nonprofits might want to add commercial activities to the portfolio of goods and services they deliver. A social entrepreneurial choice set is identified and the benefits to the nonprofit decision-maker of producing each of several different types of goods and services are discussed. This is followed by an analysis of the challenges facing nonprofits that undertake new business ventures. We then discuss the motivations for agents to fund nonprofits and their potential concerns over supporting entities that produce both for-profit and nonprofit activities. An analysis is conducted of the potential substitution effects that commercial activities might engender in the behavior of funding agents, introducing the economic concept of *crowding out* and a conceptual framework to examine its potential consequences. The next section suggests that new technologies are increasing the potential for nonprofits to create new commercial ventures and it proposes several key actions that a nonprofit might take if it wishes to be successful in developing a proactive commercial venture plan. The final section suggests several actions that might be taken to make it easier for nonprofits and their funding agents to evaluate the viability of a commercial activity. We conclude that the time is ripe for nonprofits, government, and funding agents to establish a dialogue leading to guidelines on how best to develop the blended services that society seems to require.

Why Nonprofits Consider Commercial Ventures

Except for a small minority, most nonprofits are dependent on the largesse of funding agents including donors (through donations, gifts, and bequests), government (through contracts and grants), and foundations and community organizations such as the United Way. In the last two decades, several developments have had a substantial impact on the actions of these groups: federal government cutbacks in contracts, grants, and other purchases, which started during the Reagan presidency; substantial growth in the number of nonprofits seeking support; slow growth in the dollars available from nongovernmental funding agents; and, more recently, the September 11th tragedy and subsequent downturn in the stock market. These events have dramatically reduced the ability of donors to fund nonprofits from appreciated stock, as well as having reduced the asset base from which gifts are drawn. In sum, they have forced nonprofit administrators and board members to respond to a more competitive environment while increasing the difficulties that funding agents have in meeting the needs of the nonprofit sector.

One consequence of these pressures is that some nonprofits have become more amenable to *social entrepreneurship,* that is, to behaviors that involve the finding of new and better ways to create and sustain social value (Andreason 1996, Dees and Dolby 1996, and Skloot 1998). Entrepreneurship within the sector takes such forms as creating new partnerships and alliances, attracting new funding agents, and/or developing and selling new products. Many reasons exist to engage in social entrepreneurship—to obtain additional revenues, to diversify revenue sources, and to gain greater control over programmatic decisions by lessening dependence on revenue sources that demand a strong role in decision-making (Tuckman and Chang 1994). A prime characteristic of this form of entrepreneurial behavior is the proclivity to widen the horizon of nonprofit decision-makers by encouraging them to develop new funding sources and, when necessary, undertake projects that broaden mission scope.

To understand this conduct, we use an economic model that explains the willingness of nonprofits to venture beyond their traditional choice set. In an important study of nonprofit fundraising, Gronbjerg (1993, p. 32) argues that "funding structures provide the critical context" in which nonprofit decisions take place and that nonprofits attempt to "reduce their dependency on, or increase control over specific funding sources." The analysis of nonprofit behavior presented in this paper is premised on the assumption that the desire for control is an important motivating behavior.

The Social Entrepreneurial Choice Set

Schiff and Weisbrod (1991) modified a model first introduced by James (1983). Their framework views nonprofits as potential producers of three types of goods and services. The first involves *preferred collective goods* that are the primary economic reason for why nonprofits exist. These goods are of such a nature that if they were not produced by nonprofits (or government) they would not be produced at all. Specifically, Weisbrod (1988) argues that collective goods have two properties that keep for-profits from having the means or desire to finance them. The first is that if one person uses the good it is still available for others to use and the second is that exclusion of individuals from use of collective goods is not practical. Together, these properties make it difficult for the producers of these goods to charge a price and hence to earn a profit from their production. These goods yield social utility to society but because they do not produce a profit they will not be produced by the business sector. Hence, nonprofits are needed to produce them, and this provides a theory-based explanation for the existence of the nonprofit sector. Society gains from the production of collective goods by nonprofits, and this enhances our collective welfare. Among the many outputs of the nonprofit sector that fall within this category are advocacy services, educational campaigns for disease eradication, social services, and scientific research on disease.

A second class of goods that nonprofits produce is *preferred private goods*. These are produced by the business sector and can be sold for a price, but because of their favorable social effects, nonprofits make them available to people unable to pay, usually through subsidies or outright grants. In this case, the role of nonprofits is to increase the quantity of these goods beyond what would otherwise be produced. Illustrative of such goods are scholarships to universities (a subsidy that reduces the costs of education and raises the percentage of the population educated), subsidized housing, and supply of certain pharmaceutical products at reduced cost. Yet a third type of good is *non-preferred private goods*, which are produced in the business sector. Nonprofits presumably choose to produce them because these goods generate additional revenues or enhance production of the other types of goods.

A social (nonprofit) entrepreneur who wishes to add social value usually does so by producing one or both of the first two types of goods. By nature, however, entrepreneurs are driven to seek new ground. In analyzing entrepreneurs in the business sector, Mintzberg (1973) suggests that they will examine both their own organizations and the external environment in seeking opportunities to expand and grow their business and initiating projects to bring about positive change. Similarly, social entrepreneurs engage in search behavior recognizing that their ability to create social value is limited by the revenue streams available—usually contributions, gifts, dues, etc.—and by the existing structure and culture of their organization. Seeking opportunities to expand the choice set and to acquire new revenue streams, they consider production of private goods, either directly or through partnerships or alliances with for-profit entities. Given social entrepreneurs' preferences and budget constraints, nontraditional mixes of preferred and non-preferred goods can be formulated that provide these entrepreneurs the highest level of satisfaction for the dollars available.

It is useful to highlight two essential differences between social and business entrepreneurs. The former willingly produce "profitless" public goods that create social value while using "profits" from non-preferred private goods production to subsidize the public goods. In contrast, business entrepreneurs have limited interest in goods that generate social value but focus instead on producing private goods that earn a target level of profit that benefits both them and their employing organization (Tuckman and Chang 2000).

While business entrepreneurs are unwilling to use profits to subsidize production of money-losing goods simply because these have social value, both social and business entrepreneurs have in common the need to assume additional risk in the hopes of obtaining additional net revenues; one uses earned profits entirely to subsidize an organization while the other uses them in part for personal gain (Chang and Tuckman 1990). Business entrepreneurs do use some portion of profits for replacement of equipment and expansion of the business, but their primary motivation is to acquire a share of the value generated by their enterprise. It may be argued that the intensity of the desire to earn profits differs between the two because the business entrepreneur pushes harder for personal gain, but the proposition is overly simplistic because some nonprofit entrepreneurs may have compensation schemes that enable them to share in profit-generating activity.

This explanation of why nonprofits might choose to produce (non-preferred) private goods has value for us in at least three senses. First, it uses economic theory to provide an explanation for why social entrepreneurs have an incentive to encourage nonprofits to produce non-mission-related goods. Second, it helps us to understand why goods and services totally unrelated to a nonprofit's mission may be chosen for either direct production or for some type of alliance. Third, it opens our thinking to a new revenue stream beyond the traditional set usually available to nonprofits.

Since nonprofits are not profit-maximizing, many considerations other than production of profits affect their decisions regarding which goods to produce, including whether a good has salutary effects on mission, how it affects the organization's culture, and whether they have the capacity to produce it. It is improbable, for example, that a nonprofit providing education on lung disease will sell cigarettes, despite the large profits this might produce, and a nonprofit focused on dental care will not endorse gum containing sugar. However, the decision to produce (non-preferred) private goods may, over time, cause a nonprofit to alter its behavior and drift from its mission (Tuckman and Chang 2002).

MOMA: New Revenue Mix

Initiatives by the curators of the New York Museum of Modern Art (MOMA) in 1995 led to creation of a Web site to complement the Mutant Materials exhibition then underway. The success of this effort led to construction of a more elaborate site using staff from MOMA and a new media firm at a modest cost of roughly $10,000. Subsequent positive experiences with this Web site led the museum's Department of Marketing and Communications to formalize the process of adding to the Web site and to providing guidelines for its use—which included public relations, an online gallery, research and education, and commercial activities. An online store was created in 1998 offering over 225 private products to those interested in online purchases, and the store proved to be very popular. MOMA is currently working on other online revenue generating possibilities such as the sale of art information and a system of tiered subscriptions providing certain online art projects for those who pay more. In its 2001 fiscal year, MOMA's shops, restaurants, parking garages and other commercial endeavors produced $96.6 million in revenues, or almost three times as much as its next largest source of income—admissions and membership fees. (Deussing, 2002).

The social entrepreneur's expanded choice set moves the focus of attention of nonprofit boards and administrators away from a world in which the sole type of good produced is mission-related to one where a range of new ventures is possible. Consider the simple relationship between type of good produced and funding status as laid out in Table 1.

TABLE 1. The Nonprofit Social Entrepreneur's Choice Set

	Funding Source		
Type of Good	Donor Funded	Self Funded	Other Funding
Collective	A	B	C
Preferred Private	D	E	F
Non-preferred Private		G	

The rows show the types of good produced by a nonprofit while the columns show a truncated set of funding sources, and the designation for a type of good with a particular funding agent is designated by a letter. Donors are distinguished from other funding agents because as Hansmann (1987, p. 35) points out, ". . . the donor is very likely to experience difficulty in overseeing the use made of his donation and feel the need for the kind of protection afforded by the nonprofit form." B- and E-type goods provide the most freedom from external funders' preferences, enabling nonprofit administrators to produce the goods that they see as appropriate to their mission while A and D are more typically the funding sources available to charitable nonprofits. A nonprofit that self-funds is self-sufficient and free of external control in the sense that its existing level of goods production depends solely on its revenues and the preferences of its decision-makers—primarily interest from endowments, royalties, and/or rents. An asset-poor nonprofit that lacks revenue sources is likely to rely on donations to produce A- and D-type goods, or it will move to C- and F-type goods funded by agents such as governments and foundations, giving up a measure of control of production in the process (e.g., it might write grants based on what it thinks the agent will fund rather than on what it truly wishes to do). Nonprofits that rely on a single major funding source such as donations run the risk of unstable revenues and are less likely to survive over time (Chang and Tuckman 1991).

For nonprofit administrators and boards, B-type goods are the most desirable to produce since they most closely relate to the mission of nonprofits and they provide the least external interference with governance. Because it is usually not feasible to find strictly mission-related goods that self-finance, A-type goods where donors provide major support of the enterprise, and C-type goods such as those financed by governments, are far more likely to be produced by nonprofits.

In the case of hospitals, and certain educational institutions, production may consist of collective goods (e.g., preventive health education or production of research) and preferred private goods. In this case (E-type), a price can be charged for the private goods and a judgment made as to whether to charge below market to subsidize their consumption. Hansmann (1987) labels nonprofits that primarily produce E-type goods as "commercial nonprofits." Since a price can be charged, these entities normally face for-profit and/or governmental competitors in sectors like health services, education, social services, culture and entertainment, and research (Steinberg 1987). Table 1 also recognizes the role that other funding agents play in encouraging production of C- and F-type goods, and the potential for funding through sales of private goods and/or other commercial ventures that produce revenue. E-type goods are likely more desirable than G-types in terms of mission-relatedness, but G-types can become desirable if the revenues they produce cross-subsidize mission-related goods, opening new sources of revenue from previously untapped sectors.

Each class of goods presents opportunities for social entrepreneurs interested in new ventures. And nonprofits considering production of private goods must determine if these will be accepted in the marketplace. A nonprofit that decides to produce an E-type good because it "fits" its mission may be disappointed to find that no market exists. In contrast, the Museum of Modern Art provides an example of successful profit-making from such goods: its shop in lower Manhattan sells many beautiful objects that both expand the choices of consumers and serve the mission of exposing the public to high-quality art. The large number of customers in this and other MOMA shops demonstrates that through selective sale of desired private goods a nonprofit can augment revenues while remaining true to its mission.

For-Profit Sponsors of Web Sites

A potentially lucrative way for a nonprofit to increase its income is to obtain "sponsors" for each page of its Web site. Large nonprofits have charged corporate sponsors $50,000 or more per Web site page for exclusive annual sponsorship rights to a page. Sponsors pay an annual fee and receive recognition by having their name, logo, and limited information about them prominently displayed; they may also receive recognition at the nonprofit's events. If sponsor recognition is properly designed, the income is tax-free but when the recognition violates certain parameters, the IRS can treat the entire payment as taxable "advertising income" for the nonprofit. Nonprofits contemplating this revenue raising strategy should learn which forms of recognition enable them to keep revenue tax-free. IRS guidance in this area is limited, informal, and being developed and fine-tuned. D. Benson Tesdahl, "Making Money from Nonprofit Internet Websites," copyright by Powers, Pyles, Sutter and Verville, P.C. www.ppsv.com/issues/corporatesponsors.html.

G-type production does not directly support a nonprofit's mission, but its purpose is to contribute to revenues that ultimately support mission-related spending. For example, cause-related marketing provides nonprofits with funds to carry out their mission, but issuance of credit cards to members does not directly enable a nonprofit to carry out its mission. In contrast, licensing a discovery to a for-profit may further a nonprofit's mission by exposing more people to a new product than would be feasible if the nonprofit tried to market the product itself, primarily because the licensee is better able to develop and disseminate it.

The Challenges for Social Entrepreneurs

The role of the social entrepreneur, like that of his business-sector counterpart, is to identify opportunities and to exploit these while minimizing the risks to the enterprise. Production of G-type goods with one or more for-profit partners adds complications because the social entrepreneur must find the right combination of mission- related goods to satisfy a nonprofit's leadership while, at the same time, enabling for-profit partners to meet their own needs.

Other challenges face social entrepreneurs that choose to create new business ventures, and one of the first is the mindset that nonprofit administrators bring to the table. From an economic perspective, nonprofits must struggle with balancing growth and service needs and this objective is not easy to achieve. For a nonprofit to grow, a certain portion of its existing resources must be invested, but at the same time nonprofits usually have more demands on their scarce resources than they have funds to meet those needs. A nonprofit that uses all its funds for goods or service delivery can only grow through donations or other external increases in their funds. Alternatively, a nonprofit that only invests in its future may find it difficult to find a funding agent.

Determination of the right balance becomes more complex as the number and type of goods produced increases (Galaskiewicz and Bielefeld 1998). These and related issues are not well addressed by researchers, in part because they are organization specific and, in part, because they require either business training or experience that many nonprofit administrators lack. This has opened a new area for consultants who are interested in working with nonprofits on these and related problems requiring an economic perspective.

Some administrators are not used to thinking of commercial activities and have trouble understanding where new business possibilities lie because of both a lack of training in understanding the *comparative advantage* their organizations possess and a lack of staff trained with these skills. In fact, most nonprofits have new opportunities arise from their current activities, from complementary activities that build on what the organizations do, from partnerships that leverage their reputations, milieu, or constituency, and from the launching of entirely new ventures (Tuckman 1998). For example, the ASPCA name and logo licensing program includes over 70 licensees, such as FAO Schwartz, JC Penney, and First USA. Without trained staff, astute board members or volunteers, or external consultants, these nonprofits have trouble recognizing commercial prospects, developing a business plan, and gaining the contacts that attract commercial deals and partners. A concern also arises that they may be unable to compete with more experienced for-profit firms in the production and sale of commercial goods (Weisbrod 1998).

Nonprofits have difficulty developing explicit criteria for use in deciding when to undertake commercial activities because this is not a simple task. If the primary purpose for undertaking G-type ventures is revenue enhancement, for example, the appropriate rate of return should at least equal the rate prevailing in the marketplace. Here is an example of how subtle strategic considerations come into play in setting a price for goods in the marketplace. A nonprofit that sets a price that demonstrates high profits are achievable may rapidly attract competitors. Charging a price lower than the one that maximizes its profits may extend the time during which it can earn large profits without competition. On the other hand, setting a high price may allow it to reap early profits and to use these to build a prominent position in the marketplace, making it harder for competitors to challenge it. The question of which choice to make involves sound training and good instincts and it is here that social entrepreneurs play an important role.

Social entrepreneurs may have problems assuring nonprofit staff and board members that commercial activities enhance or at least are consistent with their mission because some people believe that commercialization is tantamount to consorting with the enemy (e.g., unsavory profit-seekers care little for the public good). Entrepreneurs must demonstrate the ways that revenues earned from commercial activities enhance a nonprofit's ability to fulfill its mission. They must also show that undertaking a commercial activity does not have a negative effect on other aspects of a nonprofit's operation. Without social entrepreneurial skills, nonprofits may have trouble finding the time to plan commercial activities, particularly when they are small and understaffed. Moreover, a lack of skills may result in an inability to change the culture of the organization so as to gain board approval for new activities (Price 1963 and Middleton 1987).

Care also must be taken to insure that commercial activities do not undermine a nonprofit's tax status. A problem is posed both by the IRS's unrelated business income tax (UBIT), which is levied on what is defined as income unrelated to the nonprofit's mission. In addition, IRS rules state that too much unrelated activity can cause a nonprofit's 501(c)(3) status to be removed. While a number of different legal structures are available to deal with these concerns, nonprofits may need outside expertise to help them to understand how best to use these structures. The ability to learn how to restructure an enterprise to take advantage of existing tax laws and legal structures is an important part of social entrepreneurship.

Cash- or asset-poor nonprofits lack the ability to accumulate money to seed commercial ventures, particularly those nonprofits that run consistent deficits and those that rely on external donations for a major portion of their revenue. The problem is more severe in the case of small nonprofits with limited visibility and few resources to use for leverage. However, a glimmer of hope exists for even these entities since a possibility exists that for-profits will take on the role of funding agent. For example, the Nature Conservancy is a national organization with limited resources, but together with Georgia Pacific, it has developed a number of important initiatives in which the latter sold or donated land to the conservation agency (Austin 2000). This collaboration enabled a resource-limited nonprofit to secure the resources of a large for-profit to carry out its mission using its reputation as a means for leveraging the funds of a commercial enterprise.

An important element of social entrepreneurship is the ability to develop creative solutions that create *win-win* situations between nonprofits and for-profits. Austin (2000) suggests several elements of successful collaborations—a realistic understanding of strategic relationships, an ability to make appropriate connections, efforts to ensure strategic fit, attention to generation of value, and careful management of the relationship. While each of these involve specific skills, all are learnable and most can be found within existing staffs.

The advantages of these types of collaborations are that they can result in mutual gains. For example, nonprofits may earn revenue by endorsing products of for-profits that enhance their mission (e.g., safe toys for dogs), licensing their technologies to for-profits who disseminate them widely, and giving for-profits access to nonprofit membership lists in return for fees or monetary payments. The challenge for nonprofit managers interested in developing such arrangements is to capitalize on the things that their organization does well, or the reputation or goodwill that it has created. Table 2 provides several resources that a nonprofit decision-maker may wish to use in formulating a plan for accomplishing this.

Funding Agent Decisions to Fund Nonprofits

Nonprofit administrators have a long history of dealing with third-party funders including donors, foundations, United Way, church organizations, and governments (Hall 1987). Relationships with these parties typically involve a *quid pro quo* in which a nonprofit provides desired services and/or meets certain conditions that its funding agents set in return for funding. Funding agent motives for providing revenues to nonprofits vary according to both the goals of these agents and the goods and services that nonprofits produce. In some cases, the goal is to speed new discoveries (e.g., research on the causes of children's heart disease), in others to build institutions doing desirable things (e.g., housing for the poor), and in still others to channel nonprofit activities in desired directions (e.g., to create more social entrepreneurship).

Funding agents also differ in the extent to which they seek active control over all or a portion of the operation of nonprofits. In situations where large numbers of small donors fund a nonprofit, no one donor can exert substantial influence and nonprofit decision-makers have a large measure of freedom over their outputs; but when a limited number of donors provide financing, this group can have considerable impact on the decisions regarding what goods and services to produce. In the latter case, nonprofit administrators may have an interest in developing commercial activities, not only for the revenues they produce but also to lessen the control that powerful funding agents are exerting.

TABLE 2.

Select List of Resources Available to Nonprofits Interested in Commercial Ventures

Consultants

Authenticity Consulting, LLC
Community Wealth Ventures Inc.
McKinsey and Company
National Center For Nonprofit Enterprise

Entrepreneurship Sources

Fortune Magazine—articles of interest
Harvard Business Review—periodic articles on nonprofit sector
Inc Magazine—small business ideas
Ewing Marion Kaufmann Foundation—Many materials on entrepreneurship—
    www.emkf.org
Techsoup–-series of articles on how nonprofits can use the Internet for commercial
    activities– www.techsoup.org

Internet References

The Benton Foundation Web site—Best Practices—www.benton.org/Practice
Guidestar—Compensation and Financial Reports—www.guidestar.org
Independent Sector website—large amount of data on Nonprofit Sector—
    www.independentsector.org

News

Nonprofit Resource Center-www.nonprofitresourcecenter.com/
Nonprofit Times—www.nptimes.com

Non-University Organizations That Sponsor Nonprofit Research

Amherst H. Wilder Foundation—www.wilder.org
Aspen Institute—www.aspeninst.org
Foundation Center—www.fdncenter.org
Nathan Cummings Foundation—www.ncf.org
Nonprofit Sector Research Fund—www.nonprofitresearch.org
The Morino Institute—www.morino.org
The Roberts Enterprise Development Fund—www.redf.org
The Urban Institute—www.urban.org
W.K. Kellogg Foundation—www.wkkf.org

Universities With Nonprofit Research

Case Western Reserve University
City University of New York
Georgetown University
Harvard University
Indiana University
Yale University

A similar situation exists for foundation funding agents. Some foundations contribute with the goal of raising the amount of, or diversifying, mission-related goods, others want to support favored nonprofits or causes (or to seed new ones), and still others finance entities that promote political or social views close to their own (Hall 1987). Recently, a new class of funder has emerged. Labeled "strategic philanthropists," they fund causes related to their interests and emphasize efficient operations, frequent collaboration between funding agents and the recipients of their largesse, lengthy associations, and, in some cases, production of mission-related goods and services consistent with their views. These institutions emphasize control through carefully crafted collaborations.

Government funding agents (local, state, and federal) typically fund nonprofits to produce goods or services they wish to see produced; some place importance on both the number and type of nonprofit clients served. Contractual financing is found in the educational, health, housing, social services, research, and scientific services sectors and it may involve either public goods or preferred private goods. Moskowitz (1989, p. 86) notes that partnership with government brings "risks, responsibilities, controls, controversy, and interference." Nonprofits must decide whether what governmental entities want them to produce is consistent with their mission, and whether they can accept the controls these entities impose.

Nonprofit production of non-preferred private goods makes the marketplace a de facto funding agent because profits earned from the marketplace are used to fund products that the leadership of the nonprofit wishes to see produced. In a sense, the market "controls" a nonprofit by requiring it to produce goods and services desired by consumers at competitive prices, but this type of control may be preferred to the types described above because it allows nonprofit administrators considerable freedom in deciding which mission-related goods to produce. While all nonprofits struggle to balance the need for adequate revenues with funding agents' needs for accountability and control, some nonprofits may place heavier emphasis on freedom from funding agent preferences. These entities are the ones most likely to find commercial activities attractive and to encourage social entrepreneurship.

In contrast, a funding agent may find participation in governance (or behind-the-scenes guidance) of nonprofit activities desirable and a strategic reason for getting involved with the nonprofit. Agents interested in institution building, achieving mutual gains, or pursuing private gain may also use involvement to insure accountability and control and be unwilling to fund a nonprofit that does not welcome their active collaboration. Table 3 relates select funding agent strategic objectives to the type of nonprofit goods supported and the desire for control. The letters H, M, and L (high, medium, and low) denote levels of control and a blank indicates that a cell is not relevant; the cells in the table are not mutually exclusive; interactions may exist between funding agent objective(s) in providing support and the type of support provided (e.g., agents seeking to fund a nonprofit to achieve mutual gains may seek involvement, while those desiring higher levels of mission-related goods provision may be satisfied simply being donors).

TABLE 3. Funding Agent Desire for Control

Nature of Interaction	Funding Agent Strategic Objectives				
	Social Goods Provision	*Build Nonprofit Institutions*	*Achieve Mutual Gains*	*Represent Own Views*	*Achieve Private Gains*
Purely Financial Support	L	M	M	H	H
Consult/ Volunteer	L	M	LM	H	H
Input into Operations	MH	H	MH	H	H
Alliance/Partner	L	LM	MH	MH	H

Funding opportunities arise through partnerships with for-profits (last row of the table) without necessarily involving private goods production or volunteer participation. For example, Austin (2000) highlights a cause-related marketing arrangement where the Boys and Girls Clubs of America signed a $60 million ten-year agreement permitting Coca Cola to install vending machines at approximately 2,000 club sites. These clubs exchange access to their members for an unrestricted revenue stream involving minimal program control. Such alliances do not require nonprofits to produce commercial goods to acquire additional revenues nor do they involve heavy external control, making them particularly attractive to nonprofits that eschew controlling funding agents.

Funding Agent Concerns About Nonprofit Commercial Ventures

Recognizing that nonprofits can benefit from exposure to business practices, some funding agents encourage them to become familiar with, and comfortable with, appropriate business techniques. Improved fiscal management, better understanding of how to market their products, and greater understanding of, and fulfillment of, customer needs are areas where close attention to business practices benefits the traditional nonprofit. Anderson, Dees, and Emerson (2002) correctly note that nonprofits benefit most from market involvement when the marketplace in which they operate is well aligned with their social missions. Even if alignment is not close, a byproduct of commercial activity is likely to be exposure to business thinking and greater consciousness of business practices. Since this fosters more efficient operation, it constitutes an incentive for at least some funding agents to encourage commercial activity by nonprofits.

A major concern of the funding agents, and of scholars and policy-makers as well, is that participation in commercial activities may cause top administrators, particularly social entrepreneurs, to drift from their mission and goals (Tuckman and Chang 2002, and Weisbrod 1998). In part, this is because a concern exists that if the nonprofit's administrators act as rational businessmen, rising profits from commercial activities may cause them to devote relatively more time and energy to commercial goods production because it yields higher financial returns to their organization. This is particularly problematic if a portion of their compensation is based on the profits from the business venture. A related concern is that exposure of administrators to a commercial mindset may affect the services they deliver by causing them to lower either their quality or quantity to compete more effectively. A third concern is that if the actual deliverers of services engage in both charitable and commercial activities they will become "tainted" by the commercial approach and less effective at carrying out their charitable mission (e.g., employees of nonprofit housing organizations may be less inclined to offer free housing services once they discover that a part of their client population is willing to pay a modest sum for housing). Such values-based arguments are somewhat lessened if commercial activities are staffed by different people than those in the nonprofit. Moreover, since funding agents lack adequate criteria for determining when the commercial activities of a nonprofit have deleterious effects on their social mission, these activities may create uncertainties that make funding agents reluctant to continue to provide financial support.

We have noted that government agencies can be important funding sources, particularly in the social services and community development areas (Gronbjerg 1993). Issues arise for these funding agents when nonprofits decide on private goods production including: whether commercial activity transforms nonprofits into self-serving entities not suitable for government funding; whether added revenue from these activities reduces the need for charitable funding; whether these activities should affect the nonprofit exemption from antitrust laws; what to do about the differential tax treatment of nonprofits that have commercial ventures; and how best to guard against offering unfair advantage to the commercial parts of nonprofits (Weisbrod 1998). Since ambiguities remain in the answers to each of these questions, the potential exists for government support of a nonprofit to be negatively affected by its decision to engage in commercial activity.

Substitution Effects and Funding Agent Behavior

Given the above arguments, it is wise for nonprofit administrators considering commercial ventures to specifically consider the adaptive behaviors of funding agents. It is useful to consider Weisbrod's (1998) dichotomy between exogenous funding that comes to a nonprofit irrespective of its other activities, and endogenous funding that is affected when revenues from one source affect those raised from another. Economists recognize that human behavior is adaptive and that, for a variety of reasons, funding agents may alter their payments to a nonprofit either positively or negatively, based on what they see happening to its other revenues. It is valuable for nonprofit administrators to be aware of the insight that economics has to offer in this area.

The likelihood that adaptive behaviors exist, whatever their magnitude, means that nonprofit administrators should weigh revenue additions from commercial activities against the possibility that key funding agents may diminish their contributions as commercial revenues increase and, at a minimum, some allowance should be made for this in revenue forecasts for new ventures. For example, a foundation may be less interested in strengthening a nonprofit if it shows a healthy rise in commercial revenues and a government agency may reduce its purchases of a nonprofit's services when it finds a nonprofit receiving licensing fees.

Crowding Out. Economists use the term *crowding out* to describe what happens when growth in a revenue stream causes a cutback in another. A variety of motivations cause this to occur: a belief that commercial nonprofits can no longer be trusted, a feeling that commercial nonprofits no longer need the same amount of subsidies or donations, and/or a feeling that commercial activity reduces the quality of a nonprofit's output. It is also possible that funding from a new revenue source may cause another one to increase; for example, if an agent feels that as a result of increased revenues a nonprofit can do a more effective job of producing mission-related goods than previously. This might also happen if added revenue is taken as a proxy of success and an agent wishes to back "a winner," or if added revenues improve a nonprofit's ability to distribute its services nationally and this encourages an agent to sign more contracts with this entity.

A note of caution is in order. The observed fact that a rise in one revenue stream reduces revenues from another can result from two different sources. A nonprofit may raise revenues from one source, and this causes one or more funding agents to reduce their funding. Alternatively, a nonprofit may lose revenues from one source and scramble to substitute revenues from another. This appears to be crowding out, but it is simply adaptive behavior. The causes are different but the observed outcome is the same; and it is important not to confuse the two because in some circumstances commercial activities may be undertaken in an attempt to keep a nonprofit from financial ruin.

Limited research has been conducted on the magnitude of funding agent behavioral adjustments and no studies attempt to examine differences in the crowding-out effect by strategic objective. One study examines the interdependencies among the donations, sales, costs, and pricing revenue streams of a local chapter of the American Red Cross. Kingma (1995) finds that increases in the profits from sales of Red Cross goods and services decrease donations, supporting the crowding-out hypothesis. Increases in donations, on the other hand, decrease profits by increasing costs and decreasing the subsidized prices of Red Cross services such as health and safety classes. Kingma finds no effects from donations on either full-service prices or prices charged by "authorized providers" of Red Cross services. Another study by Okten and Weisbrod (2000) finds no evidence of crowding out from either government grants or an organization's own program services when data from seven different nonprofit industries are analyzed. These and a modest number of other studies indicate that while crowding out should be a consideration in the decision to undertake commercial activity, the order of magnitude of crowding out may not be sufficiently large to alter a nonprofit's decision as to whether to produce a good or service.

A conceptual scheme for thinking about crowding out.   Absent a set of rigorous studies, we present a conceptual schema to guide nonprofit decision-makers.

Table 4 relates the strategic objectives of funding agents as defined in specific categories of predicted behavior. A minus indicates a negative adjustment of revenues from that funding agent, an N that no action occurs, a plus a positive adjustment, and an NA that a specific cell is not relevant to the discussion. The signs presented below are designed to engender discussion and to leave room for differences in opinion about likely crowding-out effects. The table's main purpose is to stimulate thought as to the likely effect of a decision to engage in commercial activity on other revenue sources.

TABLE 4. Hypothesized Effect of Private Goods Production on Agent Willingness to Fund the Nonprofit

Type of Funding Agent	Strategic Objective of Funding Agent				
	Social Goods Provision	*Build Nonprofit Institutions*	*Achieve Mutual Gains*	*Represent Own Views*	*Achieve Private Gains*
Donor	-+	-	N+	-	-+
Corporation	-+	-	N+	-	-+
Foundation	-	-	N+	-	NA
Government	-+	-N	N+	NA	NA
United Way	-	-	-	NA	NA

The preponderant adjustment behavior hypothesized in the table is reduction in revenues from funding agents when commercial activity increases. The existence of both a minus and a plus in a given cell indicates two possible behaviors: 1) "minus," when agents content with an existing level of mission-related goods reduce their contributions, reflecting the fact that as goods levels increase their contributions are no longer needed; 2) "plus," when agents are encouraged by the rise in mission-related goods volume to fund at higher levels. Funding agents motivated by a desire to build institutions are likely to cutback because these entities have limited resources and will put funds elsewhere when they see a nonprofit successfully building its revenues from other sources. Agents seeking mutual gains are hypothesized to have either neutral or positive substitution effects since increased revenues benefit the agent as well as the nonprofit. United Way agencies are unlikely to fall in this category because the strong alternative demands for their limited funds put pressure on them to cut back revenues to successful nonprofits while augmenting the revenues of nonprofits with more limited revenues. A negative reaction is forecast for agents seeking to promote their own views because, as nonprofits develop new revenue sources, they become more independent of their previous funders and less likely to faithfully represent their views.

Two categories of funding agents are most likely to pursue private gain objectives: donors because the output of a nonprofit may be of direct help to them (e.g., a donor funding a nonprofit seeking a cure for cancer); and a corporation with a business motive for affiliating with a nonprofit (e.g., a piano company providing its product to an orchestra in return for recognition at every performance). In both cases, the predicted reaction could be in either direction.

Insights. Several insights can be drawn from this conceptual exercise. It is not a foregone conclusion that a nonprofit choosing to engage in non-preferred private goods production or other commercial activities will experience declines in its other revenue sources. Whether it does depends on the strategic objectives and the other motivations of its funding agents. Consequently, it cannot be automatically assumed that crowding-out will occur, and even if it does the effect may be small. A higher probability exists of a negative response from individual funding agents than a positive one and nonprofits should recognize this in their planning assumptions when deciding whether to engage in non-preferred private goods production. Finally, the above discussion highlights the need for further research on the substitution effects that occur when nonprofits enter commercial ventures to provide nonprofit decision-makers with a better understanding of the likely consequences of their actions

Proactive Consideration of Commercial Activities

At its core, the decision of whether to undertake a commercial venture is an economic one involving weighing the monetary and nonmonetary benefits and costs of this choice. Where a commercial activity enables a nonprofit to both gain financial stability and increase its control over its own programmatic outputs, the decision to undertake this type of activity may be an easy one. In contrast, when this activity conflicts with a nonprofit's mission or when loss of funding from other agents is likely, the decision requires careful thought and difficult trade-offs. In those cases where a nonprofit does not currently have any prospects for commercial activity, it may be necessary for it to identify new opportunities either internally or through the use of an outside consultant. A useful and important exercise for all nonprofits, irrespective of their current opportunities to produce commercial goods and services, is to give serious reflection to whether increasing their choice set might augment their effectiveness.

During the last decade, the discovery and dissemination of new technologies has created new opportunities for augmenting revenues and for nonprofit firms to successfully undertake activities once thought feasible only for for-profits (Tuckman and Chang 2002). Among the technological changes opening new commercial vistas for nonprofits are the cost-reducing delivery channels opened by the Internet (e.g., provision of health information on nonprofit Web sites), a growing appetite for the information that nonprofits have available in their data-bases, online charitable collections by third parties, and access to the members or clients of nonprofits in return for modest payments associated with member-ship cooperation (e.g., cause-related marketing). Specialized opportunities also have arisen, as in the case of the National Jewish Medical and Research Center licensing its technologies to business firms, nonprofit universities creating for-profit distance learning programs (e.g., NYU), and nonprofit research facilities creating successful revenue-yielding alliances with pharmaceutical firms (Powell and Owen 1998).

While many of these activities may not be feasible for small, resource poor nonprofits, some may be achievable if these entities are willing to find new ways to exploit their comparative advantages to find a for-profit partner. The environ-ment is currently favorable to social entrepreneurs willing to accept some risk in the hopes of creating new forms of social value. In commercial businesses a focus on core competencies (limiting companies to engaging in those things they do well) has caused non-core activities to be outsourced to service compa-nies willing to serve all parts of the economy. The services of these entities include accounting and bookkeeping, asset management, donor solicitation and other fundraising, employee benefits administration, external marketing, and public relations. Since these services are usually provided by for-profits at a cost equal to or less than what would be incurred if the nonprofits conducted the activity themselves, an economic incentive exists for nonprofits to reduce their costs by outsourcing to for-profits (see Chapter 4). Interestingly, it is feasible for nonprofits to provide the outsourcing services to other nonprofits, capitalizing on their nonprofit status to compete with for-profits. This opens new vistas for nonprofit production of services.

There are several key actions that a nonprofit must take if it wishes to be suc-cessful in developing a proactive plan to engage in commercial activities (see, for example, Emerson, Dees, and Economy 2002). It must create a strategic business plan that identifies the value its new activities will add. Within this context, it should consider the types of commercial activities it is suited to conduct, the resources it needs, competition in its new marketplace, and the impacts that a commercial venture will have on its existing programs and business structure. Its strategies should be clear and well focused. It should pay particular care to how it will integrate its new customer/client base into its daily operation and to the synergies likely to result. It should also consider how its new activities will affect its existing suppliers and what new relationships it will need to create. If the new activities increase risk then a clear risk management plan should be developed and set in motion. Its compensation scheme should be looked at both in the context of the nonprofit and for-profit outputs of the firm, identifying necessary adjustments that allow for incentive schemes and multiple funding sources when appropriate. Moreover, careful attention should be given to creating legal and marketing structures that facilitate the new mix of products, assure that commercial activity will not put the nonprofit's 501(c)(3) status at risk, and will have a high probability of succeeding.

It is equally important to recognize that the overall effect of these changes is to make it increasingly difficult for funding agents to determine which nonprofits to fund and what criteria to use in making their funding decisions. Clearly a need exists to have better information on the financial activities of nonprofits for funding agents. Because existing data sources are not sufficient for making intelligent funding decisions when commercial activities are involved, these agents will have trouble both understanding the activities of their clients and determining when to no longer fund a nonprofit. A need exists to provide these agents with better criteria for discriminating between desirable and undesirable commercial activity.

Improving the Status Quo

Several things can be done to assist both nonprofits and their funding agents in the decision-making process. These include improved data collection and dissemination, rules limiting the impact of commercial activities on mission-related activities, more explicit articulation of mission, expanded research by the academic community, and greater access to consultants who can assist nonprofits.

Improved Data Collection and Dissemination.   Form 990 and Form 990T are the prime reporting forms used by the IRS to collect data on the nonprofit sector.

Criticism of these forms focuses on the fact that they were designed as a tool for evaluating compliance with the law governing the sector rather than to provide meaningful data on the activities of the sector and its behavior. Weisbrod (1998) suggests reconsideration of these forms to eliminate nonessential data and to compile industry data representative of the outputs of the sector. Such an initiative would have great value since it would increase the transparency of activities within the sector and enable funding agents to have available a database that enhances their ability to choose which nonprofits to support.

Data dissemination has improved considerably as a result of the Internet, the reduction in computer costs, and the growth of entities interested in providing data to the nonprofit sector. Projects undertaken by the Foundation Center, Guidestar, the Independent Sector, the Urban Institute and other entities have made it easier for nonprofits to gain information about each other, and for funding agents to overview some of the activities of the sector. Unless better information is gathered, however, the uses of these databases will be limited and funding agents will either have to collect their own data or to make decisions without good data.

Rules on Commercial Activities

Commercial activities create opportunities that sometimes conflict with the mission of a nonprofit. It may not be sufficient to rely on good faith to ensure that behavior does not violate accepted standards for nonprofits; a need exists to insure that commercial activity does not compromise nonprofit missions. The primary monitor of this activity should be the nonprofit itself and one way to internalize this function is to create a standing board-based committee made up of a blend of businessmen and representatives of the general public to review commercial activities on a periodic basis. Nonprofits involved in commercial activities should also develop explicit guidelines governing the nature and type of activities that are acceptable, and whenever feasible they should use a separate legal entity for commercial goods and service delivery. At the national level, entities like the Aspen Institute, Independent Sector, and the National Center for Nonprofit Enterprise should help by developing and promoting a set of guidelines for use by social entrepreneurs and nonprofit boards.

Articulation of Mission. Many nonprofit missions are formulated in very general terms and, consequently, offer little guidance on the activities that should not be undertaken. For example, a nonprofit founded to improve the health of the American public can accomplish this in many ways, some of which may be tangential to the purpose for which it was founded, such as the sale of treadmills, sports clothing, health foods, and insurance (Tuckman and Chang 2002). Since general missions provide flexibility and hence have value, internal discussions by nonprofit boards might be a preferred vehicle for defining the boundaries for which activities are acceptable. This dialogue might take place within a traditional strategic planning framework or as part of an exercise to develop guidelines for commercial ventures. Limits might be set implicitly, as specific objectives for the enterprise are set, or explicitly through the creation of a separate set of guidelines or criteria for use in evaluating commercial ventures. The goal is not to preclude new ventures but rather to insure that they are consistent with mission.

Expanded Research by the Academic Community.   The nonprofit sector continues to have important and substantive needs for research, ranging from census-type studies of the sector, to normative and summative evaluations of nonprofit performance, to comparative studies among and across mission classifications, to international comparisons, predictive and explanatory studies of behavior, and studies that inform public policy on issues. Especially important is research enabling funding agents to better assess both where and how to place limited resources and those that offer insights for nonprofits trying to determine how much and what kind of commercial activity is appropriate. The types of behavioral studies favored by many academics also should be encouraged. For example, research on crowding-out is in its infancy and detailed studies of what happens to other revenue sources when nonprofits undertake commercial activities will inform both nonprofit strategy and social policy.

Improved Access to Trusted Consultants.   Differences in the skills of people trained in social services and those trained in business are likely to remain significant and, hence, a market will continue to exist for the provision of training and consulting services to nonprofits that lack the ability to comprehend and evaluate business opportunities. Both administrators and boards of nonprofits need advice on when to use business practices internally and how to go about seeking external ventures, with the need particularly great among small nonprofits and those that do not hire people with business skills. Efforts to meet these needs have taken the form of providing studies of best practice (for example, by the Leader to Leader Institute, formerly the Peter F. Drucker Foundation), creation of programs that offer trained management professionals for the sector (e.g., the Mandel Center program at Case Western Reserve University), conferences that bring together practitioners and academics to talk about commercial ventures (e.g., those of the Aspen and Urban Institutes), focused funding that encourages closer attention to business practices such as strategic philanthropy (e.g., the Morino Institute), and foundation funding of efforts to send consultant teams to meet the needs of less well financed nonprofits (e.g., consultation visits from the National Center for Nonprofit Enterprise). No one approach is likely to meet the diverse needs of nonprofits and this diversity of programs provides a range of choice to administrators and boards interested in developing their capacity for commercial activities.

Conclusion

Nonprofits will choose to engage in commercial activities when they have the desire and the ability to do so and their efforts will succeed when they produce desirable goods and services that consumers wish to purchase. Similarly, funding agents will finance activities that they believe are worthy and that they feel will benefit from their support. Since funding agents will normally finance activities that involve the production of public goods and services, they may feel that a decision to enter the business world by a nonprofit makes it less eligible for funding. Nonetheless, the changing environment, with its creation of new opportunities for nonprofits to produce a blend of goods and services, makes it important for these funding agents to spend more time than in the past on developing criteria for when to fund a nonprofit that engages in commercial ventures, and for nonprofit administrators to be able to demonstrate that they have established a meaningful set of guidelines for their commercial activities. Nonprofits stand on the doorstep of a new and exciting time in which unique opportunities to create social value will continue to arise. Some of these opportunities will be obvious while others will require excellent entrepreneurial skills to discover and exploit. The time is ripe for nonprofits, government agencies, and funding agents to begin a dialogue that will create a national framework to guide nonprofits as they develop packages of blended public and private goods and services that will benefit society.

References

Andreasen, Alan R. 1996. "Profits for Nonprofits: Find a Corporate Partner," *Harvard Business Review*. November–December. 47–56.

Austin, James E. 2000. *The Collaboration Challenge*. San Francisco: Jossey-Bass.

Chang, Cyril F., and Howard P. Tuckman. 1990. "Why Do Nonprofit Managers Accumulate Surpluses, and How Much Do They Accumulate?" *Nonprofit Management and Leadership*. 1(2): 117–135.

———. 1991. "Financial Vulnerability and Attrition as Measures of Nonprofit Performance." *Annals of Public and Cooperative Economics*. 62(4): 655–672.

Dees, J. Gregory and Nadine Dolby. 1996. "Sources of Financing for New Nonprofit Ventures." *Harvard Business Review*. Case Study. July. 11pp.

Deussing, Ryan. 2002. "moma.org: The Evolution of a Museum Website," http://arts.endow.gove/pub/Lessons/Casestudies/MOMA.html

Emerson, Jed, J. Gregory Dees, and Peter Economy. 2002. *Strategic Tools for Social Entrepreneurs: Enhancing the Performance of Your Enterprising Nonprofit*. New York: John Wiley & Sons, Inc.

Galaskiewicz, Joseph and Wolfgang Bielefeld. 1998. *Nonprofit Organizations in an Age of Uncertainty*. New York: Aldine De Gruyer.

Gronjberg. Kirsten A. 1993. *Understanding Nonprofit Funding*. San Francisco: Jossey Bass.

Hall, Peter Dobkin 1987. "A Historical Overview of the Private Nonprofit Sector." *The Nonprofit Sector: A Research Handbook*. Walter W. Powell (ed.). New Haven: Yale University Press. 3–26.

Hansmann, Henry 1987. "Economic Theories of Nonprofit Organization." *The Nonprofit Sector: A Research Handbook*. Walter W. Powell (ed.). New Haven: Yale University Press. 27–42

Harris, Margaret. "Nonprofit Boards of Directors: Beyond the Governance Function." *The Nonprofit Sector: A Research Handbook*. Walter W. Powell (ed.). New Haven: Yale University Press. 141–153

James, Estelle. 1983. "How Nonprofits Grow: A Model." *Journal of Policy Analysis and Management*. 2 (Spring): 350–365.

Kingma, Bruce R. 1995. "Do Profits Crowd Out Donations, or Vice Versa?" The Impact of Revenue From Sales on Donations to Local Chapters of the American Red Cross." *Nonprofit Management and Leadership*. 6(1) (Fall): 21–38.

Mintzberg, Henry 1973. *The Nature of Managerial Work*. New York: Harper Collins.

Moskowitz, J. 1989. "Increasing Government Support of Nonprofits: Is it Worth The Cost?" in Virginia A. Hodgkinson et al. *The Future of the Nonprofit Sector.* San Francisco: Jossey Bass. 275–284.

Okten, Cagla and Burton A. Weisbrod. 2000. "Determinants of Donations in Private Nonprofit Markets." *Journal of Public Economics.* 75: 255–272.

Powell, Walter W. and Jason Owen-Smith. 1998. "Universities as Creators and Retailers of Intellectual Property; Life-Sciences Research and Commercial Development," in Burton Weisbrod (ed.), *To Profit or Not to Profit.* New York: Cambridge University Press. 169–194.

Price, James L. 1963. "The Impact of Governing Boards on Organizational Effectiveness and Efficiency." *Administrative Science Quarterly.* 8:361-377.

Salamon. Lester M. 1989. The Changing Partnership Between the Voluntary Sector and the Welfare State" in Virginia A. Hodgkinson et al. *The Future of the Nonprofit Sector.* San Francisco: Jossey Bass. 41–60.

Schiff, Jerald and Burton A. Weisbrod. 1991. "Competition Between For-Profit and Nonprofit Organizations in Commercial Markets," *Annuals of Public and Cooperative Economics.* 62(4): 619–639.

Skloot, Edward. 1998. *The Nonprofit Entrepreneur: Creating Ventures to Earn Income.* New York: The Foundation Center.

Sloan, Frank A. 1993. "Commercialism in Nonprofit Hospitals," in Burton Weisbrod (ed.), *To Profit or Not to Profit.* New York: Cambridge University Press. 151–168.

Strom, Stephanie. 2002. "Nonprofit Groups Reach for Profits on the Side." *New York Times,* March 17. 32.

Tesdahl, D. Benson. "Making Money from Nonprofit Internet Websites." Copyright by Powers, Pyles, Sutter and Verville, P.C. www.ppsv.com/issues/corporatesponsors.htm.

Tuckman, Howard and Cyril Chang. 1994. "Revenue Diversification Among Nonprofit Organizations." *Voluntas* 5(3): 273–290

———. 2004. "Commercial Activity, Technological Change, and Nonprofit Mission" in Walter W. Powell and Richard Steinberg (eds.), *The Nonprofit Sector: A Research Handbook,* 2nd Edition. New Haven: Yale University Press. Forthcoming.

Weisbrod, Burton 1988. *The Nonprofit Economy.* New York: Cambridge University Press.

———. 1998. *To Profit or Not to Profit.* New York: Cambridge University Press.

CHAPTER 8

Institutional Collaboration

James E. Austin

Abstract

Collaboration with other institutions is of growing strategic importance to nonprofit organizations. Alliances are dynamic and multiple, so leaders need to think in terms of managing a *partnering portfolio* and assessing the desirability of an alliance based on relative benefits and costs. Efficiency gains and effectiveness enhancement motivate collaboration, but there are a multitude of barriers and risks. Guidelines for overcoming these obstacles, gleaned from the world of practice, are developed here for attracting partners, assessing strategic fit, generating value, and managing relationships.

Introduction

One of the major strategic issues facing nonprofit leaders is the creation of collaborative arrangements with other institutions. There is a multitude of forces fostering and even compelling collaboration. Economic pressures abound— scarcity of funds calls for eliminating duplication and achieving combination efficiencies. Problem complexity creates another imperative: societal issues have become so complex that their resolution exceeds the capabilities of single organizations. Sectoral boundaries are blurring—the traditional perceptions of a division of labor among the business, nonprofit, and government sectors are changing as roles and responsibilities are becoming more overlapping. Whereas in the past, interinstitutional collaboration was an option waiting in the wings, today it has moved to the center of the strategy stage. Alliances have become essential components of strategy formulation.

Collaborations can be intrasectoral, between nonprofits, or cross-sectoral, between nonprofits and corporations or government entities. These different types of alliances, involving organizations from two different sectors, share many common characteristics but also have some distinct aspects. Trilateral relationships also exist but will not be the focus of our examination, although many of our findings also apply to these three-way public-private partnerships. The purpose of this report is to explore the benefits from and barriers to such collaborations as well as to suggest guidelines for creating effective partnerships.

The Value Proposition

All collaborations involve an *exchange of value*. The promise of benefits accruing to the parties is the basic motivating force for their interaction. By cooperating, they are able to achieve things that they would not be able to do alone. Figure 1 presents a simplified version of a 2 x 2 Partnering Payoff Matrix that weighs the benefits and costs of collaboration. If the potential benefits to the partner are low and the costs high, then the collaboration is a Nonstarter. Of course, the mirror opposite giving high benefits and low costs is Partnering Nirvana. Those collaborations that demand little but produce little are peripheral activities of little strategic importance. The more complicated alliances almost always carry higher costs but offer greater payoffs—the Big Maybe. These require careful weighing of the costs and benefits and pose the challenge of seeking ways to design and manage the partnership so as to shift the balance positively. This matrix can appear differently to each potential partner because respective costs and benefits are generally different in magnitude and in kind, as they correspond to different needs and characteristics of the partners. Such differences can cause conflicts but they also create room for negotiation and accommodation to reach a *win-win* arrangement. Furthermore, the assessment of costs and benefits is not straightforward. Costs are not simply financial outlays but also encompass such elements as reputation risks, mission distortion, time investments, and in-kind resources; similarly, benefits go beyond funds flows and include, for example, image enhancement, strategy reinforcement, access to networks, skill development, and motivational enrichment. Collaboration value can be a complex calculation.

FIGURE 1. Partnering Payoff Matrix

Benefit

	High	Low
High	Big Maybe	Nonstarter
Low	Partnering Nirvana	Peripheral

(The left side is labeled **Cost**, with **High** at top and **Low** at bottom.)

Although the specific benefits and costs constituting a *value proposition* in any collaboration will depend on the particular characteristics and circumstances of the partners, the general nature and sources of value are discernible. These are what will fundamentally shape where one is likely to fall in the Partnering Payoff Matrix. We can classify benefits into two general categories: *efficiency gains* and *effectiveness gains*.

Efficiency Gains. Combining activities or facilities may lead to cost savings through the elimination of duplicative services or reduced per-unit costs through economies of scale from a larger volume. Capital can be more efficiently deployed by shared investments in fixed assets to be used by both partners, e.g., two nonprofit hospitals jointly invested in a single MRI machine for use by both, rather than having each purchase their separate machine and not being able to utilize its full capacity. Funding might also be generated more productively and efficiently by combining causes and fundraising resources and offering funders a more visible and larger program impact for their investment. This is one of the underlying rationales for United Way campaigns. Such benefits are more likely to accrue in intrasectoral collaborations between nonprofits with similar resources, services, and client groups. The collaborators are generating and then sharing common types of benefits. Sometimes funders may mandate such collaborations as a condition of funding. Such dowry-induced collaborations do not, however, always lead to marital bliss. An additional benefit is the potential for activities that would be beyond the resources of each partner individually. In such endeavors, the partners can collectively justify and support, for example, training efforts, Web development, or marketing research that each would never be able to do individually, and often would never think of doing alone.

Effectiveness Enhancement.   When the partnering organizations have different and complementary types of resources, their combination may improve existing services or create new services that contribute to greater effectiveness in attaining their missions. Such opportunities for synergy are particularly common in cross-sectoral alliances. The perceived types of effectiveness benefits accruing to the respective parties can be quite different, so let us examine each of the three categories of two-sector alliances, starting with businesses and nonprofit organizations.

Business and Nonprofits.   For profit-making companies, in addition to the satisfaction of contributing to the public good embedded in the nonprofit's mission, the benefits may include: image enhancement; consumer and investor preference; market and product knowledge and development; employee recruitment, motivation, development, and retention; tax deductibility; better treatment from government regulators; policy influence; and access to new relationship networks. The benefits to the nonprofit partner might include additional funds, products, services, volunteers, management skills, facilities, contacts, publicity, and credibility, all of which can contribute to superior mission attainment.

Government and Nonprofits.   In cross-sector alliances between nonprofits and governmental organizations the nonprofit may benefit from receiving a variety of public financial and other economic assets as well as helpful government regulations or actions. Nonprofits may be able to influence policy that contributes to their mission. Government entities can benefit from such collaborations by obtaining more cost-effective vehicles for delivering public goods or services. Public officials can capture favorable publicity and popular support. Both government and nonprofits can gain useful information and legitimacy from each other.

Nonprofit and Nonprofit.   Collaboration between distinct types of nonprofits can also enhance effectiveness if they bring together complementary resources or capabilities. For example, one group of nonprofits serving a common client group with different social services was able to create greater convenience for, and usage by, the target group by delivering their services in a single location. Differences in client or staff ethnicity or race or religion can create opportunities for organizational enrichment through greater diversity. Even similar nonprofits might increase effectiveness through information sharing and lateral learning. For example, Women's World Banking, a global network of independent microenterprise lending organizations, utilizes best practice workshops and peer group trainers to strengthen the performance of sister institutions.

Barriers and Risks. The potential foregoing benefits illustrate the types of value that create powerful motives for nonprofits, businesses, and governments to collaborate. But such alliances are neither automatic nor easy. There are a host of impediments to effective collaboration. They involve attitudinal, economic, political, and managerial barriers. We can depict these as the Seven C's of the Collaboration Conundrum:

Culture. There can be significant differences between the organizational cultures of entities from different sectors. This appears to be particularly so between nonprofits and businesses. Norms, values, perspectives, incentives, time frames, decision-making processes, and language can stand in striking contrast. Venturing across sectors can be as challenging as visiting a foreign country. Misunderstandings, poor communication, and frustration easily arise. The cultural gulf between nonprofits and governmental organizations seems smaller but still can be significant. Some worry about cultural contamination: interaction with companies might make the nonprofits too businesslike and erode their charitable ethos. Cultural affinity and compatibility are generally greatest between nonprofits, although differences can also exist. Many collaborations, particularly outright mergers, between nonprofits have been scuttled because of conflicting cultures, threatened organizational identities, and excessive egos.

Competition. Collaboration between nonprofits, however, often is roadblocked because they may perceive each other as competitors for funding and also for clients. It is difficult to share information, resources, visibility, or funder access with a competitor. Some practitioners believe that the pressure on nonprofits to become more businesslike in their operations in order to be more efficient may foster a more competitive rather than cooperative attitude. Nonprofits and businesses can also be competitors in some sectors, e.g., health care. Each can have distinctive competitive advantages, often fighting fiercely for market share, and this can similarly impede cooperation. However, in most instances nonprofits complement one another, with different resources, activities, and capabilities. This is also generally the case between nonprofits and government organizations, although sometimes they can be competing with similar services for the same client group. Finally, the globalization of business has increased competition between communities for the philanthropic resources of companies with civic engagements around the world.

Conflicting Goals.   Differences in basic missions can breed suspicion and mistrust. The missions of the potential partners may even be incompatible. For example, Jumpstart, a school readiness-mentoring program for preschoolers flatly rejects collaborating with any producer of alcohol or tobacco. Even where there is not outright incompatibility, nonprofits must be wary that what a business or a government entity is willing to support might not fit with the nonprofit's priorities. Hence, enticement deriving from resources can lead to drift or distortion of the nonprofit's mission. Some practitioners suggest that this is a particularly acute problem for many nonprofits with huge financial dependence as government contractors but it can also hold with foundations. Many nonprofits have become skilled in doing the Donor Dance, shifting programs or program labels to fit the tune being played by the funding piper. Both often end up stepping on each other's toes.

Confusion.   Even if there is mission congruency between the partnering organizations, the lack of clarity about the specific purpose, dimensions, and responsibilities of the collaboration can cause an incipient alliance to stumble. At an early stage in the alliance between Timberland, the boot and outdoor apparel maker, and City Year, a youth community service nonprofit, the company enthusiastically planned a big concert for City Year's annual citywide service day, only to discover that their nonprofit partners, unaware of this plan, rejected the offer because they could not fit it into the day's events. Good intentions are insufficient.

Control.   Collaboration entails ceding some control to the partner in exchange for the promise of compensating gain. But giving up control is not easy in either inter- or intrasectoral alliances. The possibility of one party dominating and exploiting the other looms as a risk. This can seem particularly great when one side is considerably larger than the other in terms of resources or power. It is worth noting that even within nonprofit organizations with affiliate structures there is resistance from the field to control exercised by the national headquarters; possible encroachment on affiliates' independence can be a source of considerable tension and suspicion. For example, United Way of America headquarters attempted unsuccessfully to mount a nationwide online giving system. The proposal encountered considerable resistance from many of the independent United Way affiliates as an imposition from the center. A subsequent effort was successfully launched by one of the local affiliates that in turn spread it to sister affiliates.

Capabilities. Creating and managing strategic alliances is a complex and managerially challenging process. It requires skill sets that are not necessarily in abundant supply, particularly in cross-sectoral partnering where experience may be relatively limited. The dynamic and evolutionary nature of such alliances may require considerable procedural flexibility, which is often particularly scarce in government organizations.

Costs. In the end, the potential partners need to weigh the collaboration benefits against the costs. The costs involve resources consumed. These are more than just money; they also include the *opportunity costs* of scarce top leadership time allocated to carrying out the partnering transactions rather than other important activities. Equally of concern are the risks to reputation and mission. Comparing these to the potential benefits delineated in the earlier section is further complicated by the difficulties in measuring outcomes and quantifying their value to the collaborators. Even if "successful" in generating benefits to the partners, collaborations may intentionally or unwittingly create a collusion that holds back the "creative destruction" of innovators who are shut out of the collaboration.

Collaboration Guidelines

Although the foregoing barriers and risks can be formidable obstacles to collaborations, we offer the following guidelines for capturing the potential benefits from partnering. They are grouped into four components of the partnering process: attracting partners, assessing strategic fit, generating value, and managing relationships.

Attracting Partners. An initial challenge for nonprofits interested in partnering is finding candidates. Given the imperfect marketplace for partnering, the search process requires a significant investment of time. Often, this process may require casting a wide net initially, then narrowing. The first priority is determining what is needed from collaboration. This will suggest criteria for the type of partner organization to seek. A further criterion is the potential partner organization's possible linkage to the nonprofit's mission, services, clients, members, image, or other assets.

Formulating and communicating a benefit proposal to potentially viable candidates begin the connection process. Entities that have a collaboration history or have worked with a common third party are more likely candidates. Using one's board member or other stakeholder connections to access candidates can often be quite helpful. One needs to study and understand a potential candidate so that meaningful dialogue can take place during the screening and courting process. A useful dimension of this due diligence process is talking with others who have worked with the prospective partner to assess its ability to deliver on its commitments and its sense of fairness and integrity in dealing with others. A getting acquainted process may take a while, but it is essential to effective matchmaking.

CARE started the development of its relationship with Starbucks by a call from CARE's Northwest Regional Director to the Vice President of Coffee to explore mutual interests given that both organizations were involved in some of the same coffee-producing developing countries. The process involved a period of conversations and participation in a public seminar organized by CARE where Starbucks could observe the nonprofit's knowledge and convening power and verify its credibility from third party participants. Similarly, CARE got to know other members of top management and assess the seriousness of the company and the nature of its underlying values and interests.

Assessing Strategic Fit.   The first step is to understand clearly how the purpose of the collaboration fits into the nonprofit's own strategy. It is important to anchor the collaboration strategically because conflicting currents and undertows may pull the alliance in various directions as it sails forth. The more complex task is ensuring that there is adequate mesh of missions, synchronization of strategies, and compatibility of values. The partners need not have complete congruency, but there should be sufficient overlap to avoid serious conflicts and promote constructive engagement. It is a question of ensuring reasonable alignment of organizational strategies and cultures. Differences will always exist; they simply need to be of manageable proportions. Having clear criteria from the very beginning facilitates achieving fit. This includes not only what each party needs from the arrangement—funding, awareness, volunteers, branding, marketing support, etc.—but also clarity about the scope and depth of the collaboration. Ensuring compatibility might require having to assess various other dimensions: 1) the brand attributes of the partners, e.g., brand images might range from stability and conservatism to cutting-edge innovation; 2) the geographic reach, which might be national or local in scope; and 3) time frame preferences, which could be very short term or multiyear commitments.

Fit will not always be obvious. One needs to invest time in getting to know the potential partner and understand its mission, strategy, and core values. This mutual discovery process needs to involve the top leadership of the organizations if the relationship is to be of strategic importance. The alliance will be more powerful if top leadership is passionate about the social cause and the strategic relevance of the collaboration. Such interest can be cultivated and developed. Exposing top leaders to the nonprofit's services and direct beneficiaries can often catalyze their interest. This examination should also assess the relative power balance that is likely to emerge between the two organizations and the risk of one being adversely manipulated by the other. It is highly desirable to formulate and share each others' purpose statements for the collaboration and to examine jointly potential points of incompatibility and control issues. Frank dialogue up front is good preventive medicine. And if this leads to the conclusion that there are irreconcilable differences, better to call off the engagement than go through a nasty divorce later. For nonprofits, it may require considerable resolve to turn down potentially lucrative monetary infusions, but sound strategy requires firm self-discipline.

Time-Warner matched up readily with the nonprofit Time to Read because there was a shared commitment to fostering literacy, which led to a collaboration in which the company provided facilities, materials, and employee volunteer tutors to combine with the nonprofit's training and client recruitment. Visa also teamed up with another literacy-promoting nonprofit Reading Is Fundamental, but there was not an obvious fit at first glance. However, the company discovered this fit from a survey it took of its cardholders to assess the types of social causes they were most interested in. The cardholders cited literacy promotion as a priority social need, and Visa used that interest as the primary criterion for seeking out a nonprofit collaborator.

Generating Value. Fundamentally, creating and sharing value is what collaborations are all about. Attracting, combining, and leveraging distinct resources from different organizations are the sources of value creation. In cross-sector collaborations particularly, it is important to understand that the resource flow is more than just the exchange of money. Financial flows are vital but skills, services, products, publicity, networks, facilities, image, and convening power can often prove even more valuable. The magnitude of value generated is dependent on the type, as well as amount, of resources invested. More value can be created when the partners are applying core capabilities to the alliance, that is, the distinctive competencies that they use in carrying out their normal activities. Furthermore, when they combine these competencies to create some new service or activity, it results in even more value because it is a unique new asset.

It is critical that the value exchange be perceived as mutually beneficial, fair, and significant. The partners should be as clear and explicit as possible about their respective contributions and payouts from the collaboration, although precision and attribution are complicated because resources are often pooled in a co-production process. Nonetheless, if the distribution of benefits or costs is lopsided, the collaboration is unlikely to be sustainable. Low returns will probably drive out one partner or lead the one bearing most of the investment or costs to exert undue influence over the alliance. It is also important to recognize that the value created initially in a partnership can depreciate over time: contributed money is spent, skills provided are learned, contacts are transferred, publicity is garnered, etc. Or, the original needs of a partner may shift such that what was valuable to it earlier no longer holds value. Consequently, one of the imperatives of sustainability is continual innovation that produces value renewal. The most valuable partnerships with the longest lives are those where the players work hard to build the next generation of collaborative activities, while growing and deepening their interorganizational connections.

One of the complications in the value exchange is pricing. There is neither a standard transaction nor a transparent marketplace for deciding how much a collaboration is worth. Consequently, there is no simple or standard answer to this piece of the partnering process. However, nonprofits tend to undervalue their assets, such as their name and reputation, their services, their client or member base, their technical knowledge, or their contacts. Price formation is often the result of informed guesses, negotiation, and willingness to pay. Values of other nonprofits' collaborations, if obtainable, can provide a reference point. Otherwise, one's own sequential partnering creates a de facto marketplace in which the pricing of previous collaborations becomes the basis for subsequent ones. In fact, where multiple partnerships exist simultaneously, competition may occur that bids up the price. Some types of collaborations that are very transactional in nature, such as cause-related marketing deals or affinity cards, are becoming sufficiently ubiquitous that their commercial value can be calculated with greater precision based on usage, audience exposure, incremental transactions, etc. For example, if during a cause-related promotion period, sales increase x percent, the company could be willing to donate to the nonprofit an amount up to incremental net profit generated by the campaign. It might even be higher, given that some percentage of the consumers captured during the promotion will likely become repeat customers for the company.

It is increasingly common for donors and social venture capitalists to think in terms of *return on investments*—both economic and social. Consequently, it is important for the partners to assess carefully the returns generated by the collaboration, not only to them but also to the larger society. This *cost-benefit analysis* should be a basis for determining if the collaboration can be justified relative to the opportunity cost of the resources invested in it. Collaboration for the sake of collaboration is seldom justified. It is important to note that measuring social value and the benefit to society is complicated methodologically and often lacks the degree of precision one would desire. Nor is there generally an external force that demands measuring the benefits to society from a collaboration. This is primarily a governance function of the partners' respective boards. Strategic alliances should be the business of boards and oversight falls within their fiduciary responsibility.

> Bayer Chemical Company faced a shortage of chemical technicians and none of the local educational institutions in Pittsburgh offered relevant training programs. The company also wanted to increase the diversity of its workforce. Bayer and other chemical companies joined together to partner with the Bidwell Training Center that specialized in training disadvantaged or unemployed minority youth. The companies combined their technical trainers and job opportunities for graduates with Bidwell's core capabilities of recruiting candidates and administering training programs. The result was an entirely new program that produced an on-going stream of graduates, new job opportunities, and a strengthened local industry.

Managing the Relationship.   The effectiveness and sustainability of a partnership is greatly dependent on how well the relationship between the parties is handled. It is through the interactions that the partners get to know and understand one another. Given the cultural terrain that needs to be crossed, it is important that each partner make a concerted effort to comprehend the other's norms, perspectives, language, and behavior. Open-mindedness, empathy, and respect are valued attributes for this process. A willingness to adapt behavior is also important. Communication that is clear, frequent, and consistent, and that is backed by actions that fulfill commitments, contributes greatly to building trust. And trust is the intangible glue that holds collaborations together, particularly when difficulties and doubts arise. New communications technology via the Internet greatly facilitates the relationship-building and maintenance processes.

It is particularly important for partners to build social networks across their organizations. These interpersonal linkages need to transcend top management and penetrate deeper into the employee ranks. Only by deepening and broadening these relationships can the organizations overcome the discontinuities that occur due to employee turnover. Given the weakness of the alliance marketplace, these networks can create compensatory mechanisms for information flows and performance assessment. In addition to network building, partners should strive to integrate activities throughout their organizations. This will not only gain and engage a variety of internal champions, but also may open the door for new resources to enhance collaboration in the future.

The stronger alliances assign explicit responsibility for managing the partnership to Relationship Managers. The task is not simply one of maintaining harmony. It is also imperative for both entities to manage expectations from the beginning—specifically, what each can bring to the table and what each of their roles and responsibilities are. Both must feel comfortable with these roles. Both being explicit about respective responsibilities and maintaining mutual accountability for delivering on commitments are essential to superior performance. However, it is important not to overtax one's resources to a point where promises simply cannot be kept. It is better to assess realistically what can be delivered and not exceed that, but it is also reasonable to ask for assistance from one's partner in order to increase one's capacity beyond existing limits.

Lastly, it is useful to build in some safeguards, such as placing clear boundaries around certain sensitive areas, such as name or logo usage, or exit clauses and procedures. A potential power imbalance between partners may result from absolute differences in organizational size and resources. Such differences do not preclude the existence of mutually beneficial collaboration opportunities, but they do require a partnering ethic that restrains the exercise of such power to coerce partners into agreements that are not in their best interests. Clear contracts can foster ethical behavior, for example, by delineating responsibilities, having clarity on "deliverables" from both sides, limiting the areas in which partners can take unilateral actions, having clarity about decision-making processes, and specifying a consultative or mediation process to handle disputes.

Partnering Dynamics

Although collaborative undertakings can be brief encounters with sharply focused activities, they can become long-lasting alliances. Table 1 presents the "Collaboration Continuum" that depicts a range of cross-sectoral collaborative relationships. Collaborations can move from *philanthropic* to *transactional* and even to a stage of *organizational integration.* The latter may appear more like a joint venture than a transactional relationship. For cross-sector collaborations, the move into such a deeper relationship generally involves corporate leaders becoming passionate about the nonprofit's mission and often joining its board of directors. In this case, there is major company employee involvement with the nonprofit and a thick social network across the organizations. These enduring relationships can be of great strategic importance and value. Frequently, collaboration breeds more collaboration, either with the same partners or others. Collaborators travel a learning curve as they work together. Partnering skills are developed on the job.

TABLE 1. Cross-Sector Collaboration Continuum

	Stage I	Stage II	Stage III
Nature of Relationship	*Philanthropic > > > >Transactional > > > >Integrative*		
Level of Engagement	Low >High		
Importance of Mission	Peripheral >Central		
Magnitude of Resources	Small >Big		
Scope of Activities	Narrow >Broad		
Interaction Level	Infrequent >Intensive		
Managorial Complexity	Simple >Complex		
Strategic Value	Minor >Major		

Source: James E. Austin. 2000. *The Collaboration Challenge.* San Francisco: Jossey-Bass, 2000.

Most nonprofits have multiple institutional relationships. The critical challenge is how to strategically manage their partnering portfolio. Different alliances can have different purposes, require distinct levels of resources, and generate varying benefits, so one needs to think carefully about how many and what types of collaboration to undertake. Furthermore, in examining one's existing relationships, a critical strategic issue is to decide which ones merit moving further along the Collaboration Continuum by developing deeper partnerships, which ones to leave at a low investment level, which ones to abandon, and which ones to avoid in the first place. It can be useful to think of the portfolio in terms of the Partnering Payoff Matrix (Figure 1): What is the existing mix of your collaborations between Nirvana, Big Maybes, Periphery, and Nonstarters and how do you want to change it?

John Garrison, the former CEO of Easter Seals, observed that his organization was able to develop deep relationships with several companies, which included not only financial contributions but also extensive involvement of employees as volunteers in the Easter Seals camps, efforts by the companies to integrate individuals with disabilities into their workforce, and participation of CEOs on the Easter Seals board. He notes that the collaboration was able to reach an "Integrative Stage" (see Table 1) by facilitating CEOs' direct interaction with Easter Seals children and other disabled clients. This approach created an emotional connection that generated deep commitment for the mission. Interestingly, when Garrison subsequently led the American Lung Association, he was able to develop many very productive cause-related marketing or "Transactional Stage" type relationships, but none achieved the depth of the Easter Seals alliances. He attributed this to the inability to elicit the same passionate connection to the ALA's advocacy and public education mission as to the Easter Seal's direct service program featuring clearly needy beneficiaries with whom the CEOs could interact. Furthermore, the companies collaborating with ALA were much larger than those with Easter Seals, and it was more difficult to gain access to the CEOs.

Conclusion: The Knowledge Quest

In the 21st century, creating and managing alliances will become ever more central to nonprofit strategies and an essential competency for nonprofit, business, and government leaders. Professional and academic institutions can contribute to developing that competency through further research on interinstitutional collaborations and by promoting the dissemination of findings. Developing partnering case studies that document smart practices, and disseminating this knowledge to practitioners, is a critical ongoing task for researchers. A clearinghouse function is needed to assist institutions in their search for potential partners. The list of readings appended to this chapter provides information sources that offer in greater detail many of the themes presented herein. This century ushers in an Age of Alliances.

References

The following information sources may be quite useful to practitioners and academics interested in pursuing collaborations.

Nonprofits and Corporations

Andreasen, Alan R. 1996 "Profits for Nonprofits: Find a Corporate Partner." *Harvard Business Review.* November–December. 47–55.

Austin, James E. 2003. "Marketing's Role in Cross-Sector Collaboration." *Nonprofit and Public Sector Marketing.*11(1): 23–39.

Austin, James E. 2000. "Principles for Partnership." *Leader to Leader.* 18 (Fall): 44-50.

Austin, James E. 2000(b). *The Collaboration Challenge: How Nonprofits and Businesses Succeed Through Strategic Alliances.* San Francisco: Jossey Bass Publishers; *Meeting The Collaboration Challenge Workbook,* Jossey-Bass and Drucker Foundation (workbook may be downloaded gratis from www.pfdf.org).

Austin James E. 2000. "Strategic Collaboration Between Nonprofits and Business." *Nonprofit and Voluntary Sector Quarterly.* 29(1): Supplement. 69–97.

Burlingame, Dwight F. and Dennis R. Young (eds.). *Corporate Philanthropy at the Crossroads,* Bloomington: Indiana University Press, 1996.

Business for Social Responsibility Education Fund. "Cause Related Marketing—Partnership Guidelines." www.bsr.org.

Cone, Inc. and Roper Starch Worldwide, Inc. "1999 Cone/Roper Cause Related Trends Report."

Cone, Inc. and Opinion Research Corporation International. "2000 Cone Holiday Trend Tracker."

Frumkin, Peter and Alice Andre-Clark. 2000. "When Missions, Markets, and Politics Collide: Values and Strategy in the Nonprofit Human Services." *Nonprofit and Voluntary Sector Quarterly*. 29(1): supplement. 141–163.

Galaskiewicz, Joseph and Michelle Sinclair Colman. 2004. "Corporate-Nonprofit Relations," in Walter W. Powell and Richard Steinberg (eds.), *The Nonprofit Sector: A Research Handbook* (2nd edition). New Haven: Yale University Press. Forthcoming.

Galaskiewicz, Joseph and Akbar Zaheer. 1999. "Networks of Competitive Advantage." *Research in the Sociology of Organizations*. 16: JAI Press. 237–261.

Gray, S. and H. Hall. 1998 "Cashing in on Charity's Good Name." *The Chronicle of Philanthropy*. July 30. 25–29.

Kanter, Rosabeth Moss. 1999 "From Spare Change to Real Change." *Harvard Business Review*. April–May. 96–108.

Kanter, Rosabeth Moss. 1994. "Collaborative Advantage: The Art of Alliances." *Harvard Business Review*. July–August. 96–108.

Nielsen, A.C.. 1999. "Good As Gold—The Stillwater/AC Nielsen Report." www.acnielsen.co.nz.

Pringle, Hamish and Marjorie Thompson. 1999. *Brand Spirit: How cause related marketing builds brands*. West Sussex, England: John Wiley & Sons Ltd.

Sagawa, Shirley and Eli Segal. 2000. *Common Interest Common Good: Creating Value through Business and Social Sector Partnerships*. Boston: Harvard Business School Press.

Smith, Craig. 1994. "The New Corporate Philanthropy." *Harvard Business Review*. May–June. 105–114.

Spillett, Roxanne. 2001 "Strategies for Win-Win Alliances." *Leading Beyond the Walls*. Frances Hesselbein, Marshall Goldsmith, Iain Somerville (eds.). San Francisco: Jossey-Bass. 261–270

Waddock, S.A. and S.B. Graves. 1997. "The Corporate Social Performance–Financial Performance Link." *Strategic Management Journal*. 18(4). 303–319.

Nonprofits and Government

Altshuler, Alan A. and Robert D. Behn. 1997. *Innovation in American Government*. Washington, D.C.: Brookings Institution.

Ben-Ner, Avner and Bendetto Gui (eds.). 1993. *The Nonprofit Sector in the Mixed Economy*. Ann Arbor: University of Michigan Press.

Boris, Elizabeth T. and Eugene Steuerle (eds.). 1999. *Nonprofit and Government*. Washington, D.C.: Urban Institute Press.

Brooks, Arthur C. 2000. "Is There a Dark Side to Government Support for Nonprofits?" *Public Administration Review*. 60(3). 211–218.

Ferris, J.M. 1993. "The Double-Edged Sword of Social Service Contracting: Public Accountability Versus Nonprofit Autonomy." *Nonprofit Management and Leadership*. 3(4): 363–376.

Frumkin, Peter. 2000. "After Partnership: Rethinking Public-Nonprofit Relations," in *Who Will Provide: The Changing Role of Religion in American Social Welfare*. Brent Coffin and Ronald Theimann (eds). Boulder, CO: Westview Press.

Gronbjerg, Kirsten A. 1993. *Understanding Nonprofit Funding: Managing Revenues in Social Service and Community Development Agencies*. San Francisco: Jossey-Bass.

Saidel, Judith R. 1998. "Expanding the governance construct: Functions and contributions of nonprofit advisory groups," *Nonprofit and Voluntary Sector Quarterly*. 27 (4): 421–437.

Saidel, Judith R 1998. "Contracting and patterns of nonprofit governance," *Nonprofit Management and Leadership*. 8,(3): 243–260.

Saidel, Judith R. 1991. "Resource Interdependence: The Relationship Between State Agencies and Nonprofit Organizations, "*Public Administration Review*. 51(6): 543–554.

Salamon, Lester M. and Alan J. Abramson. 1995. *Partners in Public Service: Government Nonprofit Relations in the Modern Welfare State*. Baltimore: Johns Hopkins University Press.

Salamon, Lester M. and Alan J. Abramson. 1997. *Holding the Center: America's Nonprofit Sector at a Crossroads*. New York: The Nathan Cummings Foundation.

Smith, Steven Rathgeb and Michael Lipsky. *Nonprofits for Hire: The Welfare State in the Age of Contracting*, Cambridge: Harvard University Press, 1993.

Collaboration Theory

Amburgey, Terry L. and Hayagreeva Rao. 1996. "Organizational Ecology: Past, Present and Future Directions." *Academy of Management Journal*. 39: 1265–1286.

Burt, Ronald S. 1997. "The Contingent Value of Social Capital." *Administrative Science Quarterly*. 42: 339–365.

Child, John and David Faulkner. 1998. *Strategies of Co-operation: Managing Alliances, Networks and Joint Ventures*. New York: Oxford University Press.

Coleman, James S. 1990. *Foundations of Social Theory*. Cambridge: Belknap/Harvard University Press.

Dacin, M.T., Mark J. Ventresca, and B. D. Beal. 1999. "The Embeddedness of Organizations: Dialogue and Directions." *Journal of Management*. 25(3): 317–356.

Ebers, Mark. 1997. *The Formation of Inter-Organizational Networks*. Oxford, England: Oxford University Press.

Gulati, Ranjay and Harbir Singh. 1998. "The Architecture of Cooperation: Managing Coordination Costs and Appropriation Concerns in Strategic Alliances." *Administrative Science Quarterly*. 43: 781–814.

Gulati, Ranjay and Gargiulo. 1999. "Where Do Networks Come From?" *American Journal of Sociology*. 104: 1439–1493.

Nahapiet, Janine and Sumantra Ghoshal. 1998. "Social Capital, Intellectual Capital and the Organizational Advantage." *Academy of Management Review*. 23: 242–266.

Portes, Alejandro. 1998. "Social Capital: Its Origins and Applications in Modern Sociology." *Annual Review of Sociology*. 24: 1–24.

Putnam, Robert. 1993. *Making Democracy Work: Civic Traditions in Modern Italy*. Princeton: Princeton University Press.

Ring, Peter S. and Andrew H. Van de Ven. 1994. "Developmental Processes of Cooperative Interorganizational Relationship." *Academy of Management Review*. 19: 90–118.

Uzzi, Brian. 1997. "Social Structure and Competition in Interfirm Networks: The Paradox of Embeddedness." *Administrative Science Quarterly*. 42: 35–67.

Williamson, Oliver. 1994. "Transaction Cost Economics and Organizational Theory." *The Handbook of Economic Sociology*. Neil J. Smelser and Richard Swedberg, (eds.). Princeton: Princeton University Press. 77–107.

Wood, Donna J. and Barbara Gray. 1991. "Toward a Comprehensive Theory of Collaboration." *Journal of Applied Behavioral Science*. 27: 139–162.

Zaheer, Akbar, Bill McEvily, and Vincenzo Perrone. 1998. "Does Trust Matter? Exploring the Effects of Interorganizational and Interpersonal Trust on Performance." *Organizational Science*. 9: 1–20.

CHAPTER 9

Internet Commerce and Fundraising

Dov Te'eni
Julie E. Kendall

Abstract

This chapter offers a framework for assessing the impact of Information and Communication Technology (ICT) in nonprofit activities and uses it to integrate current research and practical 'know how.' The assessment of ICT should consistently consider a set of criteria relevant to strategic fit, the portfolio of ICT projects, and project management. The discussion highlights the need for *business models* to optimize the use of ICT and the need for standards of ICT to enable collaborations among nonprofits and between nonprofits and for profit organizations. The primary foci are Internet fundraising and e-commerce.

Introduction

The chapter identifies the central phenomena, decisions, best practices and challenges in the areas of Internet-based fundraising services, and e-commerce—a subset of the field now known as e-philanthropy. More broadly, we address the use of ICT by nonprofit organizations. Throughout this chapter, we employ a conceptual framework that incorporates two aspects: 1) a systemic view of the marketplace in which nonprofits participate; and 2) a decision-making procedure for utilizing ICT. The systemic view includes the players, their goals, the relationships and partnerships between players, and the rules that govern these relationships. This part of the framework is used to determine the potential roles of ICT in nonprofit organizations and how it can be utilized cost-effectively. Of the many roles ICT can play, we concentrate here only on those supporting an organization's external activities, such as fundraising and e-commerce, omitting internal activities, such as human resources management. The second part of the framework addresses the decision-making procedure for investing in ICT, and it includes the decision on whether or not to outsource ICT functions.

A note concerning our method of work is in order here. In general, we worked with a task force of practitioners and academics, drawing on the literature and field reports, our own experiences, and several exemplar organizations that we selected: the World Wildlife Fund (WWF), the Robin Hood Foundation, and the Points of Light Foundation. However, we could not ignore the terrorist events of September 11, 2001, which occurred in the midst of this project. These events have dramatically affected online donations for disaster-related charities and relief organizations. According to Nicole Wallace in *The Chronicle of Philanthropy* (September 2001), more than $70 million of the $676 million in contributions have come online. Moreover, in some organizations, in particular the American Red Cross, online donations accounted for almost 30 percent of contributions. While the long-term effect of these events on online fundraising is not clear, the enormous potential of online services has been demonstrated. Furthermore, the huge increase in the number of online donors may create a new baseline for potential online donors in the future. We felt it important to learn from the use of the Internet at that time of crisis, within the broader context of nonprofits and ICT use.

A Conceptual Framework

We define e-philanthropy as philanthropy supported by advanced computer and communication technologies. The e-philanthropy market space includes several types of players: 1) nonprofit organizations, which include those that pursue particular social missions and foundations that support them; 2) consumers of services provided by nonprofits; 3) donors and volunteers who donate money and personal resources to nonprofits; 4) intermediaries, which can be nonprofit or for-profit organizations that assist nonprofit organizations in their online activities and facilitate interactions among nonprofits and their consumers and donors, for example, to enable donations; 5) for-profit organizations that collaborate with nonprofits, for example, by sharing their profits; and 6) regulators who determine a set of regulations and standards whose purpose is to govern the marketplace, for example, through income tax regulations. Figure 1 depicts a schematic summary of the marketplace with several interactions among players. While other interactions surely exist, we concentrate only on those shown in the figure. The broken lines in Figure 1 denote potential relationships through intermediaries that can be enabled or enhanced by ICT.

FIGURE 1: The Players and Their Relationships in the Nonprofit Marketplace.

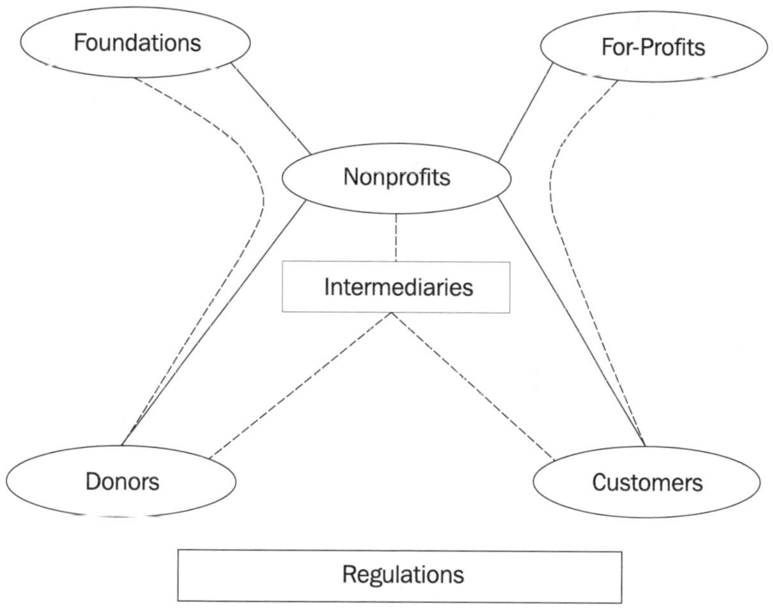

ICT can support services rendered by players and affect the relationships among players.

Broadly speaking, the impact of ICT is either in supporting services the nonprofit provides or in affecting relationships among players. The next section analyzes these impacts in detail. Given the potential impacts of ICT, nonprofits must decide whether to invest in ICT, and if so, how to acquire and utilize it most effectively. An organization's motivation to invest in ICT is related to its potential impact. Motivation to use ICT may arise for several reasons: ICT is required by a regulator (e.g., detailed records of donations must be submitted in electronic form), it represents a direct value (e.g., an online catalog charged per session), it serves the business efficiently (e.g., ticket sales), or it can be part of the organization's infrastructure (e.g., networks).

The costs and benefits of ICT depend on the motivation for its use and the type of impacts anticipated (see Lucas 1999). For example, investments in ICT infrastructure can show modest direct returns on investment but support current business and allow new programs. On the other hand, ICT that transforms organizations (e.g., enabling worldwide movements by creating virtual organizations) are usually risky but potentially can achieve ambitious missions. In any event, the assessment of ICT should generally account for three interrelated activities: *strategic alignment, prioritization of a systems portfolio,* and *development and implementation* (Willcocks and Lester 1999). Strategic alignment is the fit between business policy and utilization of the ICT resource. Prioritization of a systems portfolio is the allocation of resources among competing investments in ICT according to some criteria that take into account different impacts and risks. Finally, development and implementation consists of planning, analysis, design, implementation, and post-implementation service of an information system project. In the latter category, we will deal here only with the question of in-house development versus outsourcing.

All three assessment activities should incorporate multiple value perspectives. Willcocks and Lester (1999) suggest several interlinked measures, which represent investment criteria from the perspectives of corporate funding, project management, business processes, user involvement, organizational learning, and technical management. Clearly, some of these measures are more relevant to certain assessment activities than others, e.g., technical management is critical to development and less important to strategic alignment. However, the general idea is that there also must be some common threads running throughout the three activities of ICT evaluation. For instance, organizational learning may be a fundamental organizational policy that bears directly on strategic alignment in assessing e-learning initiatives, but it may also be relevant to prioritizing ICT projects that rely on automated expert systems, versus those that rely on internal networks of human experts. It may similarly influence decisions on whether to outsource the project or train internal personnel to develop the system. Figure 2 summarizes the decisions associated with the assessment of ICT. In the next section, we highlight some salient issues arising in these decisions.

FIGURE 2. Assesment of ICT

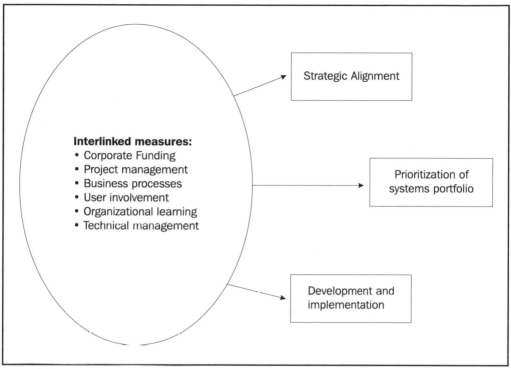

Interlinked measures:
• Corporate Funding
• Project management
• Business processes
• User involvement
• Organizational learning
• Technical management

Strategic Alignment

Prioritization of systems portfolio

Development and implementation

(adapted from Willcocks and Lester, 1999)

The Impact of Information and Communication Technology. ICT can affect the operations of an individual player in the marketplace (e.g., by supporting or even changing certain services rendered by an organization), or it can affect the relationships and interactions among players (e.g., by enabling partnerships based on automatic referral systems). Below, we elaborate on the decisions nonprofits face as a result of each of these types of impact.

ICT for Automating Services and Operations. A nonprofit can operate its own Web site (either as an in-house activity or an outsourced activity) as means of furthering its mission, interacting with its constituency, and facilitating its operations. More generally, ICT can serve nonprofits by supporting mission-related activities and supportive (non-mission-related) activities. Examples of mission-related uses of ICT include virtual communities for AIDS caregivers, support lines for suicidal individuals, e-mail access to one's local clergy, adult education by e-learning, online museums, and so on. Supportive activities are usually grouped into: 1) fundraising and other money-generating activities (e.g., sales) that will collectively be called e-commerce; and 2) other supportive functions such as administration, marketing, legal services, and so on.

ICT can also serve entire sectors rather than particular nonprofit organizations. Nonprofits can benefit from services rendered by intermediary organizations to groups of nonprofits usually within some subsector, such as providing knowledge about regulations or matching donors with charities in health care. Of course, this distinction is not always clear because some nonprofits take it upon themselves to also serve the entire community. Figure 3 shows a partial list of Internet-based functions organized as mission and supportive services of specific nonprofits, and also intermediary services provided to groups of nonprofits. The distinction between mission-related services and supportive services may be useful in analyzing idiosyncrasies (expected in mission-related functions) and commonalities (expected in support functions).

Although, we concentrate here on Internet-based fundraising and e-commerce, it is important to appreciate how ICT comprehensively supports a nonprofit to take account of the interactions between fundraising and the other types of activities—mission-related and supportive. Nonprofits are similar to for-profit organizations in the wide range of activities that ICT may support. These activities include communication, decision-making, and maintaining infrastructure that underpin the running of the organization internally, as well as supporting their interchanges with patrons, funding agencies, regulators, peer institutions, vendors, and the broader public. These information and communication technologies include e-mail, telephone networks, video conferencing, intranets, extranets, and Web-based push and pull technologies.

Moreover, it is important that Internet-based fundraising and e-commerce be examined in relation to noncomputerized activities. By and large, nonprofits are not just virtual entities, they are brick and mortar presences which undertake many normal procedures and activities. We examine how the Internet supports, extends, and influences the other types of fundraising activities done by nonprofits including mission-related services, supportive services, and services to nonprofit organizations.

Mission-related services that are undertaken at the nonprofit's site include advocacy and action, virtual volunteering, helping special populations, and e-education. In addition, there are support services at a nonprofit's site including communication with their constituencies, online donation, donor analysis, online events, and fundraising. Finally, there is a large group of services to nonprofit organizations that includes: tools and coaching to improve organizational effectiveness, event planning, the matching and management of volunteers, search engines in nonprofits, and grant services.

FIGURE 3. Mission-Related and Supportive Roles of ICT

Mission related services at nonprofit's site:

- Advocacy and action
- Virtual volunteering
- Children—youth services (special populations)
- E-education

Supportive services at nonprofit's site:

- Communication with constituency: newsletters, email, bulletin boards, chat groups
- Online donation (secured, record information including credit cards)
- Donor analysis
- Online events and fundraising

Services to nonprofit organizations:

- Improving organizational effectiveness—tools and coaching
- Event planning
- Volunteer matching and management
- Search engine in nonprofits
- Grant services

ICT can impact operations by improving and differentiating a service or by reducing operating costs. In supportive services, the availability, quality, and efficiency of service are the bases to judge improvement. The objective is to use ICT to improve and broaden services and decrease costs. In mission-related activities, ICT can help differentiate the service or carve a particular niche. As Figure 2 suggests, assessing the impact of ICT involves strategic fit, portfolio prioritization and development, including outsourcing decisions.

World Wildlife Fund

As a 40 year-old nonprofit organization, WWF is highly sophisticated and experienced in its fundraising strategies and decision-making practices overall and in its Internet fundraising in particular. The major challenges that WWF faces in its Internet fundraising include the potential loss of Internet-savvy employees to other, more lucrative e-commerce endeavors; global economic downturns that impact charitable giving; and the downsizing or loss of high-tech firms that have been high-profile partners and donors.

Another challenge is the diffusion of online offerings under WWF's structure. The WWF is program-driven, and there are 51 separate programs. Each can have online offerings, presenting a coordination problem. Additionally, there is a dynamic nature to their Web sites, and in fact there are daily meetings to discuss content. While this can be thrilling for users, it can also make strategic planning very difficult.

Developing a Systems Portfolio.   While strategic fit is of utmost importance to mission-related activities, portfolio prioritization is the essence of assessing supportive activities. For example, ICT for fundraising (such as Web sites that enable online donations) should be judged on how it increases the potential reach (number of donors that can access the site), how it makes the interaction with different classes of donors more effective (e.g., richer in information or a more convenient way for existing donors to give), how it allows organizations to learn more about their donors, and how it reduces costs (by saving on personnel and phone bills versus the service fees). These aspects improve the operations and reduce costs. ICT can often enable new or related services such as chat rooms and bulletin boards to encourage donors to communicate with one another and form a virtual community of supporters.

Building a systems portfolio and then managing the projects of each effort, i.e., the cycle of planning, developing, and implementing, require significant organizational resources and commitments. Without such investments, ICT projects are doomed to fail. The Points of Light Foundation, a nonpartisan nonprofit organization devoted to promoting volunteerism, engages in planning for ICT on an annual basis. The overall planning process uses a three- to five-year horizon, and more specific plans are made one year ahead. The plan is developed by applying a SWOT (Strengths, Weaknesses, Opportunities, and Threats) analysis to the organization's mission as it relates to ICT. After development, the plan is reviewed internally within the Administration and Technology department. Additional input is solicited from the various departments throughout the organization before the plan is implemented. Interestingly, the Web strategy is developed within the Marketing and Communications department. It begins with an evaluation of opportunities and resources and draws on the professional experience of the Web team. The ICT team is consulted closely as objectives are established, to ensure that adequate resources are available for executing the Web site plan. This process ensures that ICT planning is commensurate with business policy.

The decision on how to develop ICT is tied to the systems portfolio concept because a portfolio can be designed to reduce risks. The World Wildlife Fund (WWF), the world's largest privately supported international conservation organization, believes in managing ICT cautiously and therefore maintains a diverse portfolio of technologies for major activities. For example, fundraising continues to work through multiple channels, the Internet being only one of them. Similarly, the use of a third party for activities such as database development and maintenance, Web-site development and e-commerce infrastructure, is only part of their development strategy. WWF's approach is to evaluate which route to take for any given situation and also to ensure a mix of development routes overall.

Outsourcing. Development and implementation activities include the decisions to outsource the ICT function. Some internal ICT functions (e.g., payrolls) can be outsourced to third parties, such as Application Service Providers (ASP), without affecting the relationships between partners. In this case, partners are defined as other nonprofit, or even for-profit, organizations that share costs, expertise, volunteers, or staff in a specific fundraising project, or share with a nonprofit organization the objective of favorable tangible and intangible outcomes for both partners. For example, the World Wildlife Fund partnered with the for-profit organization Amazon.com to hold an online auction, but they outsourced the management of their member databases to a third company. The

Fund's decision to outsource did not affect their relationships with Amazon.com. However, any decision about outsourcing must begin with a full evaluation of the benefits and costs involved. The major incentive to outsource ICT functions has traditionally been to reduce costs while maintaining or improving service levels. Studies of outsourcing have shown that benefits generally accrue to a lower-risk strategy of selective rather than total outsourcing (most for-profit organizations outsource up to 10 percent of their ICT budgets). Cost savings materialize when the price of the service is low as a result of *economies of scale* enjoyed by the producer. Such economies of scale can be expected in supportive services, which are general in nature. By contrast, mission-related activities tend to be idiosyncratic. Furthermore, mission-related activities, which are core to the organization, usually involve a high rate of coordination and leadership that would entail high *agency costs* and lower control over implementation, which again would make outsourcing less attractive. (This issue is examined in depth in Chapter 4 of this volume.)

Another common reason for outsourcing is the lack of in-house technical capability. In larger organizations, the ICT department may be unskilled in some new technology or backlogged with other projects. Aspects of project management and technical management may favor outsourcing, but organizational learning may suggest the need to invest in in-house training and possibly to defer deadlines in order to build up a long-term capability for mastering the new technology. In small organizations, problems often derive from a lack of resources either to build an in-house capability or to purchase services from Application Service Providers. Very similar problems have been noted in studies of earlier information technologies, in which a lack of sufficient resources, particularly technical personnel, resulted in ineffective use of ICT by small nonprofits (Te'eni and Speltz 1992). Indeed, outsourcing proved to be a partial solution for this problem, but often organizations relied on free or very cheap hardware and software, which resulted in prohibitive maintenance and integration costs.

Development and Implementation.   The challenges in developing and implementing supportive functions such as donor management are to choose the right technologies and to determine how to develop and deploy those technologies. A related and larger challenge is to re-design the whole process of managing donors in light of the new ICT available. For example, new virtual communities of donors can be created instead of pursuing conventional fundraising approaches.

Nonprofits need to make very similar decisions about the use of ICT for interactions with consumers. Here, too, ICT can revolutionize the way nonprofits communicate and service consumers. For example, intermediaries using ICT can serve as referral agents that aggregate consumer demand across several subsectors, attracting more potential consumers than individual nonprofit organizations could do by themselves.

Although costs, quality, and availability of service are the main considerations in outsourcing supportive functions, relationships with donors and customers obviously have strategic implications. The *cost-benefit analysis* becomes more complicated when mission-related services are evaluated because their impacts are usually difficult to quantify. As a result, a full quantification of costs and benefits is rarely possible, so managers must balance qualitative and quantitative measures (see Chapter 10 of this volume). We begin, therefore, by considering the strategic fit between the organization's mission and the ICT strategy. For example, the Cleveland Play House decided a few years ago not to outsource ticketing to Ticketmaster, despite its economic attractiveness, because it wanted to control these interactions to strengthen relationships and influence customers' choices of additional services. The Robin Hood Foundation, a nonprofit organization that funds the management of other New York City nonprofits, organized a benefit concert for victims of the World Trade Center attacks. They used PipeVine, a (now defunct) nonprofit intermediary that provided charitable gift processing for online giving, to offer a Web-based call-in interface. The event raised over $53 million, and was a great economic success. However, the automatic comparison of recorded data with the credit card database was so primitive that many well-meaning citizens were e-mailed a terse note by PipeVine that their donations were rejected because their credit was denied. Recognizing a donor-relations disaster in the making, Robin Hood staff intervened using e-mail to rewrite the credit card notice sensitively, informing their donors of the problem and recovering their commitment to the cause. An organization should not outsource if it cannot be sure of a tight fit between its organizational policies and organizational culture, on the one hand, and the way operations are handled by a third party on the other.

Management of ICT must fit into the organization's business strategy in terms of function and image. While it is obvious that ICT should serve the organization's mission-related and supportive functions, it is worth noting that ICT also plays a role in an organization's public image. A Web site, in particular, projects a public image that should be commensurate with an organization's mission. For example, the Robin Hood Foundation's Web site portrays a simple, straightforward message that is characteristic of its structure and culture. The Web site tells the story of how they are different from other nonprofits. The display is consistent with the general story of Robin Hood in Sherwood Forest, with a page design rendered in earth tones of leafy green, gold, and orange. Use of ICT can affect relationships inadvertently. The Robin Hood Foundation takes particular care to monitor and ensure this does not happen.

Systems development and implementation is also about people, not just technology. Assessments of ICT need to include realistic costs of remuneration and human development. Today's world is competitive and technologically complex. An organization should encourage a learning culture. At WWF, management aims to reward employees who invest time and attention into learning the intricacies of online fundraising, understanding that their knowledge is crucial to the success of the organization's online strategy.

As nonprofits intensify the use of ICT to manage relationships with donors and consumers, they need to employ sophisticated tools for knowledge management. This is true in the for-profit world too, but it is particularly critical in the nonprofit world, which is characterized by the exchange of relatively rich information, i.e., information that includes interpretations, attitudes, and multiple perspectives rather than mere facts. Daft and Lengel (1986) define rich information as information that can overcome different frames of mind or clarify ambiguous issues within a time interval. In nonprofits, particularly in social agencies, religious agencies, and the arts, service providers exchange relatively rich information with their consumers. In personal issues, for example, there is no black and white. In social issues, opinions and notions of justice tend to be more open to different interpretations, in comparison to the more factual nature of business transactions or even complex engineering data. This type of information calls for advanced tools to manage knowledge in comparison to the relatively lean transactions found in recurring operations such as orders and sales. For example, graphics, voice, and highly interactive means of communication have proved necessary for these complex relationships (Te'eni 2001). The assessment of knowledge management technologies should account for the benefits of strong relationships with donors and customers. Rich information on customers and donors goes well beyond elementary data such as birth dates and religion to include attitudes, opinions, the history of giving, and incidents of poor interactions. Such information can be valuable in exploiting these benefits. (For more information on the relationship between the Web, organizational learning, and nonprofit arts organizations, see Abuhamdieh, Kendall, and Kendall 2002.)

Donor management is, of course, only one class of ICT for supportive services. Employee giving and campaigns are based on corporate intranet or Internet sites that can be assessed for their impacts on participation and employee retention. Another application of service support is the matching of volunteers to volunteering opportunities. Services such as Volunteer-Solutions.org, SERVEnet.org, or VolunteerMatch.org, allow recruiting centers to be open 24 hours a day, seven days a week. They help match the right volunteer with the right task faster and more efficiently than could be done otherwise. The bigger the network, the bigger the payoff. Costs of maintenance tend to be high if the system is to be effective. ICT systems for supporting events, such as broadcasts of benefit concerts or performances where donors call in to contribute, can use a Web-based system that permits volunteers to log contributors' calls and track donations. Online auctions are also promising (e.g., MissionFish and eBay). The main benefit of these systems is their ability to accept donations of physical goods that are intended essentially for liquidation.

ICT for Restructuring the Market

The broader impact of ICT is on the structure of the nonprofit marketplace. ICT impacts the marketplace by providing new possibilities for partnerships, by enabling fundamentally different ways of engaging in social action and by changing the economics of nonprofit activities. The most common use of ICT is in facilitating *business models* between partners, such as partnerships between nonprofits and for-profits in the area of e-commerce. A prerequisite for such interactions is the use of common communication protocols. In order to capitalize on such technologies, business models for profit-sharing or other systems of incentives must be developed to ensure sustainable partnerships. Consider the following possible business models for business/nonprofit collaboration:

- Advertisement on nonprofit site ("visitors click & sponsors give" in Endcancernow.com of the American Cancer Society): In several variant types of agreement, the business sponsor agrees to make a donation when the advertising effect is confirmed. (Also see the Hunger Site www.worldhunger.org which raised $3.5 million.)

- Profit-sharing: Consumers shop at sites that have committed to share their profits with nonprofits (e.g., 4charity.com and GreaterGood.com, www.free2give.co.uk).

- Referral portals (also known as Vetting portals): Nonprofits or for-profit organizations recommend and refer donors to selected charities. (For example, hmr.org of the Health and Medical Research Charities and Giveforchange.com refer to social change organizations.)

- For-profit organizations in the business of raising funds or providing other services to nonprofits (e.g., Contribute.com, Fastgive.org, Donate.net).

The forms of collaboration follow from the business models adopted. In the "visitors click and sponsors give" model, there is a clear collaboration between three parties: the sponsors, the nonprofits, and the consumers. In other business models, other arrangements are made. For instance, nonprofits can gather personal information that may be shared with sponsors. All in all, this area of business/nonprofit collaboration in e-commerce remains an important challenge, not only in terms of economic models of cooperation, but also in terms of strategic partnerships that can affect the relationships between nonprofits and their donors and consumers.

The assessment of ICT in these cases is interlinked with the value of the partnership. Initially, a nonprofit will examine the strategic fit with partners in terms of whether business policies, as well as the culture and image of a potential economic partner, match or enhance their own (see Chapter 8). A classic example was a brief auction event partnership between World Wildlife Fund (WWF) and Amazon.com. An association with saving the (natural) Amazon (part of the mission of WWF) was at first glance a perfect fit with the pioneering Internet retailer, largely due to the retailer's name and adventurous reputation. Although the auction was a success, the partnership did not continue. Once the novelty of the relationship wore off, the WWF did not find any compelling strategic or economic reasons to continue the partnership. Indeed, WWF chooses online partners and outside vendors very carefully, working with the assumption that these partnerships are long-term commitments. An important criterion in their choice of partners is compatibility of the potential partner with their organizational mission. The opportunity to take on a partner solely to make money is never sufficient motivation in their eyes. WWF also evaluates potential partners in terms of whether they possess an appropriate public image.

There are also issues of confidentiality and ethics surrounding the sharing of client and donor records when an online partnership is struck. A general organizational policy regarding partnering should be spelled out before any online partnership is entered. Some nonprofit organizations simply state that they never share donor information with partners and believe it is a violation of their client-organization relationship to do so. They may even make this a "selling point" to attract donors who are concerned about confidentiality. Another route is for the nonprofit organization to provide appropriate public disclaimers to donors on their Web sites, e-mails, and other electronic communications stating that, "These are our partners who share similar values," and, "From time to time we may share relevant donor information with them." This is typically accompanied by a list or display of the partners' corporate logos that are hyperlinked to the Web sites of their strategic partners. A third option is to display an options box on the nonprofit's Web site whereby donors are given the option of participating in data-sharing with partners or electing not to participate merely by checking a box. A forth option is some middle ground where permission is sought for a "one-time" sharing of data when a transient partnership is sought. Other nonprofit organizations skirt the issue by sharing only aggregate data, Web traffic data, and demographic descriptions with partners, without providing a mailing list that discloses individual donor or client information. The lesson one can draw here is that partners for nonprofits must be evaluated thoroughly and selected very carefully, particularly in the face of tempting technical and economic possibilities.

As noted above, the strategic fit must extend to the image and use of ICT. A good example is the metaphor created by a Web site through its icons and content. The WWF Web site uses natural colors such as bright blue (the color of oceans) and the Robin Hood Foundation uses the shades of the Sherwood forest, playing into its well-known name and extending its theme of "persuading the rich to give, and giving it to the poor."

In addition to the question of strategic fit, the costs and benefits associated with each business model must be considered, with scrutiny of qualitative as well as monetary measures, as noted above. The cost-benefit analysis is discussed here from the nonprofit's perspective. In the profit-sharing model (a percentage of profits in exchange of referrals), the primary benefits are the new sources of income for the nonprofit with a relatively low cost of providing the referrals. The benefits are usually modest because the percentage of profits is usually low (around 5 to 15 percent). The cost of coordination is also low, but the potential cost of damaged relationships with supporters may be high. Although an intangible cost, relationships are endangered because of the access to the supporters that the nonprofit provides to a third party. This is in addition to the issue of image mentioned above.

Robin Hood Foundation

Robin Hood has a single objective, which is to end poverty in New York City. One cannot but notice the Robin Hood story when entering the foundation's Web site. All of the shades of the (Sherwood) forest are present on the Web site, which is professionally rendered in gold, green, sienna and river blue. Each page has a small graphic icon, rendered in a deeper-hued color than the subdued color of the top bar (a graphic such as a leaf or a scroll). The functionality offered to the potential contributor is modest. If the user clicks an icon labeled 'Online Contributions', the system brings up familiar looking fill-in forms colored in a light yellow color with white blanks, and it is noted that transactions are secure. Transaction processing is done through a third party that specializes in online funding—helping.org.

One of the main obstacles to online contributions has been a general lack of trust in e-commerce. The disclaimer on the donation page states:

"I understand that 100% of my donation will go directly to serve those in need, since all overhead and administrative expenses for Robin Hood are underwritten in full by its Board of Directors and the AOL Time Warner Foundation is covering the transaction costs associated with my contribution."

The primary benefit of referral portals is new sources of revenue from a wider reach to supporters. On the one hand, the cost of referrals is rather low to the referring and receiving organizations. The benefit, on the other hand, has been relatively low when compared with direct visits to the nonprofit Web site. However, there are several intangible benefits that should be considered in terms of richer relationships with supporters. The information accrued in automatic referrals can be analyzed for gaining rich information about specific groups of givers. This information can later be used in building better relationships, e.g., by building virtual communities of supporters around common interests and common locations. The information of course is recorded online so that it can later feed into computerized systems that maintain relationships with supporters (e.g., invite specific supporters to events that seem relevant to them).

The fundraising sites (of third party agencies that raise money for nonprofits) also have their costs and benefits. The major benefit is additional channels for giving. These benefits are easy to quantify on the basis of predictions and contingencies in the contract between the fundraiser and recipient. The operating costs involved are rather low because the operations are straightforward, often designed as "plug and play," so that there are few adaptations to be made on the side of the recipient. The main cost is the service fee that is sometimes taken as a percentage of the gift. There is also the risk of trusting your money to a third party. Additionally, there is an intangible benefit in learning about donor prospects from an analysis of the data generated by the fundraising site.

The Points of Light Foundation derives substantial benefits from several different types of ICT partnerships. It participates in several referring portals. Most notable among these is the Network for Good. The Foundation acts primarily as a content provider for the Network, contributing information about volunteering and available volunteer opportunities. Points of Light has a different type of partnership with the United Way of America. United Way has developed an online application for centralizing volunteer opportunities in communities across the country (similar to the product offered by VolunteerMatch). The Foundation acts as a marketing partner to the United Way, helping find nonprofit users (volunteer centers) for the product and supporting it with training and resources for those users.

ICT Investment and Impact: Challenges to the Nonprofit Sector

The discussion so far has emphasized the role and assessment of ICT from the organization's perspective. This section looks at the major challenges to the nonprofit sector in both research and development of ICT applications. It is intended as a roadmap for future efforts in building the necessary knowledge for more effective use of ICT.

Previous reports on e-philanthropy (see list of Additional Resources below) have suggested several challenges in this area. The 2001 Kellogg Foundation report *e-Philanthropy v2.001* (2001) concentrates on five challenges to online activity: 1) nonprofits need better tools for selecting online services and intermediaries; 2) nonprofits need to invest strategically in ICT; 3) the nonprofit sector needs models and policies for knowledge management, beginning with policies on information-sharing and intellectual property; 4) nonprofits acting through their own Web sites or through portals need to develop ways for building trust online; and 5) nonprofits must be able to reach out to a diverse population. Another recent report to the Surdna Foundation (2001) posed several challenges that assume that ICT will indeed restructure the nonprofit sector. The challenge to individual nonprofits is therefore how to examine the potential impact of ICT, not on their current product but on the new way of operation that can emerge from clever use of the technology. The main challenges to foundations are to develop models for assessing the impact of ICT projects that serve specific nonprofits and the entire sector.

Some of these problems are not new. The scarcity of resources that most nonprofits can devote to ICT has created serious maintenance and utilization problems (Te'eni and Speltz 1992). Other problems have been discussed in the for-profit literature, e.g., the need to align ICT strategy with organizational mission and strategies (Porter 2001). This seems to be a particularly difficult task in the nonprofit sector, perhaps because of the more ambiguous goal structure of a social mission coupled with resource constraints. Such challenges also arise from the unique nature of the network economy, which is characterized on the one hand by the new business opportunities stemming from more effective communication technologies that facilitate distributed work and collaborations, and on the other hand, by considerably higher levels of turbulence and competition in the marketplace (Te'eni and Young 2003). Another area of concern is the development of ICT that will comply with national and international regulations. Related to regulations is the use of technical standards that will be important for compatibility with other nonprofits and for-profit partners. Without standardization it will be impossible to advance meaningful collaborations that rely not only on exchange of structured data but also on richer information such as procedures and organizational ontologies (dictionaries).

Finally, in the September 11th tragedy, ICT proved to be invaluable in addressing emergencies and in accommodating mass but spontaneous voluntary action, particularly the donation of money. Moreover, a new standard of accessibility for getting volunteers involved was set. The situation also demonstrated that voluntary agencies must now be able to use ICT to overcome physical distances that until now have perhaps diminished their social obligation to reach out.

Yet with all the enthusiasm for utilizing ICT, good judgment on the limitations of ICT must also be recognized. However ICT is implemented, it cannot interfere with trustworthy relationships. In a recent study of ICT in religious institutions, Berlinger and Te'eni (1999) found that some parishes refused to use ICT because they felt personal, confidential, and face-to-face communication was the only way to form the intimate relationships that are called for in religious settings. This is an extreme example, but nevertheless it shows that practitioners will need to be sensitive to the social and interpersonal impacts of ICT as well as the economic impacts.

Future Research Directions

This is a brief overview of future research directions that we believe are necessary to further extend what is known about using the Internet for fundraising and e-commerce by nonprofits and to further the study of e-philanthropy in general.

We have proposed a framework for considering these problems (Figures 1 and 2). However, any such framework is just a basis for its application to particular issues, requiring practical tools. These include decision models, techniques, and support that can help nonprofit decision-makers decide: when to outsource their Internet fundraising; how to choose an appropriate outside vendor; how to create and maintain relationships with outside vendors; how to form strategic alliances with business partners for Internet fundraising; how to use a combination of e-mail, Web, and other ICT solutions to build and maintain donor relationships; how to establish guidelines for projecting what percentage of revenue will be obtained from online donations; and many more salient topics.

The global economy is changing and the economics for nonprofit organizations are changing along with it. Furthermore, ICT is changing the nonprofit marketplace. Research is needed to predict and articulate the environment as a context for alternative decision models. One crucial research question is whether e-philanthropy will increase total giving or rather redistribute the existing level of donations. A related issue is how e-philanthropy may change the pattern of voluntary action, and how the patterns of e-philanthropists differ from their traditional counterparts. What is the nature of global philanthropy and global social action that is enabled by the Internet?

Future research issues will also need to address the impact of economic cycles (particularly slowdowns) on e-commerce in general and on online nonprofit fundraising in particular. We know that economic pressures affect the prospects for charitable fundraising in two important ways. First, in times of a weakened economy there is a diminished overall level of charitable giving caused by loss of jobs, a desire to conserve for the future, and a general business slowdown. Secondly, a recession or depression creates higher demand for services offered by nonprofits, including such essentials as food and shelter. How are these effects amplified or diminished by global ICT? One important aspect of fundraising on the Internet is the potential for global outreach. The downside is that if the global economy is in trouble, global Internet fundraising will probably suffer as well.

Summary and Practical Guidelines

The potential impact of information and communication technology on nonprofit activity is enormous. The challenges are great, the potential benefits substantial, yet the risks are high. To date, ICT in nonprofits has been underutilized and inadequately researched. We have offered a guided tour of the applications of ICT, concentrating on external activities in which the organization interacts with other agents in the marketplace. In addition, we provided a framework for decisions on investment in and development of ICT applications. Clearly, the analysis of the potential roles of ICT in both supporting operations and changing the structure of the marketplace deserves special attention if nonprofits are to reap the full advantages of ICT. The nonprofit sector should mount a collaborative effort to advance research on the effective use of ICT.

Figure 1 can be used to map out the nonprofit's potential use of ICT. ICT can play a role in supporting functions and services but it can also play a major role in enabling relationships between market players. Figure 3 provides a short list of functions, both mission-related and supportive services that ICT can support.

Managing the development and use of ICT requires a series of informed decisions that are grouped into three stages in Figure 2. Maintaining strategic fit between ICT policy and organizational policy and culture is essential. It requires resources and mechanisms to ensure appropriate fit. Secondly, there is a need to construct a portfolio of ICT projects, each of which must be evaluated according to established criteria such as those presented on the left-hand side of Figure 2. While it is usually straightforward to estimate costs of ICT projects, it is very difficult to estimate benefits. A necessary step in assessing benefits of Internet-based e-commerce and fundraising is to specify a business model. Finally, ICT-based services have to be purchased, developed, or outsourced. Outsourcing of ICT should be selective and should demonstrate strategic fit, while avoiding core activities requiring control and coordination.

As noted, Figure 1 emphasizes the role of ICT in enabling relationships between nonprofits and other players and engaging new supporters and beneficiaries. Building and maintaining trust in ICT-based interactions is paramount. As we have seen above, when nonprofits suspect that intermediaries (such as

ASPs) may weaken their relationships with donors or customers, they may decide to interact directly. Moreover, the choice of ICT-based partners must proceed with utmost caution and a major consideration will be how well they strategically fit with the nonprofit. Special care must also be given to the regulators of the marketplace. Intellectual property regulations and laws must be defined. Furthermore, standards and regulations for sharing of electronic data, providing security for confidential personal and financial records, and creating accessible and economical technological platforms, need to be developed and adopted as early as possible. These factors are necessary for collaborations within the nonprofit sector and also with for-profit organizations.

Indeed, the general consensus emerging from the field is that the management of ICT requires ongoing control and evaluation including operations and service support. Special attention should be given to clients' satisfaction with communication supported by ICT. Most ICT managers agree that human capital is an essential component of the application of ICT. It must be developed, motivated, and cherished. Along with the human aspect is the recognition that advanced knowledge management tools such as large, shared relational databases of donors, partners, and vendors, and data mining tools that permit creation of profiles of donors and their preferences, will each play a growing role in enabling organizational and collaborative activities.

References

Abuhamdieh, Ayman, Julie Kendall, and Ken Kendall. 2002. "An Evaluation of the Web Presence of a Nonprofit Organization: Using the Balanced Scorecard Approach in Ecommerce." *Information Systems: The e-Business Challenge.* Boston: Kluwer Publishing. 209–222.

Berlinger, Lisa R. and Dov Te'eni. 1999. "Leaders's Attitudes Affect Computer Use in Religious Organizations." *Nonprofit Management and Leadership.* 9(4): 58–69.

Daft, Richard L. and Richard H. Lengel. 1986. "Organizational information requirements, media richness and structural design." *Management Science.* 32(5): 554–571.

Kendall, Julie. 2002. "Adventures in Fund Raising on the Web: The Story of the Robin Hood Foundation and their Endeavors in e-Philanthropy." Case study available at www.thekendalls.org.

Kendall, Julie. 2002. "ICTs, the Web and the World Wildlife Fund: Lessons Learned in e-Philanthropy Partnerships." Case study available at www.thekendalls.org.

Lucas, Henry. 1999. *Information Technology and the Productivity Paradox: Assessing the value of investing in IT*. New York: Oxford University Press.

Porter, Michael E. 2001. "Strategy and the Internet." *Harvard Business Review*. March. 63–78.

Te'eni, Dov. 2001. "A Cognitive-Affective Model of Organizational Communication for Designing IT." *MIS Quarterly*. 25(2): 1-62. Also available online at http://misq.org/archivist/bestpaper/teeni.pdf.

Te'eni, Dov and Nicky Speltz. 1992. "Management information systems in cultural institutions." R. Hollister, D. Young, and V. Hodgkinson (Eds.), *Good Leadership and Management Practice for Nonprofit Organizations: Essays by Researchers and Practitioners*. San Francisco: Jossey-Bass. 77–92.

Te'eni, Dov and Dennis R. Young. 2003. "The Changing Role of Nonprofits in the Network Economy." *Nonprofit and Voluntary Sector Quarterly*. 32:3. 397–414.

Willcocks, Leslie P. and Stephanie Lester. 1999. "In search of information technology productivity: Assessment issues." L.P. Willcocks and S. Lester (eds.). *Beyond the IT Productivity Paradox*. New York: John Wiley & Sons. 69–97.

Additional Sources

Surveys

1) 2001 Chronicle online fund-raising survey www.philanthropy.com/premium/articles/v13/i17/17001001.htm.

2) Disconnected: The first nonprofit email survey—M. Gilbert. www.gilbert.org/disconnected .

3) Virtual promise (Internet use by charities in UK), 2001 published by Third Sector. www.virtualpromise.net.

4) Kellogg January 2001 survey (see *e-Philanthropy v2.001* below).

Publications, Periodicals

Charity Channel—E-Philanthropy Review (http://CharityChannel.com/newsletters/e-philanthropy-review).

Non Profit Express. www.npxpress.com.

Philanthropy News Digest. www.fdncenter.org.

Reports

e-Philanthropy, volunteerism, and social change making 2000 (http://www.acktknowledgeworks.net/ephil/).

e-Philanthropy v2.001 From entrepreneurial adventure to an online community. April. (http://www.acktknowledgeworks.net/ephil/).

Surdna report: More than bit players: How information technology will change the ways nonprofits and foundations work and thrive in the information age. A report to the Surdna Foundation by Andrew Blau, May 2001.

Study of Internet use in UK charities http://www.virtualpromise.net/

Regulatory issues in *The Charleston Principles* www.nasconet.org

Chapter 10

The Seven Insights of Effective Nonprofit Economic Decision-Making

Dennis R. Young

The chapters of this book have traversed a very wide spectrum of business and economic decision-making issues facing leaders of nonprofit organizations. The components in this spectrum are highly diverse, involving such varied concerns as motivating workers, ensuring access to services by people of limited income, ensuring that the quality of service is not sacrificed to economies of contracting out, ensuring the profitability of fundraising activity, accounting for risk in investments, determining the appropriate mix of profitability and loss-making in new ventures, finding compatibility with institutional partners, and positioning nonprofit initiatives on the Internet. All of these issues are of substantial interest in themselves. Indeed, books could be written (and in some cases have been written) on any one of them alone. But these separate issues also reflect a number of common themes. Some of these themes have already been articulated and have driven the book's conception and the construction of each chapter.

To reiterate briefly, one common theme is that each issue involves the allocation of valuable economic resources. That is, each of the forgoing issues relates to the larger question facing nonprofit leaders: How can I make my organization as efficient and effective as possible, given the limited resources at my command? Second, and relatedly, each of the issues is subject to analysis through a common set of tools and ideas of economic analysis and business decision-making. As signaled in the first chapter, notions of opportunity and transactions costs, cost-benefit analysis, analysis at the margin, risk analysis, and the interaction of supply and demand in markets, pepper the discussions throughout and help identify solutions for nonprofits to address their economic concerns. Third, of course, we have emphasized throughout the book that the application of these ideas, while common to those used in the business world, often leads to different solutions for nonprofits because of the special goals, mission orientation, constraints, cultures, and traditions of nonprofit institutions. In large part, this latter focus is the raison d'être for this volume, because we recognize that nonprofit organizations are serious economic enterprises that require their own special applications of economic and business logic.

In this chapter, however, we want to go beyond these initial motivating themes to explore further insights and observations that emerge when the economic analyses of nonprofit decision-making in its various facets are compared one to another. Ultimately, this approach offers some cautionary but helpful perspectives with which to approach nonprofit economic decision-making in general, no matter what the particular issue. Below, we undertake this discussion in an inductive fashion, by overlaying the patterns in each chapter and determining where they seem to converge. The result is a mix of obvious and not so obvious insights. Here, in a sequence that facilitates their discussion but implies no particular priority ordering, are what might be called, with apologies to Stephen Covey, the Seven Insights of Effective Economic Decision-making:

1. Mission is a primary concern, central to making all wise economic choices in nonprofit organizations.

This is probably the most obvious and unsurprising common theme that runs throughout the chapters of this book. Nonetheless, its importance and pervasiveness compel emphasis and elaboration. For one thing, this is what really separates nonprofit economic decision-making from business decision-making. In business, the pursuit of a mission may serve the overriding goal of profit-making. In nonprofits, the bottom line is mission achievement, with profit-making sometimes instrumental to the pursuit of that mission. As a result, decisions appropriate for nonprofits often depart from business practice because nonprofits must be willing to sacrifice profits, or consider them of secondary importance, in order to better serve mission.

Chapter by chapter, the primacy of mission shines through. Prices are set, or even avoided, in order to accommodate clients' ability to pay or to encourage mission-related behaviors, not to maximize profits. Wages are set, or even foregone, and nonpecuniary benefits cultivated, in order to attract and retain workers devoted to mission. Outsourcing of core functions is avoided where it threatens to undermine mission, even if financial savings are sacrificed. Recommended fundraising practices do emulate profit-maximizing, but only within limits that avoid damage to mission achievement and account for social (community-wide) as well as organizational efficiencies. Investment decisions consider direct mission-relevant benefits of program-related and internal infrastructure expenditures as alternatives to conventional financial returns on marketable securities.

Similarly, new nonprofit ventures may be considered worthwhile even if they generate financial losses, so long as they produce mission-related benefits and can be supported by some viable combination of income streams. Institutional collaborations are considered for their direct mission-related effects, such as wider exposure of a nonprofit's social message, their possible detrimental impacts on mission such as fall-out from association with partners that prove disreputable, as well as for any financial benefits. And Internet initiatives involve the full set of mission-related considerations associated with decisions to outsource, engage institutional partners, price services, and undertake new ventures. It is no exaggeration to state that the bottom-line question of any nonprofit economic or business decision should be: What are the impacts (positive and negative) of the various alternatives on achievement of the organization's mission.

2. As a practical matter, mission-related effects are often difficult to codify and quantify, but they should be made as precise as possible.

Having establishing the primacy of mission in nonprofit economic decision-making, one is left with a large and bothersome problem: the difficulty of implementing this principle in practice. At the very least, each chapter demonstrates that mission-related effects often cannot easily be quantified in order for mission impacts to be readily balanced with financial performance. In some cases, the concern goes further—that mission-related impacts may not even be clearly defined or easily anticipated. In all areas, however, the authors here agree that mission-related effects must be anticipated where possible, articulated as precisely as they can be, appropriately documented, and quantified where feasible. Underlying all of this is the implicit assumption that mission itself is clearly conceived and defined. However, as Weisbrod (1998) and others have observed, nonprofits often state their missions in very broad and vague terms that sometimes seem to defy operational precision. However, without a precise idea of mission, nonprofits are hampered in properly integrating mission impacts into their economic and business decisions.

Again, this concern crosses all facets of nonprofit economic decision-making. For example, in order to develop a price schedule that accommodates some groups of clients even if they have limited ability to pay, one must know how the mission of the organization translates into helping specific groups of beneficiaries. How important is it for a nonprofit preschool program, for example, to maintain an economically and ethnically diverse student body and what should the proportions of different groups of children be? Such a question can only be addressed by clarifying the mission into specific terms, e.g., goals, before trying to design the price schedule to address those goals.

Similarly, in the realm of worker compensation, how important is it for an organization such as a neighborhood YMCA or a church to address local community goals versus a broader social goal such as youth development? If local community building is a priority, it may be important to cultivate local volunteers rather than recruit professional workers, or to seek out paid workers from the neighborhood rather than the broader labor market. Alternatively, if the broader goal of youth development is more important, then offering professional wages and benefits may be in order. The appropriate wages and nonpecuniary benefits offered to workers cannot be determined without clarifying and giving more precision to how these goals follow from the organization's mission.

Outsourcing decisions require mission precision as well. One must ask, what aspects of a nonprofit organization's activities are truly central to the mission and which others can be safely outsourced without jeopardizing mission? Is part of the core mission of an art museum to encourage local artists, and if so, how would one judge success along these lines? Can this function be outsourced through a contract with a local art gallery or must it remain a function subject to the judgments of the museum's professional curators? If the latter, what criteria should those curators use to determine which artists are to be given exhibition space, and indeed how much exhibition space should be allocated to this activity? If the former, can the contract with the gallery be properly implemented by specifying the numbers and describing the characteristics of artists whose paintings are brought in for display?

Decisions to spend on fundraising also raise questions about the precision of mission. Is it the function of a social service organization to pursue its own mission as vigorously as possible, garnering whatever charitable resources can be commanded through aggressive (profit-maximizing) fundraising activity, or is the organization's mission tied to an overall social mission to improve the quality of life for less fortunate people in the community? If the latter, organizational decisions about fundraising must reflect collaboration in a wider fundraising campaign, with possible sacrifices of net revenue potential for the organization itself.

Investment and expenditure decisions reflect some of the most cogent issues around mission precision. Does the mission of the organization require that the organization survive indefinitely or does it imply that the organization should concentrate its efforts over a certain period of time in order to solve a problem in the most effective way? Almost everyone is familiar with the March of Dimes, which helped achieve the mission of curing polio, and then, after much soul-searching, turned itself to addressing birth defects. A relevant question here, with implications for contemporary nonprofits, is how resources were allocated before the cure was found (mission achieved): Were all efforts focused on that mission or did the organization try to preserve itself for other, unnamed endeavors thereafter? The same question is implicit in contemporary foundations' payout policies, as well as in the kinds of long- and short-term investments they decide to undertake. Are these foundations planning to exist indefinitely, and if so, how do their missions, precisely codified, justify investment and expenditure policies to support that decision?

New venture decisions require mission precision along multiple lines. New nonprofit ventures are intended either to make financial profits that can support the organization in its pursuit of mission, to contribute directly and positively to the achievement of mission, or both. This means that every conceivable new venture must be classifiable into one of these categories. Should a social service agency undertake to start a restaurant that would train and employ handicapped workers? One must know how much the venture is expected to contribute to the net financial support of the organization (positive or negative) and how much it is expected to contribute to mission achievement (positive or negative), before one can determine if it is a worthwhile undertaking compared to other uses of the resources it would employ. Thus, statement of the organization's mission must be precise enough to apply to any proposed venture, at least to the point of classi-fying the venture into an appropriate category.

Institutional collaborations make similar demands on the precision with which a nonprofit organization must codify its mission. What does "win-win" mean in such a collaboration? If a nonprofit receives a grant to pursue its work, and a corporation licenses the nonprofit logo to display next to its own, is this "win-win"? For the corporate business partner, the "win" is fairly clear—it is reflected in whether the profitability of the corporation is increased by virtue of its public association with the charity. For the nonprofit partner, "win" may mean a net contribution to mission and/or a net financial contribution, which can be used to advance the mission. Determining the former requires knowing when and how much the nonprofit's mission is impacted by the collaboration. The col-laboration could result in much wider dissemination of the nonprofit's social message, or it might result in mission damage if the corporation's work is at odds with the nonprofit's mission. Associating the American Lung Association with a company that makes a smoking patch is one thing; associating it with a company famous for polluting the air would be quite another. Neither positive benefits nor negative impacts can be assessed without a precise concept of the mission to begin with, and how the achievement of that mission is to be measured. For example, if a youth organization gives an exclusive contract to a soft drink com-pany to provide vending machines in its facilities, is this likely to have a positive or negative impact on mission? In part this may depend on how the mission itself is framed and measured, and where the encouragement of good nutritional hab-its fits into that mission.

All this is not to be discouraging of nonprofit-business collaborations, or indeed to argue that assessment of such collaborations is necessarily easier for business partners than for their nonprofit counterparts. (Indeed, businesses too face challenges in assessing the impacts of collaborations since such initiatives constitute only one of many factors influencing profitability.) There are many different types of institutional collaborations with a wide variety of potentially positive impacts on mission. However, the success of all collaborations requires clear-eyed and precise framing of mission so that collaborative benefits and costs can be properly assessed.

Again, Internet initiatives reflect the same variety of concerns about the pre-cision of mission that is associated with various other decisions to outsource, undertake new ventures, raise funds, price services, and engage in institutional partnerships. In particular, an Internet initiative should reflect an organization's fundamental understanding of its own purpose and how this translates into practical terms. To what extent, for example, should a nonprofit's informational Web site confine its access to members who pay fees, as opposed to providing open access to Web users? This is a question that cannot be answered in the abstract, but only in reference to a precise concept of mission. If the nonprofit's purpose is to serve a particular set of individuals or organizations that have invested in its services, then a "members only" type of venture may be appropriate. If the mission is to disseminate a social message as widely as possible, so as to achieve a certain social impact, such as the prevention of child abuse, open access to the organization's Web site and informational resources may be in order.

In summary, the primacy of mission in nonprofit organizational decision-making requires a level of precision in the codification of mission, so that mission impacts can be calculated or at least classified, and ultimately used to evaluate alternative options and choices.

To a certain extent, this concept rubs against other tenets of conventional management wisdom. Pragmatically, managers of nonprofits, as managers of all organizations, like to preserve their flexibility and "wiggle room" in the face of difficult environmental and internal challenges, often with good reason. Leaving mission vague gives them more options. Courses of action can always be justified retrospectively, even where they may not be the wisest of choices. Moreover, less precise mission statements are likely to become obsolete less quickly, perhaps helping to avoid organizational stagnation or the need to undertake the arduous and sometimes contentious exercise of mission statement revision. Certainly, efficient economic decision-making practices can recognize the benefits of flexibility but they also require internal honesty and candor, even if that information is held close to the vest. Determining the best course of action, and the allocation of resources to support such action, requires knowing what one is intending to accomplish, and then knowing how one knows if that accomplishment has been manifested. That is the reason that nonprofits must attend to the precision with which they codify their missions, if they are to use their resources effectively.

3. Qualitative as well as quantitative benefits and costs must be acknowledged.

This insight is an extension of Insight 2 above, and it highlights another very important difference between nonprofit and for-profit economic decision-making. For profit-making businesses, all that really matters ultimately becomes quantified, usually in dollar terms. For nonprofits, full quantification of (mission-related) benefits and costs is rarely if ever possible. As a result, nonprofit managers must be prepared to make judgments that balance quantitative and qualitative measures in conscious and sensible ways.

Consider again how this understanding cuts across the spectrum of nonprofit economic decisions. The impacts of pricing decisions manifest themselves not just in terms of dollar revenues but also in participation, consumption, or attendance figures that have value independent of the payments they generate. What are the benefits of ensuring that children from low-income families can attend a quality day care program, even if they can pay only a nominal fee? With effort, some of the benefits might be quantified in terms of enhanced future earnings, savings from crime avoidance, and so on. Other beneficial effects such as improved race relations, or the broadening of the social experiences of middle-class children, would be more difficult. But all of these effects may be important if the mission of the nonprofit preschool is to contribute to the health and well-being of the community and to children from all walks of life. Any analysis of the day care program's pricing policies would be incomplete without acknowledging these potential effects, quantifying them where possible, and taking them into account, at least in a qualitative way, in making choices about price schedules.

Similar observations apply to compensation decisions. Nonprofits cannot consider these decisions solely on the basis of easily measurable productivity effects, narrowly defined. In pure market terms, workers in a for-profit business would be paid a competitive wage according to what they contribute to the productivity and profitability of the corporation—the so-called *value of their marginal products*. Nonprofits too must pay attention to the prevailing market wage and to the productivity that particular workers bring to the organization. But nonprofits need also to account for more complex mission-related effects. For example, what are the impacts on the productivity of other workers if certain subgroups of individuals receive vastly richer compensation packages because of their market value? If achieving the nonprofit mission depends on high, public-spirited morale, and if morale depends on preserving a culture of equality and collegiality, as appears to be more often the case in the nonprofit setting, then wage policies need to be modified accordingly. These more subtle collective productivity impacts of wage decisions may not be easily quantified but they can nonetheless be trenchant in the nonprofit environment and need to be accounted for.

Outsourcing too requires tabulation of quantitative and qualitative effects. The relatively easy part of this decision is determining whether a given activity or function can be more cheaply produced in-house or by an appropriately specialized outside contractor. Bids can be compared with an accounting of costs of in-house operations. However, it is the more subtle benefits and costs that can be most important. The transactions costs required to effectively monitor an outside supplier may be difficult to estimate because it is hard to anticipate how much supervision a given contractor will require. Moreover, the losses that can be incurred from a contractor gone astray, or indeed from poor performance of in-house staff, may be very subtle. How does one value the loss of a donor's confidence or a consumer's trust if a function close to the heart of an organization's mission is handled poorly? Nonetheless, it is important for the nonprofit to acknowledge these possible contingencies even if it goes no further than listing them in a table of anticipated qualitative effects.

Fundraising is probably the most easily quantified of nonprofit economic decisions. However, while both the direct expenditures for fundraising and the results of fundraising are denominated largely in dollar terms, there are still several difficult-to-measure dimensions including the value of volunteer time spent on fundraising and motivational benefits of stakeholder participation associated with fundraising events. Moreover, nonprofits may need to take into account community effects outside the direct purview of the organization. Should a nonprofit forego some of its profit potential if collaboration or coordination with other charities leads to a more successful community campaign overall? And if so, what trade-offs should the nonprofit be willing to make between organizational and community benefits?

As discussed in Chapter 5, nonprofits have been somewhat remiss in recognizing that the business logic of profit-maximizing can take them a long way towards reaching efficient decisions in the realm of fundraising activity by balancing estimated dollar costs and revenues at the margin. In fairness, however, even the measurement of dollar-denominated marginal benefits and costs presents challenges. For example, to what extent should so-called "joint costs" of administrative infrastructure be attributed to fundraising, and how do these costs vary with increases in fundraising activity? And on the benefit side, how does one determine the appropriate linking across time between fundraising expenditures at time x and funds received at a later time y? These are matters that can benefit from further research that could result in practical guidelines to help nonprofit managers properly account for returns to fundraising expenditure.

Investment and expenditures from nonprofit funds is another area where conventional business logic directly applies. In particular, managers of nonprofit fund portfolios are generally obligated to be prudent investors, choosing their portfolios to maximize investment returns within specified parameters for risk and liquidity. But again, strict attention to easily quantified financial returns on investment is often too limited a view in the nonprofit context. For example, program-related investments or investments in organizational infrastructure generate mission-related benefits that can be as or more valuable than financial returns. At the same time, these alternative returns on investment may be difficult to gauge in quantitative, much less dollar-denominated terms. For instance, the return on a commercial venture designed to employ mentally challenged clientele is more than just the financial profits it may generate. It must include an accounting of the direct programmatic benefits to these workers—benefits which may be difficult to measure with great precision. Alternatively, the returns to investing in a new building where staff can work more productively are also hard to gauge. How much more productive will workers be in the new space and how will the productivity gain be assessed in terms of mission-related benefits? The measurements that nonprofits require to assess their returns on such investments go beyond financial gains, and they must be acknowledged in whatever measurement units or qualitative indicators are feasible.

Similar observations apply to decisions about new nonprofit ventures, both from the point of view of nonprofits undertaking them and the funders underwriting them. As discussed in Chapter 7, new ventures are initiated for combinations of reasons, relating to both financial returns and mission-related benefits. The latter is where measurement issues are most likely to arise. Mission-related benefits can vary as widely as missions themselves. A new arboretum can generate ticket and gift sales, educate visitors, and beautify a community. Some of these benefits are more easily quantified than others, but all are important. Nonprofit managers and "venture philanthropists" therefore face essentially the same situation as that described above for those entrusted with investing nonprofit funds: they need to quantify what they can, but acknowledge and account for all such important effects whether or not they can be reduced to numerical or dollar terms.

Institutional collaborations are another case in point. For example, nonprofits often derive financial benefits from these arrangements, such as direct grants or payments generated from sales using sponsored bank credit cards. Such financial benefits are clear and quantified. Other benefits and costs are not as easily measurable. For example, the additional visibility and exposure that a charity receives by having its name and logo included in corporate advertising may generate significant additional financial and mission-related benefits. Alternatively, the reputational damage that a charity may incur by association with a corporation that has run afoul of the law, or by causing people to think it has somehow lost its integrity and become a corporate marketing tool, may generate significant but hard-to-measure costs. But no nonprofit should enter a collaborative arrangement with a corporation without carefully assessing these more subtle benefits and costs as well as the more straightforward financial impacts. Again, this is not an argument against collaborations per se, but rather a cautionary lesson about the manner in which nonprofits should approach these arrangements.

Prospects for commerce and fundraising on the Internet magnify the foregoing considerations by expanding the range of possibilities for nonprofits to engage in new ventures and invest their resources, and by raising some additional concerns about hard to measure benefits and costs. Internet participation introduces new risks associated with computer viruses and worms, and security of the organization's proprietary information. It introduces the possibility that an organization's intellectual property could be criminally appropriated on the Internet, with possible damages to reputation and value of assets. Corporate businesses and government agencies are subject to the same kinds of risks, but they may be better prepared to handle issues of electronic security. Nonprofits have not established themselves generally as sophisticated users of technology and may be more vulnerable to these potential hidden costs.

Overall, the pervasiveness of difficult-to-measure benefits and costs of economic decisions suggests that nonprofits need to put more effort into measurement systems that can help them take all relevant impacts of their decisions into account. The danger in developing measurement systems is that they can omit as much as they manage to account for, hence inadvertently distorting decisions in inappropriate ways. One always worries that managers will focus their efforts on a few performance indicators on which they think they will be judged, just as the introduction of standardized tests in schools sometimes leads to "teaching to the test." Still, carrying forward without progress in measurement is not likely to lead to bliss from ignorance. Measurement systems must be developed that acknowledge both quantitative and qualitative effects and bring them both into the decision-making process.

In this connection, it is worth commenting on the calculus and language of *cost/benefit analysis* (CBA). CBA was developed in the context of federal government decision-making, beginning in the 1930s, precisely because the narrower private sector calculus of profit and loss was inappropriate for public sector decisions and projects (for example, see Dasgupta and Pearce 1972). Since its inception, CBA has occasionally been maligned and misused because narrowly focused analysts have sometimes put too much faith in dollar estimates and ratios, and not enough into describing the full array and distribution of benefits and costs. Nonetheless, CBA continues, especially with recent refinements, to provide a useful language and set of tools for public sector decision-makers. Given that nonprofit organizations also toil to produce collective benefits, and incur social as well as private costs in the course of addressing their missions, it is somewhat surprising that, with few exceptions, there has been little adaptation of the benefit/cost calculus to the nonprofit context (but see Young and Steinberg 1995; and Quarter, Mook, and Richmond 2002). There may be various reasons for this, including a cultural resistance to analytical and quantitative methodology in the nonprofit realm. Some "venture philanthropy" advocates are now framing their discussions in terms of "social returns to investment" although their progress has been slow to recognize the historical literature on cost/benefit analysis (for example, see Emerson, Wachowicz, and Chun 1999). Despite its limitations, adaptation of the cost/benefit rationale, framework, and methodology might go a long way towards helping nonprofits account for the varied mix of quantitative and qualitative effects that they encounter over time and across the full array of their economic decisions, and to put these effects into a common framework for allocating economic resources.

4. The tensions between mission and market must be understood and appropriately managed.

One of the early concerns about the "enterprise" movement in the nonprofit sector that emerged with some force in the early 1980s is that some advocates seem to put too much emphasis on commercial activity as a panacea for nonprofit financial stability and growth, and not enough stress on the potential risks associated with commercializing nonprofit organizations. Since that time, the voices of both advocates and critics have grown stronger, but with little convergence (see Shore 1995 and Weisbrod 1998 for contrasting views). It is not our purpose here to contribute to this debate except to observe that the integration of nonprofits into the market environment is a reality that will not soon reverse itself, and that the tensions between market opportunities and pressures on the one hand, and pursuit of social mission on the other, pervade the entire spectrum of nonprofit economic decision-making, not just decisions to undertake new ventures. As such, these tensions must be recognized and appropriately managed.

The tensions surrounding pricing are obvious. One prices one way if one's objective is to respond to market opportunities for revenue enhancement and profit generation, but often quite another way if the objective is to ensure access and a desirable mix of clientele from different rungs of the economic ladder. Similarly, with compensation decisions, one responds to the prevailing market wage if one wants to compete aggressively for the best possible talent, at least in some specialties such as technology support or financial management, but one may stress nonpecuniary benefits with a below-market wage if the objective is to attract public-spirited employees who strongly value the mission or equality and collegiality in the workplace. In the realm of outsourcing, markets offer the temptation to contract out any function for which the market offers greater cost efficiency or expertise than what can be found in-house. However, the risks of contracting out activities that are close to the heart of the nonprofit's mission are not reflected in the marketplace and require a mission awareness and valuation that must be established and guarded from within.

Fundraising is potentially one of the latter functions. There is often a direct economic temptation to contract fundraising activity to for-profit, professional fundraising firms, even if those firms sometimes keep the overwhelming proportion of the returns for themselves. If nonprofits are promised 10 percent of the gross revenue without having to spend a dime, this still looks like a good financial proposition in isolation. It takes a more subtle analysis of potential mission-damaging effects, such as possible loss of long-term donor support or reputational damage to the organization, to resist such a market-based temptation.

Investment of nonprofit funds takes place overwhelmingly in the market context and is very hard to integrate with mission-related concerns. Questions must be asked about investments that have little to do with their potential financial success, but which may have much to do with their compatibility with the nonprofit's mission. Nonprofits obviously need to resist investments that would sully their missions, even if those investments are financially superior. It would be inappropriate for a nonprofit health care organization to have an inordinate stake in a particular pharmaceutical company if the organization's mission is to objectively evaluate alternative remedies for certain diseases. Similarly, it is sometimes difficult for nonprofits to invest their funds internally when (legitimate) financial returns beckon in the marketplace. When Henry Hansmann (1990) wrote his paper on university endowments, he wondered aloud why Yale maintained such large corpuses of funds when the roof of the library in which he was working was leaking!

The various manifestations of new ventures obviously reflect the same kinds of tensions that we have already noted. Nonprofits have learned that they must be particularly wary of institutional partnerships with corporations whose propositions are heavily driven by market considerations. Corporations can offer very generous benefits, in cash or other resources, if it is worth their while in market terms. Nonprofits must ask what the real costs are to themselves and their achievement of mission. Is it worth the risk to reputation if the corporation's behavior is questionable in some way? Is it worth the cost if the corporation requests the nonprofit's association with a product that is at odds with its mission? Should a school encourage fast food in its cafeteria, for example, or a particular brand of shoe for its athletes? Is it conscionable for a nonprofit health provider to associate with the producer of a particular health care product when that of another producer might be of better quality? Should a nonprofit museum accept a large grant from a fashion designer if the implication is that the museum must favor the designer's work in its programming? Should a university accept research grants from a corporation if the corporation insists on keeping information secret until it can obtain exclusive patents? All these situations have arisen in recent years, and, although not necessarily typical, each illustrates instances where the tension between mission and market in nonprofit ventures involving corporate partners became especially troublesome.

Clearly, mission-market tensions extend to ventures and fundraising on the Internet. Indeed, technology has strongly facilitated the interaction of corporate and nonprofit interests by making their mutual transactions so much easier and faster, thus accelerating the dangers. But it is in this realm that nonprofits also have the best chance of ameliorating some of the tensions between mission and market. By recognizing the problems that are generated by informational deficits that might induce nonprofits (and other consumers) to enter into ill-advised deals, nonprofits can contribute by creating trustworthy information intermediary services (Te'eni and Young 2003). The value of nonprofit information intermediaries lies in the fact that they can be trusted in a bewildering world of commercially generated information. That can be their mission. They need to avoid market temptations to buy their favor, but this is where they can excel.

In sum, almost every nonprofit economic decision is likely to reflect the tension between mission and market. This is not to argue, however, that nonprofits should shun the marketplace in order to protect their missions. To the contrary, nonprofits must understand and adapt to the marketplaces in which they are embedded, so as to maximize their chances of mission-focused success. In all of the areas discussed above, mission-market tension is properly managed by recognizing the relationship between the particular choices at hand and the impacts of those choices on mission achievement, and then responding appropriately within the set of opportunities and constraints established by the market. For nonprofits, mission comes first but it is often hard to maintain that stance in the face of strong market pressures. Hence, this is a key dimension along which nonprofits must develop their own strong self-discipline, codes of practice, and ways of thinking about market-related choices. Properly managed, however, nonprofits can become effective players in the marketplace, drawing the resources they need from the market and putting them to service in their charitable and public service missions.

5. Diversify to manage risk.

Diversification is a well-known strategy to manage risks in an investment portfolio. So it is not surprising that the principle of diversification is prominent in our discussion in Chapter 6 of investment decisions for nonprofit funds. What is somewhat surprising is the frequency with which this theme appears in other chapters, and the alternative ways in which the principle of diversification is adapted to different dimensions of nonprofit economic decision-making.

First, a recap in the area of nonprofit investments is in order. The managers of nonprofit funds are required to be prudent investors, balancing risks against returns, much as any other responsible investors. However, nonprofit fund managers face some difficult challenges not usually associated with private investment. First, they are sometimes explicitly constrained from diversifying—often by corporate donors who do not want to see the donated stock in their companies sold in large quantities in the stock market. This is a situation that characterizes some of the largest and best known grant-giving foundations, with important consequences. In particular, the agendas and commitments of these foundations are jeopardized when their company stock takes a severe downturn, as many do from time to time. Alternatively, these same foundations are forced to make rushed, if not hasty, decisions to give grants when their rising stock rapidly inflates the value of their portfolios. Without the option of diversification, nonprofit organizations with undiversified endowments have a difficult time smoothing out the hills and valleys of prosperity and recession, and they cannot easily follow the biblical injunction of saving in fat years in order to cover the exigencies of lean ones.

Diversification of nonprofit funds is a moral and political issue in these situations, e.g., it requires judging if donors' preferences take precedence over mission-related interests. But there is also an economic dimension to this issue. On the one hand, the economic principle is quite clear—in order to best pursue their missions, nonprofits need the flexibility of investment diversification. On the other hand, if nonprofits maintained complete flexibility to diversify their assets, this might have a chilling effect on the generosity of large corporate donors. These are the two factors that nonprofit leaders need to balance in applying the principle of asset diversification to the management of their particular financial portfolios.

A second issue for investment managers is the question of risk itself. How much risk is it prudent for a nonprofit organization to tolerate in its portfolio, and how should its risk profile be determined? And should it tolerate greater financial risks in the parts of its portfolio that reflect program-related investments directly contributing to mission, compared to risks it would tolerate from pure financial investments? These are questions that need further scrutiny and research. If nonprofit managers and trustees are agents of society at large, they should not be applying their personal risk preferences so much as reflecting society's tolerance of risk or the risk tolerance of its key stakeholder groups. At the very least, nonprofit trustees need to formulate consistent risk profiles for their organizations, rather than leave this policy to the whim of particular investment managers or investment committees.

The principle of diversification arises in several other chapters throughout the book, including the discussions of outsourcing, new ventures, and institutional collaborations. In one respect, diversification as applied to new ventures very much reflects the same considerations as the investment decision. From the viewpoint of funders, support of new ventures can be viewed in much the same way as an investment portfolio. Diversification makes sense because some ventures will work out and others will not, though it is impossible to determine with certainty at the outset which ones will fall either way. Some ventures will promise potential high (social) returns but with a high risk of failure and others will seem more likely to succeed but with lower upside potential. Funders are likely to want both types of projects in their portfolios, with mixes depending on their attitudes toward risk.

Similarly, nonprofits themselves can usefully view the decision to enter new ventures in terms of a portfolio of initiatives, along both financial and mission-related lines. In terms of financial returns, they will want to have a portfolio of strategies for generating revenues, some of which can provide modest returns at lower risk, and the more risky of which can have larger upside revenue potentials. Similarly, in terms of mission impact, some programs can have fairly predictable if modest mission-related benefits while others are more likely to fail but also more likely to have large impacts if they succeed. In sum, the nonprofit manager faces a two-fold diversification challenge in connection with new ventures, to find a portfolio of programs appropriately varied along both mission-related and financial dimensions.

Outsourcing and institutional collaboration present nonprofit managers with still other risk and diversification challenges. In both these cases, the benefits of not putting all of one's eggs in one basket must be balanced against the costs of overseeing multiple relationships and the benefits of cultivating some relationships in depth. Outsourcing contracts and institutional partnerships are not passive elements in an investment portfolio. They require active, costly oversight and development. Thus, transactions costs play a large part in determining the degree to which it is worthwhile diversifying the number of alternative suppliers or external partners. At the very least, the discussion of outsourcing in Chapter 4 suggests that for non-core functions the nonprofit manager would be wise to maintain both in-house and external options, but the degree to which multiple external suppliers should be maintained depends on the costs of overseeing them as well as the nature of risks and benefits associated with each.

The discussion of institutional collaborations in Chapter 8 probes this issue further, suggesting that the more one concentrates on developing in depth, long-term collaborations, the more one is likely to obtain substantial benefits, and the more trust is likely to build between institutional partners. In other words, there is a paradox in the fact that risk itself can be reduced by in-depth cultivation of particular relationships as well as by diversifying the number of those relationships. This is a balancing problem that appears to require substantially more research and analysis. Meanwhile, it behooves nonprofit managers to consider the changes in risk and return that result from both strategies in tandem: diversifying the portfolio of institutional collaborations to some prudent extent, while developing these relationships in greater depth.

It is worth observing also that most nonprofits do have de facto collaboration portfolios, since they deal with many other institutions in various ways in the course of carrying out their work—suppliers, service contractors, partners in communitywide initiatives, professional and trade associations, and so on. But they don't necessarily recognize these sets of working relationships as portfolios, nor do they manage them strategically—appropriately balancing the risks as well as the benefits and costs of each relationship. Hence, simply conceptualizing their sets of working relationships as portfolios that need to be managed, would be a step for nonprofits towards more effective economic decision-making.

No doubt, applications of diversification can be found in other areas of nonprofit economic decision-making as well. Fundraising, as noted above, can be viewed as a multifaceted endeavor involving a portfolio of different strategies with alternative risk and return profiles. Internet ventures are a subset of the larger scope of possibilities for new ventures and fundraising strategies. Compensation decisions encompass the issue of diversification along several lines, including finding the appropriate mixes of volunteers and paid workers, and the appropriate mixes of regular staff versus contractors or consultants. Pricing decisions too reflect diversification issues. As Oster, Gray, and Weinberg observe in Chapter 2, it may be wise to maintain selected combinations of pricing policies so as to balance the risks and benefits of alternative approaches. Services can be priced at certain times during the week and offered free at others; services can be sold in bundles as well as á la carte. The reasoning that nonprofit managers can use to balance risk and return is much the same, for each of these dimensions of nonprofit economic decision-making.

6. Nonprofit organizations are pushed and pulled in different directions by multiple, diverse stakeholders. The challenge is to retain a clear focus on mission and core capabilities in light of these pushes and pulls.

In some sense, arguing that nonprofit managers must focus on mission as the bottom line for nonprofit economic decision-making is a glib, oversimplified prescription. In point of fact, nonprofit organizations are influenced constantly by multiple stakeholder groups, most which have a particular interest in, or interpretation of, the mission. As such each stakeholder group puts pressure on nonprofit leadership to orient programs or policies in the particular directions it sees as appropriate. This means that nonprofit economic decisions are laden with considerable tensions reflecting the interests of alternative stakeholders, many of whom can hold the organization to account in various ways. Perhaps the ironic solution to these tensions, as emphasized throughout this book, is to continue to sharpen, clarify, and try to achieve consensus about mission, and to clearly identify and emphasize core capabilities, so that the leadership of the organization can resist inappropriate diversions of attention and resources, and maintain an effective economic course of action.

The challenge of multiple stakeholders raises itself throughout the spectrum of nonprofit economic decisions. In the arena of pricing, for example, one is faced with the need to accommodate alternative groups of potential beneficiaries, some that can't pay much, and others that can. As a result, price schedules are likely to pit the interests of one group against another unless a consensus is reached to which both groups can subscribe. As noted in Chapter 2, such consensus is possible but often difficult. Well-off parents who wish to have their children go to school with a diverse mix of other children may willingly pay more tuition to enable that possibility. Parents of college students who are asked to pay the full price because of their higher income can buy into arguments that the resulting mix of students makes for better education for everyone, and that in any case all students are subsidized to some extent from other sources of university funds. Nonetheless, the setting of tuition schedules in such cases, requires not only agreements in principle about how the mission plays itself out in the pricing arena, but finding precisely the right price schedules that satisfactorily address mission in the minds of alternative stakeholders.

In the area of compensation, a number of stakeholder pressures come into play. Paid staff have different interests than volunteers, bringing alternative pressures to bear on the labor mix utilized by a nonprofit organization. Professional workers may stress the importance of professional standards of work and the reliability and dedication of full-time workers. Advocates for volunteers may stress the motivational benefits and spirit brought to the organization by volunteers, the cost effectiveness of this resource, and a special mix of skills that volunteers can bring (through pro bono work, for example) which might be unattainable through paid employment. The nonprofit executive must find the right mix by balancing these arguments and concomitant pressures through an assessment of how different mixes contribute to the effectiveness of the organization in achieving its mission.

Similarly, internal stakeholder pressures may manifest themselves around the issue of wage differentials among different groups of paid workers. Those with widely marketable skills will pressure for differentials to recognize their greater market value. Those with skills that are less widely marketable will emphasize the importance of fairness and collegiality, as well as their particular contributions to achieving the organization's mission. Again, the responsibility of nonprofit organizational leaders is to find the right mix that mediates these pressures through a common understanding around mission and effectiveness.

Outsourcing highlights similar stakeholder divisions. Internal staff may wish to keep work for themselves and resist policies that favor external consultants over regular employees. External providers of other inputs, including supplies, equipment, travel services, insurance, real estate, and the like, who may or may not be donors, volunteers, or even board members of a nonprofit, may pressure the nonprofit to make greater uses of their services. Conflicts of interest obviously should be avoided, but sometimes the pressures are more subtle than blatant self-dealing. Board members are often recruited because they can help a nonprofit with expertise or other resources, and usually the help provided reflects genuine generosity and confers real benefits. Still, this is an area that requires vigilance, to ensure that the organization is really getting the best deal and that the outsourcing arrangement is the most cost-effective alternative in addressing the organization's mission.

Fundraising too involves its own multi-stakeholder pressures. Fundraising often engages volunteers and is built around targeted goals. Both development staff and volunteers develop proprietary interests in those goals, and in increasing those goals over time, irrespective of whether the resources devoted to reach those goals are justified in terms of net returns. It remains for organizational leadership to modulate the development function so that it produces the largest return for the resources devoted to it.

Similarly, we have observed that nonprofits operate in a social context where competition and collaboration in fundraising may be an issue. Nonprofits may have to respond to community pressures to collaborate even where this means that a degree of success at the organizational level is sacrificed.

Investment and expenditure decisions are also lightning rods for potential conflicts among multiple stakeholders. For one thing, there may be competition for investment funds between those with responsibility for particular programs or organizational functions, and those who favor maximizing financial returns overall. Facilities managers may argue for investments to replace outmoded infrastructure as a means to increase organizational productivity. Human resource managers may argue the same for staff education and training. Program managers may seek program-related investments through commercial ventures that employ people from the organization's target clientele group. Members of the board may even argue for placing funds into particular securities or financial institutions because they believe in the integrity or competency of those investment vehicles. Potential conflicts of interest aside, it behooves nonprofit leaders in these various cases to measure alternatives by a common standard of mission-related returns to investment.

Again, new ventures reflect much the same pressures as investment and expenditure decisions. Financial managers in the organization may press for ventures that promise a strong financial return while program managers may seek ventures that contribute more directly to mission. Institutional funders may favor ventures that can promise financial self-sustenance after some period of time, so that they can set a clear "exit strategy," over other ventures that may contribute more strongly to mission but are likely to require ongoing support. Foundations or other donors with particular missions of their own will favor ventures reflecting their own philosophies and approaches. Staff involved in current programs may object to diverting resources to new initiatives that might undermine their current efforts. Consumer or client groups that feel poorly served may advocate for new programs at the expense of current ones, and so on. Again, nonprofit leaders need a compass to navigate the turbulence of these diverse pressures for action and accountability. That compass must be a sense of mission combined with a solid understanding of the organization's core competencies, so that organizational leadership can demonstrate that its favored combination of new venture possibilities is the best use of organizational resources.

Institutional collaborations offer another interesting cut to the issue of multiple stakeholders and accountability. In particular, one of the dangers of cultivating a few deep, collaborative relationships rather than a wider network of relationships is that it gives collaborators more leverage. This is the downside of decreasing risk and increasing trust through intensive, long-term partnerships—one can become dependent on collaborating partners because the stakes of breaking up can grow so much higher. As a result, the nonprofit must be careful not to have its goals displaced by its partners' priorities. If a museum finds itself excluding certain art because it would offend the top executives of its sponsoring corporation, or if a clinic avoids offering a certain drug for its patients because it is sponsored by an alternative pharmaceutical company, then one must ask if the decisions to collaborate have caused the organization to stray from a path that maximally contributes to its organizational mission.

These problematic instances, however, should not obscure the positive potentials in these accountability relationships. Partners in a strong alliance often seek ways to assist rather than constrain one another. Corporations, for example, have been known to help their nonprofit counterparts to recruit additional corporate sponsors to support their causes.

Internet commerce and fundraising also generate interesting issues stemming from stakeholder interests and pressures. As Te'eni and Kendall observe in Chapter 9, the Internet is a diffuse medium that dilutes and decentralizes stakeholder communities. Benefits and revenues of Internet initiatives are spread over very large arenas, perhaps worldwide, rather than necessarily confined to local communities. Such dispersion raises questions about how a nonprofit organization should allocate its own resources, e.g., to what extent it should it expand its view to a wider market versus continuing to serve, and raise resources from, the local community in which it may be historically associated or physically located. Nonprofit managers are likely to feel pressures from both those with local loyalties and others who see opportunity in the wider world. Again, mission as well as core competency in the form of knowledge of the culture and character of particular communities need to be the touchstones from which these kinds of economic decisions are made.

7. Economic conditions change. Nonprofit economic decisions need constantly to be revisited.

As Chapter 1 described, nonprofits operate in a dynamic economic environment that has changed dramatically and sometimes suddenly over the past forty years. While the principles of economic analysis are timeless, their application to nonprofit economic decision-making yields different answers in different circumstances. Thus, nonprofits must adopt their policies and practices over time in order to remain effective. This lesson carries across the full spectrum of nonprofit economic decision-making.

For example, nonprofit organizations have become much more embedded in a market environment, facing greater competition for their services than ever before. This affects how they price their services—specifically, it may require them to price more competitively and to limit below-market discounts. A nonprofit health care service, for example, which might formerly have priced its cosmetic surgery program at a premium in order to make a profit that could subsidize its emergency clinic, may no longer be able to do so if faced with a for-profit competitor down the street. It may need to price its cosmetic surgery competitively and reduce or eliminate its charity emergency care or fund it in another way.

Similarly, in the more competitive contemporary environment, nonprofits now need to choose their new ventures differently. No longer is it sufficient to focus on mission impact alone, relying on charitable contributions and other sources to cover costs. New ventures need to be scrutinized for both their income-generating and mission-impacting potentials, and they need to be undertaken in combinations that are financially feasible. Moreover, in an environment of greater competition, nonprofits must scrutinize their potentially profitable ventures very carefully to determine if they are likely to fall to competition from the business sector in the future. Finding that special "niche" in which a nonprofit may have a comparative advantage relative to a for-profit competitor becomes very important. That niche might involve selling products featuring the exclusive logo of a prestigious art museum, or offering training programs that promise participation of the distinguished faculty of a university. It does no good for a nonprofit to offer a commercial service whose profits will ultimately be competed away unless this is part of a plan to exploit "first mover advantage" and then withdraw. The latter might be the case with an invention whose patent will expire or whose design will take some time for competitors to copy.

Certainly the changing economic environment strongly influences how nonprofits must now compete in the labor market for staff and volunteers. Here too the competition has become much more intense. Women in particular have more options and can no longer be counted on to volunteer for large blocks of hours or to work for low pay in stereotypical "female" jobs such a teacher, social worker, or nurse. Nonprofits are having to become more competitive in the wider labor market, offering wages closer to market and, at the same time, exploiting the special character of their organizations and the work that they do, in order to offer important nonpecuniary benefits that can help offset necessary wage differentials. Again, nonprofits need to continually reexamine the comparative advantages that they embody in order to compete more effectively for the human resources they require in the context of a changing labor market.

Outsourcing is another area of nonprofit economic practice that must evolve with changing economic conditions. One consideration again is the increasing competition which drives nonprofits to become as efficient as they can be. In part, this requires nonprofits to concentrate on, and keep in-house, those functions they do well, while contracting out those functions that can be purchased more economically in the market place. In addition, the changing technological environment encourages nonprofits to outsource their activities more heavily than they might have otherwise. Information technology makes it easier to shop for services and to maintain communications and oversight with suppliers, reducing the need for in-house capacity. Indeed, nonprofits, like other kinds of organizations, are becoming more like networks themselves, engaging consultants and service suppliers over wide geographic regions in order to get their work done in the most effective way possible.

Fundraising is yet another area in which economic practices are evolving in conjunction with changing economic conditions. Certainly competition for charitable funding has become much fiercer in recent years. This competition manifests itself along several dimensions: in the labor market for development professionals, in the head-to-head rivalry among charities for the generosity of particular donor groups and grant-giving organizations, in the engagement of for-profit fundraising firms, in the development of institutional partnerships tied to charitable gifts or other revenue streams, and so on. If anything, the greater competition for charitable funding is pushing nonprofits to learn the rules of profit-making, so as to design their development strategies to maximize net revenues. In the process, however, nonprofits are also having to learn how to modify the strategies of profit-making in order to take account of special concerns in the nonprofit sector, including donor backlash from aggressive solicitation by telemarketers or from revelations of high fundraising costs. In addition, nonprofits are having to modify institutional arrangements for community fundraising once taken for granted, especially in light of the increasing assertiveness of donor groups. The monopoly of United Ways has given way to multiple federated campaigns within particular communities, and indeed the market share of community-wide fundraising has declined over all. Moreover, community foundations are now having to compete with for-profit securities firms for the investment of donor-advised funds intended to give donors control over how they distribute their savings to selected charitable causes.

Clearly technological change is affecting economic decision-making in relation to fundraising as well. The Internet facilitates multiple schemes for tying the purchase of goods and services from corporations with donations to charitable causes, for advertising nonprofits on for-profit Web sites and vice versa, and for allowing nonprofits to reach out more directly and extensively to the donor public. All this has changed both the cost and the revenue structures of nonprofit fundraising operations. Nonprofits must still ask the same basic question— will expenditure of an additional dollar on fundraising initiatives continue to yield more than a dollar in return—but both the level and types of expenditure are changing with the expanding options offered in the present network environment.

Nowhere is change more evident than in the evolving institutional collaborations in which nonprofits increasingly engage with business and government. Again, we can attribute the changes to underlying shifts in the competitive and technological environments, as well as to changes in the public policy arena. In a fundamental sense, the proliferation of collaborations is one strategy that allows nonprofits to become more competitive. As noted above, some collaborations allow nonprofits to outsource functions which can be executed better by others, so as to concentrate on functions in which they excel. In part, collaborations also reflect the more competitive environment of charitable fundraising, driving nonprofits to seek arrangements with corporations or government that promise new or increased revenue streams. Interestingly, the more stringent public sector and business environments drive nonprofit institutional collaborations from the other side of the market. Reduced budgets and privatization policies have led government organizations to contract out more of their services, frequently seeking nonprofits as reliable and trustworthy partners for doing so. Similarly, corporations faced with increased, often global, competition have sought a new competitive edge, and have learned that nonprofit organizations can add to their marketing luster, help motivate their employees, or bring other competitive benefits. While the fundamental considerations haven't changed, multiple changes in the economic environment, including reduced public sector commitments, global competition in the business world, new technological possibilities, and more intensive competition for resources within the nonprofit world, have converged to encourage nonprofits and their counterparts to explore and cultivate a variety of new arrangements for collaboration.

Finally, perhaps the most significant change has taken place within the nonprofit world itself, having to do as much with a shift in attitudes as with changes in the resource environment. While they were always implicitly entrepreneurial, nonprofits have now come out of the closet as an entrepreneurial sector, and no longer shun a businesslike image. No longer are words like entrepreneurship, marketing, competition, strategy, venture, returns to investment, and commercial revenue foreign to the nonprofit vocabulary as they were just twenty-five years ago. These concepts have virtually lost their negative connotations as icons of an inappropriate business mentality. And certainly they have lost their obscurity in the nonprofit world. Indeed, in some quarters they have become mantras. Therein lies both the potential of the nonprofit sector as well as the dangers it will face in the years ahead.

Clearly the nonprofit sector is served well by the view that its leaders and managers must be energetically engaged in finding new and better ways of doing things, and in using the resources at their disposal more creatively and effectively. An entrepreneurial orientation driven by mission and engaging a variety of personal, organizational, and social motivations has injected energy and realism into the sector. This view recognizes that nonprofits are serious economic enterprises with certain comparative economic advantages that serve important societal objectives, and that it is just as important for these enterprises to use their resources effectively as it is for business or government to do so. Indeed, for reasons discussed in Chapter 1, it may be even more important for nonprofits to be responsible and aggressive economic stewards because they serve vulnerable groups and because they are peculiarly entrusted with resources by the general public and by those who have been personally generous with their time and money. This responsibility is by no means inconsistent with the notion of an entrepreneurial nonprofit organization. Research on entrepreneurship and its history in the nonprofit sector shows that entrepreneurship is a generic process driven by multiple personal and organizational motivations; it is by no means confined to personal wealth enhancement by self-serving venturers (Young 1983).

However, danger lies in the mistaken but common notion that becoming an entrepreneurial nonprofit economic enterprise means becoming just like an aggressive, corporate business enterprise. Certainly at this point in the early 21st century, one cannot say that corporate business is serving well as a model for nonprofit emulation. If anything, the recent accounting scandals serve as cautionary tales of what can happen when institutions entrusted with public confidence betray that faith. The nonprofit sector is built on trust. Trust lies at the core of why these institutions are granted their special status in public policy. Accordingly, nonprofits must responsibly demonstrate their trustworthiness by applying sound economic principles to their business decision-making—in the service of achieving their social missions rather than selfish or self-serving ends. This is a constant that transcends whatever changes take place in the environment of nonprofit organizations over time.

Concluding Comments

Principles of economic and business decision-making are generic. They can be employed in the service of profit-making and private gain, as they usually are in the wider world of commerce, or they can be employed in service of the more nuanced missions of nonprofit organizations. Sometimes economic practices carry over from business to the nonprofit world in a fairly straightforward way. For example, while fundraising does entail some intangible benefits and costs, it is fundamentally an exercise in profit-making that can benefit substantially from a business approach. Investments should examine financial returns within an appropriate risk profile. Outsourcing decisions must consider fundamental cost parameters and comparative advantages, whether those decisions are made by a nonprofit or a business. Within certain boundaries, nonprofits must compete in the same labor markets as businesses do, bearing in mind the prevailing market wage. And so on.

But nonprofits require a much more sophisticated set of guidelines for practice that take into account both their unique social missions, goals and constraints, and also the peculiar factors and conditions that affect the market venues in which they do their special work. Not least among these are the difficulties of interpreting and measuring mission impacts, including the various qualitative and as well as quantitative benefits and costs associated with mission, the multiple stakeholders to whom nonprofits must respond, the special trust placed in nonprofits to uphold their missions, and the challenges of adapting basic economic reasoning to a moving target—the nonprofit organization in the highly dynamic economic and social environment of the early twenty-first century. Nonprofits will succeed by becoming competent economic enterprises but only if they also maintain their special character and identities and shape the rules of enterprise to fit them appropriately. We trust that the chapters of this book have begun to demonstrate how this can be done.

In the eighteenth century, Edmund Burke said: "Government is a contrivance of human wisdom to provide for human wants. Men have a right that these wants should be provided for by this wisdom" (Oxford, 1979, p. 111). A similar observation could be made for contemporary nonprofit organizations—they are clearly a creation of men and women to address worthy social objectives, established with the clear expectation that those entrusted with the resources of these organizations will employ them to best possible effect. While they are indeed human contrivances, nonprofit organizations do also reflect an underlying wisdom—that the energies of economic enterprise can be channeled in such a way, through economic incentives, legal constraints, and noble human aspirations and motives, so that they can effectively serve important social causes and interests rather than private gain. The rules for engaging economic strategy in support of this wisdom are still evolving, but they have a clear basis in economic and business principles mobilized in service of social welfare.

References

Dasgupta, Ajit K. and D.W. Pearce. 1972. *Cost-Benefit Analysis: Theory and Practice.* London, England: MacMillan Press.

Emerson, Jed, Jay Wachowicz, and Suzi Chun. 1999. "Social Return on Investment: Exploring Aspects of Value Creation in the Nonprofit Sector." Chapter 8 in *The Roberts Enterprise Development Fund, Social Purpose Enterprises and Venture Philanthropy.* San Francisco: The Roberts Foundation. 2: 13–173.

Hansmann, Henry. 1990. "Why Do Universities Have Endowments?" *Journal of Legal Studies.* XIX: 3–42.

Quarter, Jack, Laurie Mook, and Betty Jane Richmond, 2002. *What Counts.* Upper Saddle River, NJ: Prentice-Hall.

The Oxford Dictionary of Quotations. 1979. New York: Oxford University Press.

Shore, Bill. 1995. *Revolution of the Heart.* New York: Riverhead Books.

Te'eni, Dov and Dennis R. Young. 2003. " The Changing Role of Nonprofits in the Network Economy," *Nonprofit and Voluntary Sector Quarterly.* 32:3. 397–414.

Weisbrod, Burton A.(ed.). 1998. *To Profit or Not to Profit.* New York: Cambridge University Press.

Young, Dennis R. *If Not for Profit, For What?* 1983. Lexington: D.C. Heath and Company.

Young, Dennis R. and Richard Steinberg. 1995. *Economics for Nonprofit Managers.* New York: The Foundation Center.

About the Authors

James Austin holds the John G. McLean Professorship of Business Administration at the Harvard Business School and serves as the Chair of the School's Initiative on Social Enterprise.

Avner Ben-Ner is Professor and Director at the Industrial Relations Center, Carlson School of Management, University of Minnesota.

Joseph Cordes is a Professor of Economics and International Affairs at George Washington University in Washington, D.C.

Marion Fremont-Smith is Of Counsel at Choate, Hall & Stewart and Senior Research Fellow at Harvard's Hauser Center for Nonprofit Organizations, Harvard University.

Julie E. Kendall is an Associate Professor in the School of Business-Camden, Rutgers University.

Sharon M. Oster is the Frederick Wolfe Professor of Entrepreneurship and Management at the Yale School of Management.

Anne E. Preston is an Associate Professor of Economics at Haverford College.

Patrick M. Rooney is Director of Research for the Center on Philanthropy at the Indiana University and an Associate Professor of Economics and Philanthropic Studies, Indiana University–Purdue University in Indianapolis.

Dov Te'eni is a Professor on the Faculty of Management, Tel-Aviv University.

Howard P. Tuckman is the Dean of the Rutgers Business School: Newark and New Brunswick and P2 Professor in the Department of Economics.

Lawrence J. Wilker is the Co-Founder, President and CEO of Show on Demand, Inc. and Theater Dreams. Previously, he was the President of the John F. Kennedy Center for the Performing Arts.

Dennis R. Young is founding CEO of the National Center on Nonprofit Enterprise and a Professor of Nonprofit Management and Economics at Case Western Reserve University.

About NCNE

The National Center on Nonprofit Enterprise, a 501(c)(3) charitable organization headquartered in Arlington, Virginia, helps managers and leaders of nonprofit organizations by offering current and relevant knowledge on critical economic and business decision-making issues. Through an extensive network of academic, business and nonprofit practice leaders, and managers and consultants, NCNE consolidates, interprets, synthesizes, and disseminates theory, research, and practical managerial advice. NCNE's comprehensive program of helpful services and activities make state-of-the-art knowledge accessible to practicing nonprofit managers and leaders. Visit NCNE's Website at www.nationalcne.org for more information.

National Center on Nonprofit Enterprise
3401 N. Fairfax Dr. MS 3B1
Arlington, VA 22201-4498
703-993-4994
703-993-8215- fax
ncne@nationalcne.org

Index

AAFRC Trust for Philanthropy, 95
Adelphi University, 116
advertising, 129, 179
agency problems, 72–74, 76, 176
AICPA. *See* American Institute of Certified Public
    Accountants
ALA. *See* American Lung Association
alliances. *See* collaboration, institutional
Al Sigl Center for Rehabilitation Agencies, Inc.,
    80
Amazon.com, 175–176, 180
American Institute of Certified Public Accountants
    (AICPA), 88
American Law Institute, 105
American Lung Association (ALA), 162
American Red Cross, 30, 138, 168
Art Institute of Chicago, 112
ASPCA, 130
assets
    fixed and special, 108–109
    values, 16, 158
    See also investments
Association of Fundraising Professionals, 89
asymmetric information, 78–79
average costs, 13–14, 90–91, 114

Ballen, John, 110
Bayer Chemical Company, 159
Better Business Bureau (BBB), Wise Giving
    Alliance, 85
Bidwell Training Center, 159
Black, Scott, 110
boards of directors
    compensation decisions made by, 60
    compensation of, 58
    conflict of interest policies, 116

finance or investment committee, 110, 111,
    113
    outsourcing decisions and, 209–210
    roles in investment management, 109, 110–
    111, 112, 113, 116
Boston University, 116
Boys and Girls Clubs of America, 135
Burke, Edmund, 217
businesses
    charitable donations by, 95–96
    comparison to nonprofits, 6–7, 8–10, 13–17,
    18–20, 192, 216–217
    compensation of employees, 50–51, 73
    competition from nonprofit commercial
    ventures, 5
    cost-benefit analyses, 103
    entrepreneurs, 125
    expenditure policies, 102–105
    Internet companies, 180, 182–183
    investment policies, 102–105
    outsourcing by, 68, 141
    sponsorship of websites, 129, 179
    See also collaboration, institutional
business ventures of nonprofits. *See* commercial
    ventures

Cahen, Robert, 35–36
CARE, 156
Case Western University, 52
charitable donations
    by corporations, 95–96
    growth of, 3, 95–96
    as percentage of nonprofit revenues, 3–4, 84
    perceptions of fundraising costs and, 85, 91,
    94
    See also fundraising

Charles Schwab, 6
Chicago Symphony Orchestra, 42
Chronicle of Philanthropy, 60, 61
City Year, 154
Cleveland Jewish Community Center, 33, 40
Cleveland Mandel Jewish Community Center, 35–
    36
Cleveland Playhouse, 177
Coase, Ronald H., 80
Coca Cola, 135
collaboration, institutional
    among nonprofits, 152–154
    barriers and risks, 153–155
    continuum of, 161–162
    costs and benefits, 150–153, 155, 159, 181–
        183
    depth of relationship, 162, 211
    diversification in, 21–22, 207
    economic analysis of, 20–22
    economic environment, 214
    effectiveness gains, 152–153
    efficiency gains, 151–152
    forces fostering, 149–150
    with for-profit businesses, 20–22, 129, 131–
        132, 135, 152
    with government, 152, 154, 214
    guidelines, 155–161
    in Internet ventures, 169, 179–183
    managing relationships, 160–161
    motives, 150
    multiple relationships, 162
    objectives, 196
    opportunity costs and, 155
    partnering dynamics, 161–162, 180
    Partnering Payoff Matrix, 150–151, 162
    qualitative costs and benefits, 200–201
    risks in, 21–22
    stakeholder pressures, 211
    tensions between mission and market, 203–
        204
    value proposition, 150–153, 158–159
collective goods, 128
    See also public goods
commercial ventures
    benefits of, 123
    comparative advantage and, 130, 141
    compensation related to, 136, 141
    competition with for-profit businesses, 5
    consistency with mission, 131, 143–144,
        195–196
    consultants, 144
    crowding-in, 19, 138

crowding-out, 19, 137–140
    debate on, 202
    decision criteria, 114, 130, 140
    diversification in, 206–207
    economic environment, 212–213
    evaluating, 143–144
    for-profit partners, 129
    funding agent concerns, 136–137
    impact on mission-related activities, 143–144
    opportunities, 140–141
    planning, 141–142
    product differentiation, 19–20
    qualitative costs and benefits, 200
    resources on, 132
    as revenue sources, 4–5, 123, 130, 134
    skills needed, 130, 131, 144
    stakeholder pressures, 210–211
    taxes on income, 131
    tensions between mission and market, 203
    types of goods, 124–126
    variations, 122
    See also fees; Internet commerce and
        fundraising; prices; social
        entrepreneurship
Commissioners of Uniform State Laws, 105
Commonfund, 116
comparative advantage
    commercial ventures and, 130, 141
    Internet commerce and, 23
    outsourcing and, 12, 72
compensation
    attracting employees, 51–54, 60, 63–64, 213
    deferred benefits, 55–56, 61, 64
    determinants, 53, 61–63, 198
    of directors, 58
    excess, 49, 59
    of executive directors, 56, 58–63
    in for-profit businesses, 50–51, 73
    gender differences, 61–62
    goals, 51
    guidelines, 63–64
    incentive plans, 10–11, 56–58, 59, 61, 64, 73,
        141
    increases in, 3, 60
    of information technology staff, 178
    issues for nonprofits, 48–50
    market forces, 10, 48, 203
    mission as context for, 49, 53, 194
    nonpecuniary benefits, 48, 50, 52, 53, 54, 55–
        56, 63–64
    regulations on, 48–49, 55, 56, 59, 60
    related to commercial ventures, 136, 141

retaining employees, 55–56, 64
stakeholder pressures, 209
variations within organization, 49, 53
computer systems. *See* information and
communication technology
consultants
on commercial ventures, 144
fundraising, 89
contracting-out. *See* outsourcing
contract law, 77
core competencies, 72, 78
cost-benefit analyses
in business, 103
for institutional collaboration, 159
for investments, 17, 199–200
measurement systems, 201
qualitative costs and benefits, 197–202
use of, 201–202
costs
average, 13–14, 90–91, 114
of collecting fees, 31
direct program, 36
fixed, 36, 37, 38
marginal, 14, 90–91, 98, 114
overhead, 36, 38, 89
prices and, 36–37
qualitative, 197–202
semi-variable, 37
variable, 37
See also expenditure policies; fundraising
costs
Council on Foundations, 109
crowding-in, 19, 138
crowding-out, 19, 137–140

differencing technique, 98
differential pricing, 29, 39–41
directors. *See* boards of directors; executive
directors
diversification, 205–208
in institutional collaboration, 21–22, 207
of investments, 107–108, 205–206
donors
information on, 178, 181
virtual communities of, 176
See also charitable donations; funding
agents; fundraising

earned income. *See* commercial ventures; prices
Easter Seals, 162
e-commerce, 35
See also Internet commerce and fundraising

economic decision-making
differences between nonprofits and for-profit
businesses, 8–10, 14–16, 18–20, 192,
216–217
revisiting, 212–216
similarities between nonprofits and for-profit
businesses, 13–14, 16–17
themes, 24
economic environment
change in, 212–216
effects on fundraising, 185–186, 213–214
for investment, 102
economies of scale, 176
EMI, 35
employees
attracting, 51–54, 60, 63–64, 213
graduate training courses, 52, 144
hiring, 53
labor donations, 50
loyalty, 73
motivation of, 50, 51, 56–58
retaining, 55–56, 64
women, 3, 50, 51
work environment, 54
See also compensation
endowments, 5–6, 103, 109, 112, 205
See also investments
entrepreneurship, 125
See also social entrepreneurship
e-philanthropy, 168
See also Internet commerce and fundraising
excludability, 75
executive directors
compensation, 56, 58–63
women, 61–62
expenditure policies
comparison to for-profit businesses, 102–105
coordination with investment decisions, 113
cost-benefit analyses, 103, 114
integration with mission, 195
internal investments, 16–17, 114–115
stakeholder pressures, 210
See also costs
externalities in consumption, 31

federated fundraising appeals, 15, 151
fees
collection costs, 31
as percentage of nonprofit revenues, 28
See also commercial ventures; prices
Fidelity Investments, 6, 110
fixed costs, 36, 37, 38

Form 990, 59, 96, 142
Foundation Center, 142
foundations
    motives for grants, 134
    payout policies, 17
    See also funding agents
Franklin, Benjamin, 2
funding agents
    adaptive behaviors, 137–140
    commercial ventures and, 127, 128, 136–137, 142
    information needed, 142
    motives, 132–135, 138–139
    relationships with, 132
    See also charitable donations; donors;
        foundations; governments
fundraisers, professional
    consultants, 89
    increases in, 96
    online services, 182–183
    results, 94, 203
    solicitors, 89–90
    turnover of, 93
fundraising
    business principles applied to, 13–14
    combined with educational activities, 88–89
    competition among nonprofits, 86, 95
    contribution to net financial resources, 87
    disclosure issues, 96
    diversified strategies, 207–208
    economic environment of, 185–186, 213–214
    evaluating, 93
    federated appeals, 15, 151
    investments in, 93–94
    major and planned gifts, 93
    opportunity costs and, 14, 89
    outsourcing, 13
    public oversight of, 86
    as revenue strategy, 93–94
    stakeholder pressures, 210
    tensions between mission and market, 203
    visibility of, 84
    See also charitable donations
fundraising-contribution ratio, 87, 90–91
fundraising costs
    accounting standards, 88, 96
    allocation of joint costs, 88–89, 96
    average, 13–14, 90–91
    comparisons, 96–97
    disclosure of, 96
    effects of online fundraising, 214

    limiting, 85
    marginal, 14, 90–91, 98
    measuring, 87
    mission as context for, 195
    necessity of, 84
    qualitative, 199
    recommendations, 97–98
    reported versus actual, 88–90
    seen as excessive, 85
    timing of, 93
fundraising efficiency, 14–15, 85–86
    measures of, 87, 96
    private, 86, 87–93
    results, 87–88
    social, 86, 94–97
fundraising-expense ratio, 87, 88–90

gains from trade, 17
Garrison, John, 162
gender
    differences in compensation, 61–62
    See also women
Georgia Pacific, 131
gifts. *See* charitable donations
governments
    collaboration with nonprofits, 152, 154, 214
    funding from, 4, 134, 137
    outsourcing by, 214
Guidestar, 61–62, 115, 142

Hallock, Kevin, 61, 62
hedge funds, 109, 112
Herzberg, Frederick, 50, 56

ICT. *See* information and communication
    technology
income. *See* revenues
Independent Sector, 142
Indiana University/Purdue University, 52
information, rich, 178
information and communication technology (ICT)
    automation of services and operations, 171–173, 176, 179
    conceptual framework, 168–170, 185
    costs and benefits, 170, 178
    development and implementation, 170, 176–179
    future challenges, 183–185
    impact, 169, 171, 179–183
    investment in, 169–170
    knowledge management, 178
    limitations, 184–185

motivation for use of, 169–170
outsourcing, 175–176, 177
planning, 174–175
strategic alignment, 170, 184
supportive services, 171, 173
systems portfolio prioritization, 170, 174–175
See also Internet commerce and fundraising
institutional collaboration. *See* collaboration, institutional
Internal Revenue Code, 113
Internal Revenue Service (IRS), 48, 49, 59, 96, 129, 131, 142
Internet
free services, 35
information on nonprofits available on, 142–143
Internet commerce and fundraising
business models, 22–23, 179–180
challenges, 174
collaborations, 169, 179–183
comparative advantage and, 23
confidentiality and privacy issues, 180–181
corporate sponsors of websites, 129, 179
effects of September 11 attacks, 168, 177, 184
effects on nonprofits, 214
evaluating impact of, 174
for-profit service providers, 180, 182–183
future challenges, 183–185
future research directions, 185–186
intermediaries, 168 169, 172
market space, 168
mission-related uses, 172, 196–197
potential, 168
profit-sharing, 179, 181
qualitative costs and benefits, 201
referral portals, 180, 182, 183
regulation of, 169
stakeholder pressures, 211–212
tensions between mission and market, 204
trust issues, 182
volunteer matching services, 179, 183
websites of nonprofits, 126, 171, 174, 177–178, 181
investment advisers, 6, 109, 110–111, 112
Investment Fund for Foundations, The (TIFF), 116
investment managers, 109
investments
alternative, 15–16, 108
choices, 109

comparison to for-profit businesses, 102–105
coordination with spending decisions, 113
cost-benefit analysis and, 17, 199–200
diversification, 107–108, 205–206
economic environment, 102
endowments, 5–6, 103, 109, 112, 205
fixed and special assets, 108–109
improving policies, 115–116
integration with mission, 15–16, 113–116, 195
internal, 16–17, 114–115
legal framework, 105–106, 109, 113
losses, 112, 116
modern prudent investing, 106–109
Modern Prudent Investor Rule, 105–106
policies, 15, 16–17, 111, 116
professional advisers, 109, 110 111, 112
program-related, 113–114, 206
reporting on, 111
risk management, 205–206
role of board members, 109, 110–111, 112, 113, 116
stakeholder pressures, 210
tensions between mission and market, 203
total return, 15, 103, 105, 107
IRS. *See* Internal Revenue Service

Jumpstart, 154

Kellogg Foundation, 183
Kennedy Center, 35, 38–39
knowledge management, 178

labor market, 10, 48, 52, 213
See also compensation
law
contract, 77
Modern Prudent Investor Rule, 105–106
trust, 103, 105
Lynch, Peter, 110

make-or-buy decision. *See* outsourcing
March of Dimes, 195
marginal benefit, 98
marginal costs, 14, 90–91, 98, 114
market forces
effects on compensation, 10, 48, 203
tensions with mission, 202–205
See also labor market
market risk, 108
Maslow, Abraham H., 50, 56
Merrill Lynch, 6

Metropolitan Museum, 28
Metropolitan Opera, 43
mission
    centrality of, 6–7, 192–193
    commercial ventures consistent with, 131,
        143–144, 195–196
    compensation decisions and, 49, 53, 194
    difficulty of quantifying, 193–197
    impact of commercial activities, 143
    information technology supporting, 171, 172,
        173
    investment policies and, 15–16, 113–116,
        195
    pricing decisions and, 30, 38, 194
    tensions with market forces, 202–205
Modern Prudent Investor Rule, 105–106
MOMA. See Museum of Modern Art
Mothers Against Drunk Driving, 31
motivation, 50, 51, 56–58
Museum of Fine Arts Boston, 110
Museum of Modern Art (MOMA), 126, 128

Napster, 35
National Association of College and University
    Business Officers, 109
National Center for Charitable Statistics (NCCS),
    59, 115
National Jewish Medical and Research Center,
    140–141
Nature Conservancy, 131
NCCS. See National Center for Charitable
    Statistics
Network for Good, 183
New Era Foundation, 112
new ventures. See commercial ventures
New York Public Theater, 116
nonexcludability, 75, 79, 124
non-preferred private goods, 124, 125, 134
nonprofit organizations
    comparison to for-profit businesses, 6–7
    core functions, 8–12
    data on, 142–143
    differences from for-profit businesses, 8–10,
        14–16, 18–20, 192, 216–217
    new strategic directions, 18–23
    number of, 96
    organizational cultures, 154
    permanent status, 103–104
    resource development functions, 13–17
    resource management by, 1–2, 6
    similarities to for-profit businesses, 13–14,
        16–17

tax-favored status, 104, 131
    theoretical explanation of existence, 124
    trust in, 216
nonrivalry, 75, 79, 124

opportunity costs
    fundraising and, 14, 89
    institutional collaboration and, 155
    outsourcing and, 11–12, 72
organizational cultures, 154
outsourcing
    activity types, 11–12, 68–70, 72, 78–79, 81,
        176
    agency problems, 72–74, 76, 176
    benefits of, 68, 80–81, 141, 176
    comparative advantage and, 12, 72
    contracts, 77–78
    decisions, 80–81, 177, 194–195, 198–199
    definition, 67
    disadvantages, 68, 80–81
    diversification in, 207
    economic environment, 213
    employee cooperation with, 72–73
    in for-profit sector, 68, 141
    fundraising, 13
    by governments, 214
    increases in, 67–68
    information technology services, 175–176, 177
    management of, 70–71
    to nonprofits, 79–80, 141, 214
    opportunity costs and, 11–12, 72
    principles for decision-making, 69–71
    specialization and, 71–72
    stakeholder pressures, 209–210
    tensions between mission and market, 203
    transactions costs, 12, 74–78, 80
overhead costs, 36, 38, 89

partnerships. See collaboration, institutional
performance measurement, 29, 57–58, 103
PipeVine, 177
Points of Light Foundation, 174–175, 183
preferred collective goods, 124
preferred private goods, 124, 128, 134
Premier Inc., 76
Preston, Anne, 3
price discrimination, 9, 39–41
prices
    across services and products, 38–39, 41–42,
        208
    advantages of, 31–33
    arguments against, 29–31

bundled services, 9, 42–44
  costs and, 36–37
  cross-subsidization, 38–39
  decision to use, 28, 29–34
  demand to base, 42
  differential, 29, 39–41
  economic environment, 212
  effects on client behavior, 32–33
  functions, 8–9
  future challenges, 44–45
  mission as context for, 30, 38, 194
  promotional, 33
  setting, 28–29, 35–36, 130–131, 198
  stakeholder pressures, 208–209
  tensions between mission and market, 202–203
  transition issues, 34–35
  See also fees
principal-agent problems. *See* agency problems
private fundraising efficiency, 86, 87–93
private goods, 75–76, 124, 125, 128, 134
product differentiation, 19–20
production inputs, 69–70
  See also outsourcing
program-related investments, 113–114, 206
programs
  costs, 36–37
  cross-subsidization, 38–39
  relationship to mission, 30
  revenue-generating ability, 30
  See also prices
Prudential Securities, 112
public goods, 75–76, 79, 124, 128, 134
public-private partnerships. *See* collaboration, institutional
purchasing agents, 75–76

Reading is Fundamental, 157
referral portals, 180, 182, 183
resources, scarcity of, 2–6
revenues. *See* charitable donations; commercial ventures; fees; governments; prices
risks
  diversifiable, 108
  management of, 205–208
  market, 108
rivalry, 75
Robin Hood Foundation, 177–178, 181, 182

salaries. *See* compensation
securities firms, 6
semi-variable costs, 37

September 11 terrorist attacks, 168, 177, 184
Slate, 35
Smith, David H., 1–2
social entrepreneurship
  challenges, 129–132, 136
  choice set, 124–129
  differences from business entrepreneurs, 125
  environment, 141
  forms, 123
  increase in, 215–216
  motives, 123
  opportunities, 124–125
  See also commercial ventures
social fundraising efficiency, 86, 94–97
Sony, 35
specialization, 71–72
stakeholders, 208–212
Stanley, John, 110
Starbucks, 156
Steinberg, Richard, 98
strategic philanthropists, 134
suppliers
  asymmetric information, 78–79
  contracts with, 77–78
  relationships with, 74, 76, 77
  reliability, 76, 77
  trust in, 76
  See also outsourcing
Surdna Foundation, 184

Taxpayer Bill of Rights, 48–49, 55, 59, 60
technology
  opportunities for new ventures, 140
  See also information and communication technology; Internet commerce and fundraising
Temple University, 116
terrorism, 168, 177, 184
Ticketmaster, 177
TIFF. *See* Investment Fund for Foundations, The
Timberland, 154
Time to Read, 157
Time-Warner, 157
total return, 15, 103, 105, 107
transactions costs, in outsourcing, 12, 74–78, 80
trustees. *See* boards of directors
trust law, 103, 105

UBIT. *See* unrelated business income tax
Uniform Management of Institutional Funds Act (UMIFA), 106
United Way campaigns, 15, 151

United Way of America, 154–155, 183
unrelated business income tax (UBIT), 131
Urban Institute, 115, 142

Vancouver Public Aquarium, 33
variable costs, 37
venture philanthropy
    growth of, 18
    return on investment, 18–19, 202
Visa, 157
volunteers
    fundraising by, 89
    online matching services, 179, 183
    as scarce resource, 2–3
    value of time, 3, 89

wages. *See* compensation

Wallace, Nicole, 168
websites. *See* Internet commerce and fundraising
Weisbrod, Burton, 4, 5
Wilker, Lawrence, 38
William Penn Foundation, 58
Winston, Gordon, 39–40
Wise Giving Alliance, 85
women
    compensation, 61–62
    executive directors, 61–62
    as nonprofit employees, 3, 50, 51
Women's World Banking, 153
workers. *See* employees; volunteers
World Wildlife Fund (WWF), 174, 175–176, 178, 180, 181

Yale University, 30, 203